D0904422

Understanding the Qur'anic Miracle Stories in the Modern Age

Understanding the Qur'anic Miracle Stories in the Modern Age

ISRA YAZICIOGLU

THE PENNSYLVANIA STATE UNIVERSITY PRESS
UNIVERSITY PARK, PENNSYLVANIA

LIBRARY OF CONGRESS CATALOGING-IN-PUBLICATION DATA

Yazicioglu, Isra, 1978–
    Understanding the Qur'anic miracle stories in the modern
age / Isra Yazicioglu.
        p.   cm — (Signifying (on) scriptures)
Includes bibliographical references and index.
Summary: "Explores the implications of Quranic miracle stories
for the modern era. Examines the medieval Muslim debate
over miracles, and connects its insights with early and late
modern turning points in modern Western thought as well as
contemporary Quranic interpretation"—Provided by publisher.
ISBN 978-0-271-06156-6 (cloth : alk. paper)
1. Miracles (Islam).
2. Miracles.
3. Qur'an—Hermeneutics.
4. Islam—Doctrines—History.
I. Title.

BP166.65.Y39 2013
297.1'226—dc23
2013023135

WITH GRATITUDE,

to my parents, Selma and Osman,
and to my teachers, Yamina and Ali

CONTENTS

ACKNOWLEDGMENTS

I would like to thank Saint Joseph's University for a 2011 summer research grant, which enabled me to make major progress on this book. It is a pleasure to be part of this university, and I am grateful for the collegial department in which I work and all the support I have received over the years.

I am grateful to the Penn State Press editors. The series editor, Vincent Wimbush, like press director Patrick Alexander, has supported this project from early on and has also provided precious feedback. I also offer deep thanks to Tazim Kassam and the anonymous reviewer of this book, who have offered immensely helpful suggestions and constructive criticism. Kathryn Yahner and her team have been so professional and helpful in wading through the publication process. I am especially thankful to Charlee Redman, who answered my endless queries. And I am extremely grateful to Julie Schoelles for incredible, patient, and fine-tuned editing. Thanks also to all of our student assistants at Saint Joseph's, including Dana Saraco and Christopher DeMille. Thanks to Hakan Gülerce at the Istanbul Foundation for Science and Culture for his kind assistance in locating several conference proceedings about Nursi's works. I also appreciate Martin Nyugen and Ayse Polat for generously answering my questions on fine points on such short notice.

I am deeply indebted to various mentors and teachers I have had the privilege to learn from throughout my academic and personal journey. Peter Ochs introduced me to Charles Peirce's works and enriched my thinking about issues of interpretation and religious thought in the modern era. He read the earlier versions of my chapters and provided extremely helpful feedback. Peter also introduced me to Scriptural Reasoning. I've learned a lot from many great colleagues in this interfaith study group, who nurtured the new horizons of scriptural reading that Nursi's work had opened up for me. The late Daniel Hardy was one of these wonderful scholars, and his memory and encouragement I shall always cherish.

Jamie Ferreira taught me how to refine my philosophical arguments, and she provided very helpful comments, especially on Hume's thought. In addition, Mehdi Aminrazavi and Timothy Gianotti read and provided expert advice on earlier versions of some chapters. I am also very grateful to Sait Özervarli for both his helpful scholarly advice and his encouragement. I am also indebted to Abdulaziz Sachedina for his generous support. I would also like to mention one of my dear teachers, Ibrahim Abu-Rabiʿ, who passed away not long ago. May he be rewarded abundantly for his warm encouragement and guidance of all his students, including myself.

Two people introduced me to Islamic studies and have shared lasting insights on Islamic theology, Qurʾanic interpretation, and philosophy of religion: Ali Mermer and Yamina Bouguenaya Mermer. It was also they who introduced me to Said Nursi's works and offered tremendous help in understanding his thought. I am grateful for the countless hours they have spent with me discussing fascinating texts and topics as well as for their unwavering encouragement and personal support. Yamina also graciously worked with me through the challenges of writing this book. I am glad to be able to dedicate the book to them. Needless to say, I alone bear the responsibility for its shortcomings.

This book is also dedicated to my dear parents, Selma and Osman Yazicioglu, who have done so much for me throughout my life. I am so grateful for their unfailing compassion, patience, support, and generosity. Being their daughter has been such a blessing for me.

I have been blessed with other wonderful family members and friends, who encouraged me in this book project in various ways. Thank you very much to ammi and abbu -Ghazalah and Masood Sheikh- and to Latife and Rıdvan Yazicioglu, Nese Ulker-Cepni, and other family members. I am also grateful to our "Beam-Up" team, including Aliaa Khidr, Andrea Dzibuek, and Zuleyha Colak. Many thanks to dear Sarra Tlili for her very kind advice and encouragement.

Last but not least, I am deeply grateful to my dear husband Faraz Sheikh, my life companion, who has made the task of writing this book so much easier and more pleasant with his cheerful support and presence. I am also thankful to him for being such a caring father to our son, Isa, when I stayed extra hours in my office.

Many other people have contributed to this project in different ways. May the merciful God, who keeps the record of all good deeds, bless and reward them and all. *Wa kāna allahu shākiran ʿalīma.*

In the transliteration of Arabic, this book uses the style of the *Journal of Qur'anic Studies*, with the following exception: in order to make the book more accessible to nonspecialists in Islamic studies, I have often skipped elongation marks and other diacritics in the text. (The note citations and bibliography contain full diacritics.) Thus, for instance, I have used "Ghazali" instead of "Ghazālī," "Qur'an" instead of "Qur'ān," and "Niza-miyya" instead of "Niẓāmiyya." I have also left out the diacritics in several terms that have entered into English usage and are listed in the *Concise Oxford Dictionary*, such as *sharia* (instead of *sharī ʿa*).

In citing Turkish, I took the work of the late Professor Ibrahim Abu-Rabiʿ in Nursi studies as my precedent. Said Nursi, who is discussed in the final chapter, wrote in Arabic, Ottoman Turkish, and Persian. Although these are all different languages, I have used Arabic transliteration for the terms originating in Arabic. When I occasionally referred to Turkish terms, I prefaced them with "Tk." Where Turkish and Arabic terms appear together, I also used "Ar." to distinguish the latter. In the text and the references, I have used the following Turkish characters as they would appear in modern Turkish script:

c = j, as in *job*
ç = ch, as in *chop*
ğ = unpronounced, elongates the preceding vowel
ı = as in *io* of *station*
ö = as in French *peu*
ş = sh, as in *shop*
ü = as in French *rue*

INTRODUCTION
THE QUR'ANIC MIRACLE STORIES:
A PUZZLING MOTIF?

Moses said, "Pharaoh, I am a messenger from the Lord of all the Worlds, duty-bound to say nothing about God but the truth, and I have brought you a clear sign from your Lord." . . . So Moses threw his staff and—lo and behold!—it was a snake, clear to all. . . . The leaders among Pharaoh's people said, "This man is a learned sorcerer!"

—Qur'an 7:104–9

This book was born out of a casual conversation that first puzzled and then intrigued me. Years ago, I was talking to one of my relatives, and the topic of the virgin birth story came up. My aunt made a remark that has stayed with me since. She said, "I believe in this miracle narrated in the Qur'an, but I must admit that if a pregnant woman comes to me now and says, 'No man touched me but I am pregnant,' it will be very difficult for me to believe her." I was taken aback. At first, I thought that such a remark simply missed the point. After all, even the most enthusiastic believers would not think that the story was about being incredulous of virginity claims, would they? Yet her comment was also intriguing: she was raising a crucial question about the actual implications of a cherished miracle story. What was such a miracle story really telling its reader? She was asking, in effect, "What does this text want me to do with it? If the point is to be gullible and give the benefit of the doubt to a pregnant woman who claims to be a virgin, I am afraid I will fail to do that."

Obviously, such a question about implications can be raised for other miracle stories in the Qur'an, in which various other figures—such as Noah, Abraham, Moses, Solomon, and Jesus—are presented as performing miracles. For instance, when Abraham is thrown into fire, the fire miraculously becomes "cool and safe" for him (Q. 21:69).[1] Similarly, Jesus heals the blind and sick with his touch and revives the dead (Q. 5:110), while Moses's staff goes through instant metamorphosis, becoming a snake, or performs unusual feats, such as parting seas (Q. 7:117–19, etc.). Likewise, Solomon understands the language of the birds (Q. 27:16), has miraculous means of transportation (Q. 34:12), and so on. These miracle stories are quite similar to biblical stories in content, though, of course, there are also some crucial differences, especially in the explicit emphasis placed on edification and the amount of detail (or rather the lack of it) provided in the Qur'an.

Such miracle stories in the Qur'an, and in the Bible, may sound strange to many of us in this day and age. It is often thought that one either believes in the historical accuracy of these stories or rejects them as figments of imagination. In fact, miracle stories are often viewed in popular culture as a clear case of the clash between faith and science. It is as if the readers of miracle stories divide into two exclusive camps—believers versus unbelievers, people of faith versus people of reason and science. Yet, as this Muslim woman's remark shows, the picture is much more complicated than such a binary. Indeed, even for someone who believes a story to be factual, the question of what to do with its narration in the Qur'an can remain. The aim of this book is precisely to engage with this oft-neglected question of what to do with these miracle stories.

To be sure, questioning the relevance of Qur'anic miracle stories is not a uniquely modern phenomenon. In fact, during the very emergence, or the revelation, of the Qur'an in the seventh century, such questions regarding prophetic narratives were raised by the opponents of Prophet Muhammad. They claimed that these stories were simply irrelevant stories of the ancients (asāṭīr al-awwalīn). In contrast, the Qur'an insisted that these stories offered profound guidance for those willing to heed them. Believers also raised the question of what to do with these narratives. As the Qur'anic reception history attests, in the centuries after Prophet Muhammad lived, generations of believers engaged with them. This book will offer a glimpse of the ways in which meaningful implications have been drawn from these apparently strange narratives, in both the premodern and modern eras.

This book, focused as it is on the case of miracle stories, also aims to go beyond these specific passages to reflect more broadly on the issue of interpretation of the Qur'an. The case of miracle stories shows how seemingly irrelevant Qur'anic passages can occasion the discovery of new horizons of meaning and practice—a hermeneutical tip that can be applied to other scriptural texts as well. In fact, this book is intended not only for readers interested in Qur'anic interpretation but also for those interested in scriptural hermeneutics in general. The case of interpretation of miracle stories reveals once again that the relations between texts and their readers, reason and revelation, and faith and science are complex. In the process of interpretation, critical thinking and fidelity to the scriptural text are often much more intertwined than is often assumed.

By revealing the unexpected ways in which scriptural texts can elicit meanings and have repercussions for human life, this book contributes to the broader conversations about scriptural interpretation in the modern age. As part of the Signifying (on) Scriptures series at Penn State Press, it offers another compelling illustration of how the meanings of scriptures go beyond words on a page. That is, in order to appreciate the scriptural meanings, one needs to pay attention not only to their content but also to the ways in which they interact with and inform human perception, praxis, and social institutions.[2]

As I alluded to earlier, the Qur'an as scripture shares numerous similarities with other scriptures—especially with the Bible—that warrant extending the insights gleaned from its interpretation to them. However, there are also a number of features of the Qur'an that make the task of interpreting its miracle narratives a distinctive challenge, as well as an opportunity. As is well known, the purported narrator throughout the Qur'anic text is God, who is understood as addressing people through the "final human messenger," Prophet Muhammad. These passages, which were revealed to the Prophet via the angel Gabriel over a period of about twenty-three years (610–32 C.E.), form a discourse that is quite unexpected for an ear attuned to biblical style. The Qur'an does not follow a particular chronology: unlike the Old Testament or the Tanakh, it does not start with a creation story and move along a trajectory of salvation history. Nor does it offer a biography of Muhammad's life or a story of his ministry, unlike the Gospels. The Qur'an usually does not contain extended narratives either. While it mentions many of the figures who are also mentioned in the Bible—such as Adam, Noah, Moses, and Jesus—their stories are never told in one place. Instead, each of these figures appears and reappears throughout the text; snippet stories about each are presented elliptically and placed in an exhortational or prayer context. The story of Moses, for example, is told in more than fifty different places in the Qur'an. Each instance provides an excerpt or an episode of Moses's life and ministry and serves to illustrate central

Qur'anic themes, such as the oneness of God or belief in life after death. In addition to these distinct features in style, the Qur'an presents us with a curious situation in the case of miracle stories. To clarify what I mean by that, I will first give a general background on the prophet stories in the Qur'an and then focus on the theme of miracles within them.

One of the major claims of the Qur'an is that the creator of the universe has spoken to humanity throughout time and across different lands. Starting with Adam and ending with Muhammad, countless prophets and messengers of God have been sent to disclose meaning of life and divine purpose to humanity (e.g., Q. 4:164, 40:78). These prophets and messengers are presented as exemplary human beings bearing a universal message that was reiterated in different vocabularies across the ages. The Qur'an repeatedly notes that they were mere humans: they had needs for food, shelter, and security, they had desires, and they were mortal (e.g., Q. 3:114, 11:31, 12:24, 12:67, 25:20, etc.). The Qur'an presents their humanity as an advantage rather than as a shortcoming. In response to those who demand a suprahuman messenger, the Qur'an argues that human messengers can offer the best examples for people on earth (e.g., Q. 5:75, 15:20).

It is within these prophetic narratives that the Qur'an talks about the miracles performed by these messengers—as signs given to them to support their mission. The Qur'an is very clear that such miracles do not signify that the prophets are endowed with any superhuman qualities. Rather, it is God who enables the prophets to perform the miracles at specific times during their mission and, at times, to their own surprise (e.g., Q. 19:8, 27:10). Thus, for instance, the following verse narrates Jesus's miracles with a clear emphasis on God's will as the agent behind them: "[Jesus said:] I have come to you with a sign from your Lord: I will make the shape of a bird for you out of clay, then breathe into it and, *with God's permission*, it will become a real bird; I will heal the blind and the leper, and bring the dead back to life *with God's permission*" (Q. 3:49, italics added).

The Arabic term for miracle, *mu'jiza*, comes from the root ʿajaza (to be overwhelmed) and literally means that which overpowers, overwhelms, and paralyzes. The traditional Islamic theology has come to define the term "miracle" as the event by means of which a prophet of God overwhelms his opponents. As we shall see in the next chapter, a "miracle" in the traditional discourse was considered to be a change in the normal course of nature, which served as a confirmation of the sincerity of God's messenger before his audience. While the classical discourse, quite justifiably, referred to Qur'anic miracles with the term *mu'jiza* and defined it primarily within the context of a prophet's ministry, the term itself is not used in the Qur'an. The term used for miracles in the Qur'an is *āya*, meaning literally "a sign." In fact, the Qur'an refers to various "signs" of God and lays different emphasis on each. There are signs that are natural, such as the rain, the blossoming of the spring, or the growth of a human being in the womb. There are also signs that are unusual, though still natural, such as earthquakes and droughts. Finally, there are "supranatural" signs—the miracles—"that are apparently *against* the course of nature."[3]

According to the Qur'an, one of the excuses that Muhammad's contemporaries gave for rejecting his mission was that they wanted to see a supernatural event, a miracle, confirming his sincerity:

> They say: "We will not believe for you [Muhammad] until you make a spring gush out of the ground for us; or until you have a garden of date palms and vines, and make rivers pour through them; or make the sky fall on us in pieces, as you claimed will happen; or bring God and the angels before us face to face; or have a house made of gold, or ascend into the sky—even then, we will not believe in your ascension until you send a real book down for us to read." (17:90–93, also see 6:8–10, 52:44–45, 6:33–35, etc.)

The Qur'anic response to such a demand is very interesting and instructive. First, it highlights the real task of the prophet. He is not meant to be a wonderworker; rather, he is merely a human being whose duty is to convey a message revealed to him, inviting people to recognize their one God: "Say, 'Glory to my Lord! Am I anything but a mortal, a messenger?'" (Q. 17:93); "Say, 'I am only a human being, like you, to whom it has been revealed that your God is One'" (Q. 18:110). The message that the messenger brings is a sufficient sign in itself, validating the truthfulness of the messenger who proclaims it. In fact, the Qur'an describes itself—the very revelation of this enlightening message to an "unlettered" man—as a sign that points to God (Q. 2:23, 17:88, etc.). The Qur'an repeatedly challenges its audience to produce such a discourse on their own: "If you have doubts about the revelation We have sent down to Our servant, then produce a single sura like it—enlist whatever supporters you have other than God—if you truly [think you can]" (Q. 2:23). And in a provocative way it reframes the challenge: "Say [Muhammad], 'Even if all mankind and jinn came together to produce something like this Qur'an, they could not produce anything like it, however much they helped each other'" (17:88; see also 10:38, 11:13, 52:33–34).

At other times, the Qur'an responds to the demands for a supernatural event by noting that previous people often did not believe even when they saw miracles (Q. 5:110, 10:75–77, 17:59, 27:10–13, etc.). As Fazlur Rahman put it, it seems that the Qur'an deems miracles as almost "out of date."[4] The disbelievers will still not believe even if they see the miracles they demand: "Even if We had sent down to you [Prophet] a book inscribed on parchment, and they had touched it with their own hands, the disbelievers would still say, 'This is clearly sorcery'" (Q. 6:7). Similarly, "even if they saw a piece of heaven falling down on them, they would say, 'Just a heap of clouds'" (Q. 52:44).

Finally, the Qur'an responds to the demands for miracles from Muhammad by citing natural phenomena. The idea is that nature contains sufficient evidence for the central claims of the Qur'an, namely the reality of God and life after death. Indeed, the term the Qur'an uses for miracles, āya, is the same term used for natural phenomena (e.g., Q. 2:264, 7:107–8, 13:3, 16:65–72, 29:42, 30:20–27, etc.). The Qur'an repeatedly talks about natural processes—such as the rain, wind, stars, sun, moon, grains, fruits, growth of an embryo, production of milk and honey, sailing of ships on water, variety of human races, and so on—as signs, āyāt, that disclose a transcendental source of mercy, power, and wisdom. For instance, "In the creation of the heavens and earth; in the alteration of night and day; in the ships that sail the seas with goods for people; in the water which God sends down from the sky to give life to the earth when it has been barren, scattering all kinds of creatures over it; in the changing of the winds and clouds that run their appointed courses between the sky and earth: there are signs [āyāt] in all these for those who use their minds" (Q. 2:164, italics added). The presentation of natural phenomena as signs of God is actually a major theme in the Qur'an; nature is "the prime miracle of God, cited untiringly."[5]

The Qur'an claims that these "natural signs" are visible and clear, and yet one still needs to be trained in order to recognize them. Just as an illiterate person can see a piece of writing clearly but will not be able to read it until he is taught how to read, the signs of God in the world become intelligible only through the teaching of the prophets. Indeed, according to the Qur'an, deciphering the signs of God in nature is the very function of the revelation. Hence, the Qur'an employs the same word, āya, not only for natural events and miracles but also for the message proclaimed by messengers of God. The "signs" or "verses" of the revelation recited by the prophets disclose the "signs" in the universe.[6]

To be sure, the Qur'an is explicit about the *relational* aspect of signs of God. Despite the clarity of the signs of scripture and signs in nature, these will be signs only in relation to someone who is open to considering them as such. If one refuses to consider them, the signs cannot force themselves on that person: "However eagerly you may want them to, *most men will not believe* [in this message]. You ask no reward from them for this: *it is a reminder* for all people and there are *many signs [āyāt] in the heavens and the earth* that they pass by and give no heed to" (Q. 12:103–5, italics added). From a Qur'anic perspective, the relational aspect of the sign does not make the sign less powerful. As Rahman put it, "The signs do not become subjective . . . because many do not 'see' them, any more than the sun becomes subjective because animals habituated to darkness cannot see it."[7]

By stating that previous people did not believe despite seeing miracles, and by arguing that the natural world is more worthy of being used as evidence for faith, the Qur'an offers a critical response to the demand for miracles. So the question remains: If natural phenomena and the revelation of the Qur'an to the gentile Prophet are sufficient as signs of God, why narrate miracle stories about ancient prophets at all?

One way that the traditional Muslim scholars made sense of the apparently puzzling juxtaposition of the miracle stories about ancient prophets and the de-emphasis on miracles in Muhammad's case was through appealing to the differing needs of different audiences. They maintained that the major miracle of each prophet was tailored to the needs of his times.[8] Thus, for instance, they believed that God gave Prophet Moses miracles that would outdo magic because in his time people were interested in magic, and the sorcerer was the priest of the Egyptian religion during that period. Similarly, Prophet Jesus was given healing miracles because in his time medicine was held in high regard. The idea was that if a people were good at some skill, they would be able to recognize when a prophet surpassed that skill through a miracle. Hence, when the sorcerers of Pharaoh saw Moses perform a miracle, they immediately knew—being the experts in their field—that his feat was something qualitatively different than what could be achieved through magic (see Q. 7:106–22, 26:41–48). As for Prophet Muhammad, the traditional view maintained that he was given the Qur'an as a miracle of eloquence since his very first audience in seventh-century Arabia highly valued eloquence.[9] Indeed, as is well known, Muhammad "recited to an audience that had developed one of the most finely honed and scrutinizing tastes in the history of expressive speech."[10]

Moreover, according to the traditional view, the Qur'an was an appropriate miracle for the *final* prophet of God, whose audience was to continue until the end of time. Thus, unlike the supernatural events gifted to earlier prophets, God granted Prophet Muhammad the Qur'an as an "ongoing miracle." That is, the Qur'an was a sign that could be witnessed by generations who lived after the prophet until the end of the world.[11]

This traditional account explains how it could be justified within the Qur'anic perspective that physical miracles were not central to Muhammad's mission.[12] It does not quite address, however, what the audience of the Qur'an is to make of the miracle stories *in* the Qur'an. To be sure, it has been often suggested that the miracle stories indicate God's power and thus induce the reader to have awe of God and heed the message of the prophets.[13] Yet such an interpretation must still respond to a crucial question: How does the *narration* of a miracle count as evidence of God's power? In other words, what the audience of the Qur'an witnesses is a miracle story being narrated; the reader does not actually witness the miracle itself. Unlike the Qur'anic discourse about signs of God in nature or in scripture, which can be immediately accessed (or questioned) by turning our attention to the natural events or the text itself, the Qur'anic mention of miracles does not seem to be open to such an encounter for the reader. The sign of such miracles is, rather, inaccessible for direct witnessing. Given that the Qur'an clearly acknowledges that it is *not* addressing bygone communities in the pre-Muhammad period (see Q. 3:44, 11:49, 11:100, 12:102), why would it narrate these stories repeatedly for a people who would never see them? Could there be a deeper significance than merely reporting past events? Since the Qur'an repeatedly presents itself as offering guidance (Q. 2:2, 2:185, 3:138, 10:57, 16:64, etc.), it is fair to wonder about how these miracle stories serve its purposes of edification.

Not surprisingly, such questions about the relevance and the significance of miracle stories in the Qur'an did not go ignored in the Muslim tradition, and the reception history contains some remarkable engagement with them. This book intends to offer some of the poignant examples of this engagement, without any claim to exhaust them. (For instance, a noteworthy genre that unfortunately does not receive sufficient elaboration in this book and deserves a separate study is Sufi exegesis of the Qur'anic miracles.) In each of the following chapters of this book, we shall encounter a crucial thinker whose approach to miracle stories will contribute to our search for their potentially relevant implications. In every chapter, I shall first introduce an interpreter and then turn to the ways in which he probes the meaning of miracle stories.

At the center of our interpretive venture will be a lively medieval debate that was occasioned by Qurʾanic miracle stories. Chapter 1, entitled "In Defense of a Literal Reading of Miracles: Ghazali's Case for Contingency and Grace," forms the first thread of the debate. It discusses how Ghazali, the famous medieval Muslim theologian and mystic, makes a compelling case for reading the Qurʾanic miracle stories literally. With impressive philosophical acumen, he challenges the rationalistic and necessitarian assumptions about natural causality and concludes that Qurʾanic miracle stories can be read literally without any logical contradiction. This chapter also discusses Ghazali's theory of Qurʾanic interpretation, highlighting that Ghazali is not a thoroughgoing literalist in his approach to the Qurʾan and argues for the need to read the text metaphorically when it seems to clash with logic. Furthermore, Ghazali does not always consider miracles as strong proofs for faith; some of his remarks strikingly parallel the Qurʾanic criticism of the need for miracles. Given all these caveats, his insistence on a literal reading of miracles is intriguing: What is at stake for Ghazali in defending the literal interpretation of miracle stories? We discover that cru-cial implications are concealed beneath it. It turns out that his insistence on upholding the plain sense of miracle stories bears the fruit of a profound existential attitude toward life. Moreover, it brought about a breakthrough in medieval thought that would later form the backbone of our modern epistemology and science.

In chapter 2, "A Cautious Approach to Miracle Stories: Ibn Rushd's Case for Rationalism and Divine Wisdom," we encounter Ghazali's opponent Ibn Rushd, the famous twelfth-century Muslim philosopher and jurist. Ibn Rushd strongly disagrees with Ghazali's contention that the current natural order is contingent and that natural causality may be interrupted on certain occasions. He defends Aristotelian rationalism and realism, arguing that natural causality is a self-evident logical relation that cannot be suspended even in the case of miracles. He also finds Ghazali's approach theologically misled. For Ibn Rushd, admitting the contingency of natural order would undermine the appreciation of the profound wisdom in natural order, mak-ing any reference to divine wisdom meaningless. In this chapter, I also analyze Ibn Rushd's theory of Qurʾanic interpretation. Ibn Rushd draws a distinction between different classes of Qurʾanic readers, and while he allows a literal reading of miracles for the common person, he suggests that a literal interpretation would not be permissible for a nuanced philosopher. Through Ibn Rushd's resistance to miracle stories, we witness a very different practical implication drawn from the very same texts. Unlike Ghazali, Ibn Rushd sees a real danger in reading miracle stories in the Qur'an literally. He is worried about subversive readings that might lead to a disruption of common sense and scientific inquiry. Thus, Ibn Rushd's approach is very instructive about what these narratives may *not* imply, if we are to take the scripture seriously.

Having observed how interpretation of Qur'anic miracles occasioned such profound discussions about nature as well as human experience in the case of this medieval Muslim debate, the book will then make a perhaps surprising detour into modern thought. Even though engaging with the relevance of Qur'anic miracle stories is not an exclusively modern phenomenon, the contemporary age provides a new context that cannot be ignored. Modern successes in predicting and controlling natural processes both challenge and enrich the discussion of scriptural miracle stories. On the one hand, there is the challenge aptly voiced by David Weddle: "Why should anyone, living at the dawn of the twenty-first century, be interested in miracles?"[14] In this day and age of science and technology, in which we know how to describe various natural processes in detail and utilize them for human benefit, such stories simply seem obsolete. At the same time, these stories are less strange today: after all, we now read the virgin birth story in an age of reproductive technology, in which some babies are indeed conceived outside of the usual sexual intercourse. Thus, a reading of Qur'anic miracles in the modern age inevitably takes place against the background of, among other things, scientific and technological leaps, as well as the many Enlightenment philosophical notions attached to them. Our detour into early and late modern Western thought, surprising as it may well be, will therefore prove extremely useful.

This section of the book, "Reframing the Debate on Miracles in Modern Terms," turns to David Hume (1711–1776) and Charles S. Peirce (1839–1913), both of whom introduced drastic changes in the way Western philosophy conceived of the natural order and also displayed very interesting attitudes toward miracle narratives. Attention to their insights enables us to reframe the medieval Muslim debate over miracle stories in modern terms and facilitates an appreciation of what is at stake in a contemporary reading of Qur'anic miracles.

Chapter 3, "David Hume on Empiricism, Common Sense, and Miracles," discusses Hume, whose empiricist and agnostic approach has had a crucial impact on modern thought, both in epistemology and in philosophy of religion. Hume's position as an early modern thinker reflects an interesting combination of Ghazali's and Ibn Rushd's approaches to Qurʾanic miracles. His renowned challenge to rationalist assumptions about natural causality effectively affirms Ghazali's break from Aristotelian rationalism through the defense of miracles, and it leads to a defining moment for modern thought. However, unlike Ghazali, Hume also argues against miracle stories in his famous *A Treatise on Miracles*. His surprising insistence that miracle reports should not ever be taken seriously is reminiscent of Ibn Rushd's plea for science and rationality in his own response to Ghazali. Embodying, as it were, Ghazali's and Ibn Rushd's diverging concerns in an early modern context, Hume's stance helps us raise the crucial question of whether one could have it "both ways." Could one take miracle stories seriously, as Ghazali insightfully did, and yet resist their subversive readings, which Ibn Rushd worried about? Could a fallible epistemology, which recognizes that there is nothing logically necessary about current natural order, escape skepticism and make room for science? To this call, we find a response in the thought of a late modern scientist and philosopher.

Chapter 4, "Charles S. Peirce on Pragmatism, Science, and Miracles," discusses how Peirce, as a scientist and a thinker, offers an interesting reconciliation of the challenges and promises that lurk behind miracle stories. On the basis of his scientific training and his commitment to experience, Peirce makes room both for a fallible epistemology (in the style of Ghazali and Hume) that concedes the contingency of natural order, and for realism (as did Ibn Rushd and Hume). That is, his scientific approach suggests that natural laws cannot be regarded as absolute (as miracle stories may provocatively remind us) and also recognizes that regularities in nature are real rather than merely imagined by the human mind (hence such stories cannot be read in a way that undermines common sense and science). Peirce also traces a scientific implication of miracle stories: they alert the scientist to be open to unprecedented possibilities in her inquiry.

Bolstered with insights from the medieval Muslim debate and modern Western discussions about miracle stories, we then turn to contemporary reception in the final chapter, entitled "Said Nursi's Contemporary Reading of Qurʾanic Miracle Stories." Nursi (1877–1960) offers an insightful illustration of how these narratives could be read in relevant ways in the modern age. His hermeneutics of the Qurʾan is significant in that he insightfully focuses on the implications of the sacred text for a believer. His work fruitfully responds to our question of "what to do" in response to the Qur'an. According to Nursi, anything in the Qur'an has a message relevant for any believer in any age, and miracle stories are no exception. In Nursi's interpretation, not only are Ghazali's and Ibn Rushd's divergent insights reconciled, but the apparent contradiction between the natural and the miraculous in the Qur'anic discourse turns out to be a profoundly meaningful motif. Given that Nursi is such an important but understudied figure in current Qur'anic studies, and that his approach offers an exemplary culmination of the issues that will emerge in our interpretive journey, I will spend a bit more time on his work.

In sum, this book will illustrate how raising the question of "So what?" in response to the Qur'an and its reception history can uncover surprising insights. The venture into miracle stories sampled in this book will complicate the simplistic images of conflicts between faith and reason, and science and scripture. It shall disclose how seemingly intractable tensions between reason and revelation can give way to enriching and complementary perspectives on human existence, nature, and science. Indeed, under this hermeneutical lens, which we might label—inspired by Peirce's pragmatism, which is quite different from popular notions of pragmatism—"pragmatic hermeneutics," apparently dead or irrelevant scriptural texts can quicken to a life of meaning and relevance, just as Moses's dead staff turned into a lively serpent!

PART 1

A MEDIEVAL MUSLIM DEBATE

IN DEFENSE OF A LITERAL READING OF MIRACLES: GHAZALI'S CASE FOR CONTINGENCY AND GRACE

Abraham said, "How can you worship what can neither benefit nor harm you, instead of God? Shame on you and on the things you worship instead of God. Have you no sense?" They said, "Burn him and avenge your gods, if you are going to do the right thing." But We said, "Fire, be cool and safe for Abraham."
—Qurʾan 21:66–69

Ghazali (Abū Ḥāmid Muhammad al-Ghazālī), born in Tus, Persia, in 1058, is arguably one of the greatest scholars of classical Islam. He has had a major influence on various aspects of the tradition. Islamic theology, for instance, is divided into two periods—before and after Ghazali (al-mutaqaddimūn and al-mutaʾakhkhirūn). Similarly, Islamic mysticism gained new impetus through Ghazali, and Islamic jurisprudence incorporated formal logic through his works. In addition to his immense contribution to classical Muslim tradition, Ghazali had some influence in medieval Europe, where he became known as Algazel. More important, his thought remarkably anticipates a number of turning points in modern thought, including Cartesian and Kantian revolutions in Western philosophy. Ultimately, however, Ghazali's greatest achievement was his attempt to unify different religious disciplines, from Islamic jurisprudence to theology and Sufism, in light of the Qurʾan.[1] His preoccupation with understanding the Qurʾan in both intellectual and existential contexts makes him a good candidate for our analysis of the classical reception of Qurʾanic miracle stories.

Ghazali studied with Imām al-Ḥaramayn ʿAbd al-Malik al-Juwaynī (d. 1085), who was at the time a leading scholar of Islamic theology.[2] After the death of his teacher, Ghazali went to the court of Nizam al-Mulk (d. 1092), the Seljuq vizier who had opened universities throughout Asia Minor and Afghanistan, promoting religious learning. Ghazali, in his thirties, was appointed professor of law at one such university, the Nizamiyya College in Baghdad. It was during his four-year tenure there that Ghazali penned his crucial texts of theology and philosophy, including *The Standard of Knowledge* (*Miʿyār al-ʿilm*), an exposition of Avicennan logic; *Moderation in Belief* (*Al-Iqtiṣād fī l-iʿtiqād*), an important theological work; and *Incoherence of the Philosophers* (*Tahāfut al-falāsifa*), a critical engagement with early Muslim philosophers such as al-Farabi and Avicenna.

As he recounts in his autobiography *Deliverance from Error* (*Al-Munqidh min al-ḍalāl*), written toward the end of his life, Ghazali went through a profound crisis around the time he arrived in Baghdad. This crisis was the culmination of the critical attitude he had held toward formation of belief since his youth. He had always been dissatisfied with basing one's beliefs on the authority of others (*taqlīd*) and now began to seriously question what one could rightly possess as knowledge.[3] He first attempted to scrutinize all of his beliefs on the basis of sense perception and self-evident principles of logic, which seemed to him the only certain foundations of knowledge. However, he soon began to doubt sense perception as well as logical axioms: On what basis could one trust them? How could one really know that they were not simply illusions? Having lost all grounds for certainty, Ghazali had a nervous breakdown that lasted for about two months. He wrote that he finally emerged from it not by "systematic demonstration or marshaled argument" but rather through an intuitive assurance, which he felt was sent to him by "God's mercy." The breakdown had taught him that there was no way to "prove" the intuitive grounds of human knowledge: "First principles are not sought, since they are present and to hand; and if what is present is sought for, it becomes hidden and lost."[4]

A few years later, Ghazali went through another crisis, this time an existential one. He wondered whether he was authentic in his faith. He questioned whether his religious career was indeed for the sake of God and not simply for fame and recognition.[5] He was also dissatisfied with a mainly intellectual approach to religion and felt that he needed to recover a deeper connection to faith. He left his position in Baghdad and for the next eleven years lived as an ascetic in Damascus, Jerusalem, Hebron, Medina, and Mecca. This was a time of focus on spiritual growth. And, while he continued to teach in private, he vowed not to ever take any government posts; such positions not only deluded the ego with fame but were also paid out of a royal treasury that misappropriated the people's funds.[6] While Ghazali had been exposed to Sufism earlier in his life, it was only during this decade of seclusion that he finally embraced it and found his peace in it. It was also during this period that Ghazali composed his magnum opus, *Revival of Religious Disciplines* (*Ihyā' 'ulūm al-dīn*), in which he presented the cleansing of the heart and the cultivation of a personal connection with the divine as central goals for *all* believers—not just for the spiritual elite but also for the commoners.

Before his death, Ghazali briefly resumed his official teaching career at Nizamiyya College in Nishapur and then in Tus (1106–9), cities in what is now Iran. His return to teaching was occasioned by the "strict orders" of the state; a refusal would probably have cost him his life. It is clear that Ghazali accepted the position reluctantly, but not without the hope that God was calling him to share what he had learned in his eleven years of seclusion. He resigned from this post two years before his death. During his last years he wrote his final works, including *On Legal Theory of Muslim Jurisprudence* (*Al-Mustashfā fī 'ilm al-usūl*) and *Restraining the Uneducated from the Science of Theology* (*Iljām al-'awām 'an 'ilm al-kalām*). Ghazali died in Tus in 1111, leaving behind a major intellectual and spiritual legacy that included a comprehensive written literature, composed of no fewer than fifty titles.

Not surprisingly, reading a crucial figure such as Ghazali is not an easy task. Not only was he a prolific author whose works span a wide spectrum—including legal, philosophical, theological, exegetical, and esoteric genres[7]—but his views seem to have matured over the course of his life. Moreover, Ghazali tailors his discussion according to his intended audience; for instance, in his philosophical critique of Muslim Aristotelians in *Incoherence of the Philosophers*, he sometimes makes use of arguments that he elsewhere rejects. He makes it clear from the beginning that his aim in the book is to show the "incoherence" of certain philosophical views, and not to explain his own views. If one wants to learn about Ghazali's own stance on metaphysical issues, then one must turn to his theological works, such as *Moderation in Belief*, which he wrote as a sequel to *Incoherence of the Philosophers*.[8] Yet there is a caveat even for reading the relatively straightforward theological writings of Ghazali, for he repeatedly reminds us that theological discussion is inadequate for articulating profound truths. At best, theology brings one to the doorstep of gnosis, but it is not able to help one enter the abode of true knowledge.[9] And when we turn to Ghazali's esoteric works in order to glimpse what he holds as profound truths, we encounter yet another limit: he insists that not everyone can understand and grapple with the full implications of truth. In fact, Ghazali deems it imperative not to disclose them to the unprepared, who will inevitably misconstrue them.[10]

However, one need not be discouraged with the apparent opaqueness of Ghazali's corpus. As Montgomery Watt and Michael Marmura have pointed out, Ghazali's emphasis on the limitations of theology should not be overestimated. His mystical understanding is not set in opposition to the theological core; rather, it is presented as a deeper dimension of it. Moreover, we know that his personal maturation over the years did not translate into any radical breaks in his views.[11] To be sure, there are some seeming contradictions, but as I shall demonstrate, these are actually the result of a nuanced treatment of a complex issue. In fact, as we shall see, the ambivalence Ghazali displayed toward the issue of miracles provides the hermeneutical key for releasing the apparent tension in the Qurʾanic treatment of miracles. In what follows, we shall first look at Ghazali's ostensibly straightforward comments on miracles and then turn to his seemingly contradictory interpretation of the same passages.

Ghazali on the Evidentiary Value of Miracles

In his theological works, Ghazali argues that miracles constitute major evidence for the veracity of prophets, a position that had become standard in Muslim theology by his time. For instance, in *The Criterion for Distinction* (*Fayṣal al-tafriqa*), Ghazali argues that Muhammad's authenticity as a messenger sent by God is established by "the impeccable transmission of his appearance and his quality and his miracles which violated custom— such as the splitting of the moon and the praise of the pebbles and the welling up of water from between his fingers and the miraculous Qurʾan which he challenged the eloquent to rival and they could not."[12] Similarly, in *The Foundations of the Articles of Faith* (*Qawāʿid al-ʿaqāid*), from the *Revival*, Ghazali notes that the belief that God *can* send and *has* sent "His apostles and showed their veracity through explicit miracles" is essential to Islam. Just as the truthfulness of a physician is known by experiencing the results of his treatment, the truthfulness of a prophet is known by witnessing his miracles.[13] Similarly, in *Moderation in Belief*, Ghazali explains the appropriateness of referring to the miracles of Muhammad in discussions with Christians and Jews as evidence for Muhammad's legitimacy as a prophet; after all, the prophethood of Jesus and Moses is also supported by their miracles.[14]

In all of these texts, Ghazali's position is similar to that of other Muslim theologians before him, such as Abu'l-Ḥasan al-Ashʿarī (d. 936), Muḥammad ibn al-Ṭayyib al-Bāqillānī (d. 1013), ʿAbd al-Qāhir al-Baghdādī (d. 1037), ʿAbd al-Malik al-Juwaynī (d. 1085), and Abu'l-Yusr Muḥammad al-Bazdawī (d. 1099). All deemed miracles an essential requirement for a messenger of God.[15] The idea is that since a prophet is a human being like anyone else, the prophet's audience needs to be able to distinguish between a real prophet and a pretender. These theologians agreed that such a distinguishing mark should be some extraordinary event or a feat that cannot be performed by an ordinary human being.

While classical Muslim theologians agreed that miracles play an important role in establishing the validity of a messenger, they disagreed over *how* miracles carry out this evidentiary role. The disagreements regarded whether miracles constitute customary/contextual evidence (*dalīl ʿādī*), conventional evidence (*dalīl waḍʿī*), or rational evidence (*dalīl ʿaqlī*).[16] Only a minority of theologians argued that miracles provide rational proof (*dalīl ʿaqlī*) for prophecy.[17] In contrast, many, including most Ashʿarite and Muʿtazilite theologians, rejected the idea that the jump from miracles to the veracity of the prophets is a logical inference. There is no logically necessary relation between an extraordinary event and the premise of being a messenger of God. It is *logically* (and even theologically) conceivable that extraordinary things happen without the presence of a prophet and vice versa. Among these scholars who rejected the idea that miracles provide *dalīl ʿaqlī*, some argued that miracles instead provide contextual evidence, or *dalīl ʿādī*.[18] That is, a miracle may constitute evidence for the veracity of a prophet only when it takes place within a particular context: (1) a claim of prophecy must be made by the person who performs the extraordinary event, and (2) no one is able to perform a similar extraordinary act in response to his challenge (*taḥaddi*). In such a situation, the miracle provides customary or contextual evidence. Thus, as Ibn Taymiyya notes, the prophet, like the physician, is recognized by his actions and accomplishments in certain contexts, and this recognition is based on *ʿāda*, or custom.[19]

Other theologians regarded miracles as providing conventional evidence (*dalīl waḍʿī*), arguing that they have indicative power only on the basis of an unspoken yet implicit convention of communication between God and humanity. Just as verbal communication is possible because of language conventions, the confirmation of a prophet through an extraordinary event is possible because of an implicit symbolic convention. That is, by changing his usual way of creating upon the prophet's verbal request, God nonverbally confirms a prophet's claim. A common explanation offered in classical theological texts uses the parable of a king who sends a messenger to his subjects. While in the presence of the king, the messenger declares that, as proof that he is the king's special envoy, the king will perform an unusual act contrary to his royal protocols. If the king acts in accordance with the messenger's claim, that act is a clear indication of the king's approval of the claim. Likewise, if, upon the request of a prophet, God temporarily changes a pattern in the way he normally creates things, introducing a change in the natural order, it signifies the confirmation of the prophet by the master of the universe. These theologians argued that even though there is no prior explicit agreement between humankind and the Creator that "if someone performs X, know that he is my messenger to you," it is fair to assume it implicitly.[20] Given that human beings do not expect to hear the voice of the Divine directly—for if they could, there would be no need for a special messenger—they can only expect the Divine to "speak" through actions visible to them.[21] In *The Foundations of the Articles of Faith*, from the *Revival*, Ghazali notes his agreement with this metaphor:

> Whatever is linked [sic] by the Prophet with a challenge enjoys the same position as that to which God says "You are right." This is like the case of the person who, standing before the king announces to the subjects that he is the king's messenger, and in order to prove that he is right asks the king to stand upon his throne and sit down three times contrary to his usual practice. The king obliges and the subjects know, beyond the shadow of doubt, that the king's action takes the place of his saying "You are right."[22]

Obviously one can draw an analogy between a king changing his protocol and the interruption of the natural order by the master of the universe only on the assumption that such a similarity between a human king and the king of the universe can be justified. This method of using the seen or "witnessed world" (al-shāhid) to gauge the unseen (al-ghayb) has certain legitimacy, yet it may at times also be quite misleading. In fact, Ghazali himself criticized the frequent misuse of this type of analogical reasoning (*qiyās al-ghayb ʿalā al-shāhid*). By looking at a house, for instance, one could infer that it has been built by an agent, even though one has not actually seen that agent. Ghazali notes that this argument is valid in the sense that by looking at the *witnessed* world one *can* make *certain* inferences about the *unseen*. Yet he warns about the limits of application of this inference; one should always keep in mind that we cannot really speculate too much about the nature of the unseen. Ghazali notes, for instance, that one can also infer by looking at a house that its builder must have a body, but can this be universalized? Just as one says that any artifact has a maker, can one say that all makers have a body? For Ghazali, the answer is, of course, "no"; one should rather say that "all of the agents I have seen and analyzed have a body." And since we have not seen the one who made the universe, we cannot judge whether he has a body.[23]

However, while we should be wary of unwarranted jumps in reasoning, some analogy between human and divine must be allowed if one is to speak of any communication between God and human beings. It is fair to expect that a wise creator who wishes to communicate with human beings will take human conventions into account. This must be a reason why, despite his critique of the overuse of the analogy between the witnessed world and the unseen world, Ghazali endorses the king metaphor in understanding the role of miracles in affirming prophethood.[24]

As he argues for the evidentiary value of miracles in his theological works, Ghazali adds that they are not the only evidences for the truthfulness of a prophet. Rather, a miracle counts as evidence only when the person who claims to be a messenger proclaims a message that makes sense.[25] As noted in his preface to *Incoherence of the Philosophers*, according to Ghazali there are two fundamental principles that make up the core of any genuine prophet's message: faith in one God and faith in the afterlife. These two core pillars are confirmed by reason, and the details of prophetic messages that are rationally neutral (i.e., neither disproved nor proved on the basis of reason) can be accepted without any tension.[26] Miracles would have no value if the prophetic message had no logical consistency to begin with, and in the case of an absurd claim, even the most impressive miracle cannot serve as evidence: "I know very well that ten is more than three. If anyone tries to dissuade me by saying, 'No, three is more than ten,' and wants to prove it by changing in front of me this stick into a serpent, even if I saw him changing it, still this fact would engender no doubt about my knowledge. Certainly, I would be astonished at such a power, but I would not doubt my knowledge."[27]

Ghazali's reference to a staff turning into a serpent is noteworthy since it is one of the most mentioned miracle stories in the Qur'an (Q. 7:117–19, 20:17–20, 20:65–70, 26:43–46, 27:10, 28:31). Ghazali is thus announcing a context in which even that celebrated miracle of Moses has no value: even the most astonishing miracle cannot substantiate an illogical claim. A pertinent question is, of course, how we decide what is illogical. In fact, for many—including Ibn Rushd, the famous Muslim thinker who strongly disagreed with Ghazali on the issue of miracles—the concept of a miracle in the sense of a change in the usual course of nature is an affront to logic. In contrast, Ghazali insists, with impressive philosophical acumen, that miracles are logically possible. This defense of a literal reading of miracles is central to Ghazali's interpretation of Qur'anic miracles, to which we shall now turn.

Ghazali on the Plain Sense of Miracle Stories and Natural Causation

Ghazali's famous defense of miracles is found in his *Incoherence of the Philosophers*, which he composed to refute the philosophical views that he deemed to be irreconcilable with tenets of the Islamic faith. He singles out two Muslim Aristotelians, al-Farabi (d. 950) and Ibn Sina (Avicenna) (d. 1037), as the targets of his criticism. His goal is to show that their supposedly demonstrative views that clash with faith are actually not demonstrable, and that in fact some of them are self-contradictory.[28] Among the views that Ghazali criticizes is an exclusively metaphorical reading that rejects the plain sense of the miracle stories in the Qur'an: "Whoever renders the habitual courses [of nature] a necessary constant makes all these [miracles] impossible. [These philosophers] have thus interpreted what is said in the Qur'an about the revivification of the dead metaphorically, saying that what is meant by it is the cessation of the death of ignorance through the life of knowledge. And they interpreted the staff devouring the magic of the magicians as the refutation by the divine proof, manifest at the hand of Moses, of the doubts of those who deny [the one God]."[29]

According to Ghazali, the philosophers explain away the plain or literal sense of miraculous accounts because of their unverified assumption that the connection between a natural cause and its effect is necessary (*iqtirān talāzama bi al-ḍarūra*). Thus, these philosophers maintain that "it is within neither [the realm of] power nor within [that of] possibility to bring about the cause without the effect or the effect without the cause."[30] Based on this assumption, for instance, fire and burning are necessarily connected, and therefore it would be absurd to take the miracle story of Abraham surviving in fire literally (Q. 21:69). Ghazali thoroughly criticizes such assumptions in *Incoherence of the Philosophers*. Before we begin analyzing his critique, however, we must make note of his general stance on literal interpretation of the Qur'an.

Ghazali's insistence on reading the miracle stories literally is note-worthy because he is not a thoroughgoing literalist in his approach to the Qur'an. Rather, he interprets many Qur'anic verses (and sayings of Prophet Muhammad) metaphorically.[31] Indeed, in principle, Ghazali's approach is not dissimilar to that of his opponents; he agrees that when the literal sense of scriptural text contradicts reason, the text should be interpreted meta-phorically. In *The Foundations of the Articles of Faith*, he defends the need for metaphorical interpretation as follows:

> The knowledge that . . . there are inner meanings, which differ from the outward significations, can only be determined by either ratio-nal or legal [sic] evidence. The rational is when any interpretation according to the outward meaning is [logically] impossible, as in the words of the Prophet when he said, "The heart of the believer lies between two of the fingers of the Merciful [God]." When we exam-ine the hearts of the believers we shall not find them surrounded with fingers, and consequently we shall know that the words are used metaphorically for power, which is inherent in fingers and consti-tutes their hidden life. Furthermore, power was metaphorically rep-resented by the fingers because such a metaphor conveys the idea of power more completely.[32]

Similarly, the Qur'anic verse "When We [God] will something to happen, all that We say is, 'Be,' and it is" (Q. 16:40) may not be interpreted literally, for in that case it would be absurd: "The outward meaning of this verse is not possible because if the saying of God 'Be' was addressed to the thing before that thing came into existence, then it would simply be an impos-sibility since the non-existent does not understand address and, therefore, cannot obey. And if it was addressed to the thing after the thing has come into existence, then it would be superfluous, since the thing is already in existence and does not need to be brought into being." Thus, the verse must be interpreted as a metaphor for "conveying the idea of greatest power."[33] What Ghazali seems to mean is that things coming into being as an instant response to God's command is an effective imagery for articulating God's immense power, before which there is no resistance from anything. The verse thus expresses that the willed thing is brought into existence by God without any trouble or delay.

As he defends the necessity of interpreting certain passages metaphorically, Ghazali cautions that when the literal meaning is possible, one should *not* substitute a metaphorical reading in its place. One should beware of the excesses of metaphorical reading as well as literalism.[34] Here, Ghazali must be understood as cautioning against an *exclusively* metaphorical reading. For, as someone who affirms the polyvalence of the Qur'anic text, Ghazali actually agrees that other layers of meaning can coexist with literal meaning.[35] Indeed, despite his caution against the excesses of metaphorical interpretation, Ghazali maintains that there are situations in which the literal sense is *possible* and yet *not* intended. These are passages "where concrete words are used figuratively. The feeble-minded will regard the literal and exoteric meaning sensible and will not go beyond it; but the man who has an insight for realities will comprehend the secret it contains."[36] As an example, Ghazali refers to the following Qur'anic passage about the creation of the heavens and the earth: "Then He [God] turned to the sky, which was smoke—He said to it and the earth, 'Come into being, willingly or not,' and they said, 'We come willingly'" (Q. 41:11). To be sure, it *is* possible for a believer to take the verse literally: God has the power to make the heavens and earth speak, just as, one might say, he makes the flesh (i.e., living beings) speak. And yet, even though it is possible, the literal interpretation is *not* the appropriate reading in this context for Ghazali. Only a person with insufficient understanding would interpret the verse as saying "that both the Heaven and the earth possess life, intellect, and the ability to understand speech. He would also assume that they were addressed by a speech of actually enunciated words which both could hear and reply to with enunciated words saying, 'We come obedient.' But he who has insight would realize that this was a figurative [use of language], and that God only expressed the idea that the Heaven and earth are subject to His will."[37] Ghazali gives as another example the verse "There is not a single thing that does not celebrate His praise" (Q. 17:44). The person without understanding could interpret the verse as saying that inanimate beings are praising God by literally uttering words of praise. By contrast, he who has insight would know that no actual utterance with the tongue was meant by that, but merely that everything, through his own existence, praises God, and in its own essence sanctifies Him and attests to His unity. As has been said [in a poem]: "In everything He has a song / Which declares that He is one." In the same way it is said, "This masterpiece testifies that its maker possesses fair ability and perfect knowledge." . . . [That is,] through its form and state, [it testifies to the ability and knowledge of its maker]. Similarly everything does, in itself, stand in need of a creator to create and sustain it, to maintain its attributes and to move it to and fro in its different states. And through its need it testifies to its Maker by hallowing Him. Such a witness is comprehended by those who have insight, not those who stand still and venture not beyond externals.[38]

Ghazali adds that it is because of this difference in people's level of insight that God said, "But you [O men] fail to grasp the manner of their glorifying Him!" (Q. 17:44).[39] In these examples, Ghazali is not arguing for a metaphorical interpretation because the literal reading would be rationally inadmissible. Rather, he argues for a nonliteral reading because it is more insightful. (It is significant that in cases where Ghazali prefers a nonliteral meaning of the verse, the edification of the reader is at stake. In other words, the more insightful reading is the one that can have more impact on the reader's faith and practice. For instance, when the verse that states that everything glorifies God is interpreted to mean "in the way things happen, there are signs that point to God," there is an implication for a believer's everyday practice. Such a reading encourages the reader to pay attention to the praise enacted in the things happening around her. On the other hand, the literal interpretation that suggests that things somehow praise God in voices we cannot hear makes the verse too mysterious to be relevant for everyday life. We shall return to this consideration for edification in interpretation later.)

Now, given that he was not a thoroughgoing literalist, in principle Ghazali could have argued that miracle stories in the Qurʾan are not to be taken literally. Yet he did not do so, and the question is why Ghazali took such pains—as we shall see below—to defend the literal reading of these miracle narratives. Is it simply because he has idiosyncratically decided to uphold the literal sense of miracles? Or is it because he sees that there is an insightful message at stake? To answer this question, we must first look at his defense of the literal meaning of miracles and then turn to his personal engagement with miracles.

Ghazali's Critique of the "Necessity" of Natural Causation

In his critique of Muslim Aristotelians with regard to the issue of miracles, Ghazali aims to show that natural causality is not an irreversible pattern: "The connection between what is habitually believed to be a cause and what is habitually believed to be an effect is not necessary, according to us [*laysa ḍarūriyyan ʿindana*]."[40] Rather, for Ghazali, "the connection of these things is due to the prior decree of God, who creates them side by side, not to any inherent necessity in these things that would render their separation from each other impossible. On the contrary, it is within God's power to create satiety without eating, death without decapitation, to prolong life after decapitation and so on in the case of all concomitant things."[41] Here, Ghazali's critique of a "necessary" connection between habitual causes and habitual effects is mainly a deconstructive analysis: he argues that such a claim simply is *not* rationally demonstrable. He launches his critique in two ways, arguing that the necessity of the connection between natural causes and their effects has neither empirical verification nor rational justification.

Necessity of Natural Causation Is Not Empirically Verifiable

Ghazali's contention that we do not see necessary causal connections between things sounds counterintuitive. Do we not *see* links between events with our own eyes every day? Do we not see that water gives life to a plant, parents make the baby, fire consumes objects, and so on? Ghazali's answer is that we only observe a certain sequence of events, a constant *conjunction*; we do *not* observe *causal* connections between them. One indeed observes that a piece of cotton starts burning when it comes into contact with fire, but one does *not* actually see that fire produces the event of burning. All that one observes is that burning happens in the presence of fire, "with it" (*maʿahu*); one does not observe that burning happens *through* or *because* of it (*bihi*).[42] And to exist *with* something does not necessarily establish being made *by* it.[43]

One may ask: Even if we do not actually observe such an essential link between fire and burning, can it not be justly inferred from observation? After all, not only is fire always accompanied by burning, but the "effect," burning, does not occur in the absence of the "cause," fire. Ghazali's answer is still in the negative because the transition from the observation that "Y does not exist in the absence of X" to the judgment that "X therefore produces Y" is not a rationally warranted inference. Ghazali explains the unwarranted leap with an example that his opponent would follow:

> If a person, blind from birth, who has a film on his eyes and who has never heard from people the difference between night and day, were to have the film cleared from his eyes in daytime, [then] open his eyelids and see colors, [such a person] would believe that the agent [causing] the apprehension of the forms of the colors in his eyes is the opening of his sight, and that, as long as his sight is sound, [his eyes] opened, the film removed, and the individual in front of him having color, it follows necessarily that he would see, it being incomprehensible that he would not see. When, however, the sun sets and the atmosphere becomes dark, he would then know that it is sunlight that is the cause for the imprinting of the colors in his sight.[44]

Ghazali uses this example to demonstrate that the absence of Y (here, seeing colors) in the absence of X (removal of film from the eye) does not prove that X (removal of film) is the maker of Y (seeing colors). Ghazali thereby shows that the observation of the co-existence and co-absence of two things—such as fire and burning, or a healthy eye and seeing—does not prove the existence of an invariable causal connection between them. Obviously, the example is only a tool to make his point, for in Ghazali's ultimate scheme of causation, even the sunshine cannot be the real cause of eyesight.

According to Ghazali, not only does the derivation of causal necessity between natural events lack sufficient empirical evidence; there is additional empirical evidence that suggests the contrary. That is, the so-called "natural cause" does not display the required qualities to be the agent of its alleged effect. For instance, a spider weaves a delicate web. Although it seems that the spider is the cause of the web, upon closer examination one sees that the insect does not display the intelligence and knowledge required to design and execute such a delicate matter. Hence, the real agent of the web cannot be the spider, even if it initially appears to be so due to its temporal and spatial proximity to the web.[45] Ghazali gives another illustration for making the distinction between spatiotemporal proximity of two things and the causal relationship between them: "[Think of] a person taken to be beheaded, yet when the king sent a decree annulling and dismissing the process, he began to concentrate on the ink, the paper and the pen which were involved in the decree staying [his execution] saying: 'Were it not for the pen, I would not have been released.' It is as if he thought his salvation had come from the pen and not from the one moving the pen, yet this would be the height of ignorance."[46] In other words, the pen cannot be the real cause of the person's deliverance, since it does not display the appropriate qualities to cause such a result. That is, it is obvious that a pen lacks the knowledge, wisdom, authority, volition, and mercy to save someone's life. Therefore, "whoever knows that the pen does not move by itself, but only moves as an instrument in the hand of a writer, does not even consider the pen but directs his *thanks* to the writer alone." Likewise, "the sun, moon, and stars, as well as rain, clouds and earth, along with all living and non-living things, are but instruments in the grasp of the divine decree [qudra], as a pen subservient to the hand of an author."[47] Here, it is noteworthy how Ghazali connects the proper identification of the genuine cause of an event with the proper direction of gratitude. Just as the man in the example ought to show gratitude to the king instead of the pen, a human being who recognizes the one acting behind nature will be grateful to God, instead of natural causes themselves. We shall return later to this connection between gratitude, a central concept in the Qurʾan, and Ghazali's critique of the notion of natural causation so as to better understand his approach to miracles.

Ghazali's deconstruction of what Aristotelian thinkers took to be self-evident about natural causality is not only remarkable but also challenging. It is not surprising that Ghazali's counterintuitive conclusions provoked charges of irony and incoherence. For instance, Fazlur Rahman argued that Ghazali is inconsistent in affirming God as the cause of the world, having denied the effectiveness of natural causes: "Whereas Hume denies that there is *any* causation at all, al-Ghazali says that there is but one cause of every event, viz. God. In this Hume is obviously more consistent than either al-Ghazali or Malébranche, although their arguments are similar. For if events carry in themselves no evidence that they are caused by a cause, they obviously carry no evidence that they are caused by God."[48]

While Rahman is right in considering Hume's and Ghazali's positions as similar (which we will also highlight in chapter 4), it is inaccurate to portray Ghazali as saying that things give no clues that they are caused.[49] On the contrary, Ghazali clearly accepts the "causal maxim," or the "causal principle," according to which any new existent requires a cause for its existence, and the perfection of a result points to the capacity of its cause.[50] Ghazali simply argues that what are habitually called "causes" actually *lack* evidence that they are genuine causes, for they do not possess the will and knowledge needed to plan and execute an orderly event associated with them.[51] Indeed, it is essential that we make a distinction between two positions: one can accept the concept of causality without being forced to accept a certain application of it.[52] Hence, in the above example, Ghazali's rejection of paper and ink as lifesavers did not contradict his acceptance of the king's command as the cause of the person's deliverance.

Contrary to Barry Kogan's critique, which is similar to that of Rahman, there is no irony in Ghazali's stance at all.[53] For Ghazali is not rejecting causality altogether. His challenge to an Aristotelian thinker who attributes causal powers to fire is *not* "How did you come up with a notion of a cause? Why do you think we need a cause for burning?" Rather, his challenge is along the lines of "How do you come to assume that fire is an agent when it does not have any free will or the knowledge to recognize and act consistently according to its substrate?"

In sum, while he accepts the very concept of causality as a nonnegotiable notion in itself, Ghazali argues that given the empirical evidence, what we habitually think of as a cause in nature cannot be the real cause. Hence, the alleged necessity of natural order cannot be rationally justified on the basis of experience, via a posteriori reasoning. He also argues that the necessity of natural causation cannot be established on a priori grounds, on the basis of pure logic, either.

Necessity of Natural Causation Is Not Rationally Justifiable

In his criticism of the necessity of natural causality on a priori grounds, Ghazali is again content to deconstruct the necessity claims. He does not try to prove a priori that fire cannot burn, water cannot give life, a spider cannot be the real maker of the web, and so on. Rather, he simply argues that the necessity of the connection between these events cannot be proved on a priori or logical grounds. Ghazali's central argument for the logical possibility of the interruption of natural causality is as follows:

> [With] any two things, where "this" is not "that" and "that" is not "this" and where neither the affirmation of the one entails the affirmation of the other nor the negation of the one entails the negation of the other . . . it is *not a necessity* of the nonexistence of the one that

the other should not exist—for example, the quenching of the thirst and drinking, satiety and eating, burning and contact with fire, light and the appearance of the sun . . . and so on to [include] all [that is] observable among connected things in medicine, astronomy, arts and crafts.[54]

In other words, as long as what we habitually name as a "natural cause" and "its effect" are not identical events, then affirming one and rejecting the other cannot be logically contradictory.[55] The fact that they have always been observed to be together is not a reason to declare their separation logically impossible. Therefore, for instance, the Qurʾanic story of Abraham's miraculous survival in fire poses no logical problem; it is logically possible that fire may not burn. Similarly, no other miracle narrative in the Qurʾan contradicts logical rules.

As Majid Fakhry noted, Ghazali is prepared to accept three types of logically necessary relations. The first is the "relationship of reciprocity," according to which the negation of one concept necessarily entails the negation of the other—such as right and left, above and below, and so forth.[56] The second is the "relation of antecedence and consequence," which is the relation between condition and the conditioned. For instance, "if we find the knowledge of the person follow upon his life and his will upon his knowledge,"[57] it is necessary to conclude that knowledge may not exist without life and that free will cannot occur without knowledge. Here, Ghazali notes, it is not because life *makes* knowledge that they must go together, but because life is assumed to be the necessary condition of knowledge. The third necessary relation is that of cause and effect, "whereby the negation of the cause necessitates the negation of the effect," if the effect has only one cause. Or, if it has more than one cause, negation of all the causes necessarily negates the effect.[58]

According to Ghazali, the third type of necessary relation—the causal relation—is not proven in the case of what are deemed to be natural causes. For instance, Ghazali notes that the severance of one's neck and his death occur together, but one cannot say that the former necessarily entails the latter unless one *already* knows that there is a necessary link between the two, which is, needless to say, the very thing in question. Thus, one cannot declare any relation between two objects or events to be logically necessary without circular reasoning or a claim to have exhaustive knowledge of all the causes of a given effect. As a result, as Fakhry notes, for Ghazali we can only talk about "two modes of necessary relationship which are logically valid: logical implication and conditional correlation. The transition from these two categories to the category of causality, as an ontological princi-ple—as we have seen, is illegitimate, as is all transition from the order of thought to the order of being."[59]

Ghazali's philosophical defense of miracles through a challenge of the necessity of natural causality was, in fact, a turning point, for it "explode[d] the notion that causal necessity, as the philosophers understood it, and logi-cal necessity are different sides of the same coin."[60] Indeed, by making a clear distinction between logical and empirical statements, and the realms of the intelligible and the actual, Ghazali introduced a radical shift in the way modalities were conceived in ancient Greek and medieval Muslim phi-losophy. The latter followed a statistical model according to which the pos-sibility of a thing was defined in terms of temporal existence:

A temporally unqualified sentence like, "Fire causes cotton to com-bust," contains implicitly or explicitly a reference to the time of utter-ance as part of its meaning. If this sentence is true whenever uttered, it is necessarily true. If its truth-value can change in the course of time, it is possible. If such a sentence is false whenever uttered, it is impossible. In Aristotelian modal theories, modal terms were taken to refer to the one and only historical world of ours. For Avicenna, fire necessarily causes cotton to combust because the sentence "Fire causes cotton to combust," was, is, and will always be true.[61]

In contrast, Ghazali's defense of the possibility of miracles introduced a new conception of modalities that is "closer to our modern view of the modalities as referring to synchronic alternative states of affairs. In the modern model, the notion of necessity refers to what obtains in all alterna-tives, the notion of possibility refers to what obtains in at least one alterna-tive, and that which is impossible does not obtain in any conceivable state of affairs."[62] Thus, that which has never obtained in our world does not cease to be a possibility, and that which has always obtained in our world does not become logically necessary. With his dissolution of Aristotelian "iso-morphism of the domains of reality, possibility and intelligibility," Ghazali brought about a breakthrough that broadened the horizons of imagination and creativity.[63] And it is this breakthrough that lies at the heart of modern epistemology.[64]

Taking the literal sense of Qurʾanic miracle stories seriously has enabled Ghazali to be a pioneer in the way we conceptualize the world around us today. As we shall also see in chapters 4 and 5, such a synchronic view of modalities enables the conception of possibilities that have not been experienced in the past and thus propel the progress of science. This novel step, however, also needs to brace for an important objection: In admitting the contingency of natural order, are we giving up our common sense? As we shall see in the next chapter, Ibn Rushd feared that Ghazali's vision would unleash far-fetched fancies in our daily reasoning and thereby undermine scientific enterprise completely. After all, if the current natural order is utterly contingent, why should one rely on past experimentation and observation to predict the future? Why bother to study natural order if it is logically possible for it to change at any minute? While making room for miracles and a new epistemology, are we sacrificing our sense of stability and the possibility of scientific knowledge? In what follows, we shall observe how Ghazali anticipates such concerns and responds to them.

The Possibility of Science and Common Sense Within Ghazali's Scheme of Causality

As discussed in the next chapter, Ibn Rushd argued that no human knowledge is possible if we cannot admit necessary connections between objects in nature. Ghazali was not unaware of this line of critique, and in *Incoherence of the Philosophers* he provides a summary of such an objection, which is worth quoting at length:

> This [rejection of the necessity of natural causation] leads to the commission of repugnant contradictions. For if one denies that the effects follow necessarily from their causes and relates them to the will of their Creator, *the will having no specific designated course but [a course that] can vary and change in kind*, then let each of us allow the possibility of there being in front of him ferocious beasts, raging fires, high mountains, or enemies ready with their weapons [to kill him], but [also the possibility] that he does not see them because God does not create for him [vision of them]. . . . Or if he leaves a [servant] boy in his house let him allow the possibility of his changing into a dog; or [again] if he leaves ashes, [let him allow] the possibility of its change into musk, and let him allow the possibility of stone changing into gold and gold into stone. If asked about any of this, he ought to say: "I

do not know what is at the house at present. All I know is I left a book in the house, which is perhaps now a horse that has defiled the library with its urine and dung, and that I have left in the house a jar of water, which may have turned into an apple tree. For God is capable of everything and it is not necessary for the horse to be created from the sperm, nor the tree to be created from the seed—indeed, it is not necessary for either of the two to be created from anything. Perhaps [God] has created things that did not exist previously."[65]

In addition to such colorful examples, Ghazali's opponent offers another hypothetical case: if Ghazali is arguing for the contingency of natural order, then he should admit that a dead man, who can neither see nor think, can compose meaningful texts. After all, Ghazali contends that there is no logical link between natural causes and their effects, and God can connect any two things if he wishes. And yet such an admission in turn will destroy the basis for any kind of coherent inference in daily life.[66] In anticipating the future, Ghazali's approach seems to open the door to all kinds of wild fantasies; if there is no necessity in the current order, then anything can be expected at any moment.

As Blake D. Dutton notes, "Ghazali's response to all of this is instructive. Standing firmly upon his Ashʿarite convictions, he does not deny that any of these conjunctions and transformations *could* take place. They are all perfectly possible according to his view. Instead, he argues that these possibilities need not lead us into skepticism."[67] In other words, Ghazali resists giving up his philosophical breakthrough for the sake of soothing our common sense. Of course, he still defends common sense, but not by collapsing ontological and logical statements back together. Instead, he first notes that although in theory these fantastic things *are* possible, it does not mean they are probable or should be expected to happen. He argues that we need not and ought not take all hypothetical possibilities into account in everyday life.[68] For if it were "established that the possible is such that there cannot be created for man knowledge of its nonbeing, these impossibilities would necessarily follow."[69] In other words, if it was proven that one can *not* ever confidently disregard a theoretical possibility, then indeed one would have to dread the possibility of all kinds of strange things happening at any moment. And yet this is not proven. There is no logical inconsistency in conceding the hypothetical possibility of an event *while* expecting it not to happen, or even being *certain* that it will not take place. This is similar to the way one may know for sure that a person will not arrive in town today, even though it is theoretically possible that he could.[70] In the same way, we might add, the possibility that we may die tomorrow does not stop us from making plans for the future. Thus, Ghazali's reply to the example of the dead man admits its hypothetical possibility and yet insists that it should not be taken seriously:

> As for God's moving the hand of the dead man, setting it up in the form of a living person who is seated and writes so that through the movement of his hand ordered writing ensues, [this] in itself is not impossible as long as we turn over [the enactment of] temporal events to the will of a choosing being [i.e., God]. *It is only disavowed because of the continuous habit of its opposite occurring.* Your statement that, with this, *the well-designed act ceases to indicate the [existence of] the knowledge of the agent is not true.* For the agent now is God, who is the performer of the well-designed act and [the] knower of it.[71]

Thus, Ghazali admits the *logical possibility* of a dead man being made to compose a text *so long as* we posit another being (who is alive, willing, and knowing) as the real agent who does the composing. There is no logical impossibility that an agent with appropriate qualities of power and knowledge could make a dead man an instrument of such a coherent work—perhaps not unlike a pen, in itself ignorant and lifeless, being an instrument of an alive, willing, and knowing author. Ghazali consistently adheres to his distinction between the logical and the empirical, and between causal maxim as a logical principle and causal judgments made on the basis of past experience.[72] And, because of this distinction, he can confidently reject the claim that a dead man was seen composing articles: since realms of logic and realms of empirical reality are distinct, affirming one and negating the other may be perfectly feasible. Thus, the example of the dead man is a logical possibility that is to be rejected as an empirical claim.

To be sure, Ghazali's demonstration of the non-contradiction of these two statements solves the problem only partially. He has yet to explain *on what basis* one can expect the natural order to continue. This brings us to Ghazali's alternative scheme, which forms his second answer to the fantasy question. According to Ghazali, to deny that there is a logically necessary link among things in nature does not mean that the current order is the result of chance, nor does it mean that there is no stability in the observed order. On the contrary, the fact that so far one has observed consistency in the behavior of things and in the sequence of events suggests that the events are *not* happening haphazardly as a result of blind chance. This state of affairs has a "hidden syllogistic power" (*qūwa qiyāsīyya khafīya*) in suggesting that, if the order were "coincidental or accidental, it would not have continued always or for the most part without deviation."[73] Indeed, Avicenna, Ghazali, and Ghazali's famous opponent Ibn Rushd all agree that there is a hidden syllogism suggested to us by our observation of the natural order. And yet they differ on what the hidden implication of this is. For Ghazali's opponents, it is the "inherent causal properties of things and events" that enable such a consistency in nature.[74] In contrast, according to Ghazali, the consistent patterns in nature can be attributed neither to chance nor to an inherent necessity among things themselves. Rather, they call for something else—namely, a conscious, willing, and powerful creator. The intentionality manifested in the natural order belongs to this ever-present being called "God."

For Ghazali, then, the order is explained by the will, power, and knowledge of a divine being. There is consistency in events—for example, the burning of cotton following contact with fire—because *someone* chooses to create consistently in that way. Ghazali names this concept *ijrā* al-ʿāda, which literally means "carrying out the habit." It refers to God's "habitual" execution of the acts of creation according to a plan devised by him. According to this concept, which was held by Ashʿarite theologians in general,[75] events happen in a certain way because God chooses to create them in that particular way. To give another example, a stone always falls when left unsupported because God decreed in pre-eternity that he would create the falling under these circumstances and does so each time. The *ijrā* al-ʿāda concept affirms the order in the universe and thereby allows the predictability of future events, without subscribing to a necessary causation between the events.[76] As Marmura aptly summarizes, according to Ghazali, "there is order, to be sure; indeed, there is connection" between natural events, yet "the source of this order and of the connection is elsewhere," not inherent in nature itself but in the divine will, which creates according to certain patterns.[77]

For Ghazali, the basis for anticipating the order that will continue is the consistent plan of the maker, God. Thus, in the *Standard of Knowledge*, he confidently notes that a reasonable person will not suspect the order to change at any minute. If, for instance, you are informed that your son has been beheaded, you can be sure that he is dead—"no rational man would doubt this." An occasionalist theologian's assertion that there is no necessary connection between decapitation and death does not in any way oppose such certainty because

> the theologian admits the *fact* of death, but inquires about the *manner of connection* between decapitation and death. As for the inquiry as to whether this is a necessary consequence of the thing itself, impossible to change, or whether this is in accordance with the passage of the custom (*sunna*) of God, the Exalted, due to the fulfillment of His will that can undergo neither substitution nor change, *this is an inquiry into the mode of connection, not into the connection itself*. Let this be understood and let it be known that to doubt the death of someone whose head has been severed is nothing but seductive suggestion [of the devil] and that belief in the death of such a person cannot be doubted.[78]

Therefore, Ghazali's stance is quite different from speculative occasionalism, in which fancies are given serious consideration.[79] Indeed, an essential aspect of Ghazali's understanding of natural causality is the grounding of natural sciences—that is, the successful prediction of future events on the basis of past experience, including experimentation.[80] We shall return to Ghazali's notion of stability in nature in the next chapter, when we consider Ibn Rushd's objections to it. In what follows, we shall analyze one last objection to Ghazali's view that natural order is a contingent entity fully dependent on divine power at all times. This objection and Ghazali's answer to it will summarize Ghazali's a priori and a posteriori critiques of natural causality and further clarify his understanding of logical impossibility, which goes along with his reading of Qur'anic miracle stories.

Observation, Logic, and Natural Causation

In *Moderation in Belief*, Ghazali notes another objection to his argument that all things in existence are dependent on divine power:

> If it is said [in opposition to us]: "How do you claim that the [divine] power pertains in general to all beings that originated in time? For, the events in the world and most of things like that are born out of each other, and some of them necessarily [*bi al-ḍarūrā*] produce [*yatawalladu*] the other ones. For instance, the movement of the hand

necessarily brings into being the movement of the ring [on the finger], and the movement of the hand in water produces the movement of the water. *This is before our eyes [mushāhid] and also known by reason [al-ʿaql ayḍan yadillu ʿalayh]. If the movement of the ring and the water were [happening] by creation of God,* then it would have been possible for Him to create the movement of the hand without the movement of the ring and the movement of the hand without water."[81]

Here, the opponent expects Ghazali to demonstrate that the interruption of a particular sequence is logically possible so as to prove that the events in a particular series are *not* connected with one another intrinsically. Ghazali had offered such an analysis in the case of causal relations such as the relation between fire and the burning of cotton, but with regard to the cases noted in this example, it is not likely that Ghazali can prove that. The challenge is this: Can Ghazali argue that the ring on the finger *does not have to move* when the finger moves or that water *does not have to move* when the hand moves in water? If he cannot, then he has to admit that movement of the hand necessarily produces the movement of the ring, and similarly the movement of the water is caused by the movement of the hand in the water. And one need not refer to God's agency to explain either of these consequences; they are known through both observation and logic.

Ghazali replies by first demanding a clarification of the term *tawallud* (literally, begetting or producing), which is the term the opponent used when he stated that things in nature beget each other.[82] Ghazali says that the word "beget" can mean two different things: being *produced* by something or *coming out of* it. This distinction is important to understanding Ghazali's position; let us discuss it in two points.

First, Ghazali accepts the word "begetting" in this context only in the sense of a thing *coming out of* another thing. Thus, for instance, one can say that the baby is coming out of the womb and that plants grow out of the soil. It is in this sense of the word that one witnesses begetting clearly in the world, and Ghazali has no dispute with such a claim. Yet, this sense of the term "begetting" (*tawallud*) does not apply to the examples given by his opponent. The movement of the ring is not coming out of a "depository" within the movement of the hand; thus, the term *tawallud* is not applicable here in the sense in which Ghazali understands it.

Second, the term *tawallud* can also be used in the sense of a thing *producing* another thing. This is not at all obvious or observed, as the opponent claims. It is this sense of the word that Ghazali is objecting to. Thus,

Ghazali would question the claim that the baby is produced *by* the womb or that the plants are made *by* the soil. Similarly, the opponent cannot show how he witnesses the movement of the ring being produced by the movement of the hand: "For, it is only possible to observe that the movement [of the ring or the water] is *with* the movement of the hand. Yet, it is not possible to observe that this movement *is born out of* the movement of the hand."[83]

Ghazali's clarification is helpful and parallels his argument in *Incoherence of the Philosophers* that the event of natural causation is not actually observed "out there" but is an interpretation that we posit. Yet the opponent's argument is still not fully addressed. Even though Ghazali can conceive that the plant--soil relationship or the burning effect of fire can be altered in theory, he admits that he cannot conceive that the hand-water relationship can be altered: it does seem that moving the hand without displacing any water is impossible, for "two things cannot occupy the same space at the same time."[84] But, then, how can Ghazali argue that this inevitable result requires God's power, rather than being produced by the very nature of things?

According to Ghazali, this argument that "if the movements of the ring and the water were created by God, then it would have been possible for him to create one without the other" is not a sound argument. This is because it is tantamount to saying that if knowledge were not born out of will, then it would have been possible for God to create will in a man without creating knowledge, or to create knowledge without will. In other words, the fact that one cannot conceive of God reversing or modifying a particular relation does not automatically mean that such a relation is taking place without the immediate need for God's power, and because of natural causes. Even if there is an unchangeable relation between an antecedent event (e.g., movement of the hand) and its consequent (e.g., movement of the ring), this does not prove that the former is causing the latter. Thus, again we see Ghazali prepared to confer *logical necessity* to conditionals (e.g., my life is a condition for my knowing) but not to natural causation (e.g., my life is a cause of my knowledge).

It is important to make this distinction, for it shows how Ghazali defines logical necessity. As he notes in *Incoherence of the Philosophers*, Ghazali concedes that God's power, despite being absolute and all pervasive, does not pertain to that which is logically contradictory: "The impossible thing is not within the power [of being enacted]" (*inna al-muḥāl ghayr maqdūr ʿalayhi*). And he explains what he understands to be logically impossible:

"The impossible consists in affirming a thing conjointly with denying it, affirming the more specific while denying the more general, or affirming two things while negating one [of them]. What does not reduce to this is not impossible, and what is not impossible is within [divine] power."[85] In sum, Ghazali does accept a category of "logical impossibility" and also affirms that logically contradictory situations do not pertain to God's power. He simply does not consider natural causality as a logically necessary relation. Hence, its modification in the rare case of miracles is perfectly acceptable from a logical point of view.

Thus, Ghazali made a compelling and nuanced case for reading miracle stories literally and also argued that such acceptance of a possibility of change in the natural order need not disrupt our common sense—we can go about our everyday business without any expectation of radical raptures. The crucial hermeneutical question here is whether such an approach has any direct implication for a believer's life. That is, if one is to go about her life as usual, what is the point of assenting that miracles narrated in the Qur'an literally took place or that natural order is a contingent process? Recall the anecdote I mentioned earlier: If a reader believes in the virgin birth story in the Qur'an, would it make any difference in her life? Ghazali would agree that surely such a miracle story is *not* about giving the benefit of the doubt to pregnant women who claim to be virgins, but, then, does such a miracle story offer *any* other implication for the reader? This question takes us right into an apparent contradiction that emerges in Ghazali's attitude toward miracles in general.

Ghazali's Insightful Ambivalence: An Existential Reading of Miracle Stories

As will be recalled, in his theological and philosophical works Ghazali argued that miracles play a key role in proving the authenticity of a messenger of God, albeit with the caveat that miracles work as proofs only if the basic message proclaimed by the prophet makes sense. However, Ghazali introduces more disclaimers to this position in his later works, to the point of almost reversing what he had said earlier.

His first disclaimer is that miraculous events have no value when accompanied by *a claim that is irrelevant*. If, for instance, someone claims to have mastered a particular subject, it would be convincing if that person demonstrated his knowledge by presenting what he knows. If he instead wants to prove it by walking on water, it does not count as evidence, for the evidence is irrelevant to what is sought to be proven.[86] Such a qualification of the evidentiary power of miracles sounds quite fair, of course. What is surprising is that Ghazali goes further, voicing a complete suspicion of miracles. Alluding again to the celebrated miracle of Moses in the Qur'an, Ghazali notes that it is possible that the turning of the staff into a serpent may be a deception or an illusion, or "at most a remarkable feat" with no religious significance whatsoever.[87] Indeed, in his autobiography, while reflecting on the role of miracles in strengthening faith, Ghazali almost reverses what he had said earlier in *Faysal* and *Iqtisād*: "I believe in the veracity of Muhammad—Peace be upon him!—and in the veracity of Moses—Peace be upon him!—not by reason of the splitting of the moon, and the changing of the staff into a serpent: for that way is open to ambiguity and one may not rely on it. [It cannot be trusted]." He even goes on to say that the one who believes in the prophet simply because of the "changing of the staff into a serpent" ends up "worshipping the golden calf"—an allusion to the idolatry incident mentioned in the Qur'an (Q. 2:51, 2:93, 7:148, 20:85–91).[88] Thus, the value of miracles in strengthening faith may be quite weak. Instead of miracles, Ghazali adds, one should analyze the consistency and truthfulness of the prophetic message. Only then is one's knowledge of the prophet assured, and it becomes a *necessary knowledge*; the conviction is clearer than the conviction that would result "were he [the prophet] to change a thousand sticks into snakes."[89]

Scholars have been puzzled by Ghazali's apparently contradictory remarks. For instance, Richard McCarthy relates that Arend T. van Leeuwen finds it irreconcilable that in *Deliverance from Error* Ghazali insists that miracles do not count much for the formation of one's religious convictions, while in *Incoherence of the Philosophers* he strongly defends the literal sense of miracle stories.[90] This stance of Ghazali is indeed surprising, but actually not contradictory. Ghazali's defense of the possibility of miracles need not be about defending the evidentiary value of miracles in general. After all, these two issues have different registers; while the logical possibility of an event can be applicable across ages, the evidentiary value of miracles is highly contextual. For instance, as Ghazali clearly recognizes in his discussions of the reliability of reports from Prophet Muhammad, there is a crucial difference between a person who actually witnesses a prophetic miracle and the one who lives centuries later and only receives written or oral reports of such extraordinary events. The former experiences something directly and has to discern whether it is a genuine miracle or an act of sorcery or illusion, while the latter has a different challenge: he is called to assess the claims of a distant generation and faces the additional question of the historical reliability of the reports. Given these differences in context, it is obvious that there cannot be one general attitude toward the miracles in general, as far as their evidentiary value is concerned.

In fact, Ghazali's defense of the literal sense of miracles has a purpose other than simply upholding the evidentiary value of miracles. In the process of arguing for the possibility of miracles, Ghazali makes the case for a new existential perspective on the universe. To accept the *possibility* of miracles is to accept that the natural order is not a logical *given* but a *gift*. Provoked by these stories, therefore, the believers admit the utter contingency of the world around them and reach out for a deeper awareness of their vulnerability. Such awareness then translates into admitting human indebtedness and gratitude to the creator of a dynamically created and regular, yet contingent, universe. In other words, Ghazali's "metaphysics of contingency" is linked to a "metaphysics of grace." Since "the world could have been constructed in a way radically different from the way it was" and "might just as well be utterly annihilated in the very next moment, or in the moment after that, it is only proper that we prostrate before this vision of utter contingency."[91] For Ghazali, the world around us is a gift, its orderliness is a gift, and even our ability to habitually expect the natural order to continue is a gift.[92] It is out of God's mercy that we are able to experience regularity around us as well as feel confident about our predictions of the future on the basis of consistency and continuity in our past experiences.

Ghazali's nuanced epistemological and existential engagement with miracle stories also provides a key to the hermeneutical puzzle in the Qurʾan that I suggested in the introduction. As will be recalled, the Qurʾanic discourse harbors a curious juxtaposition: it includes not only miracle narratives but also a criticism of the demands for miracles and a repeated claim that the natural world contains sufficient evidence for faith. From a Ghazalian perspective, the presence of miracle narratives within a discourse that de-emphasizes the miraculous is indeed coherent. For the miracle stories are not told primarily to provide evidence for faith; rather, they are told to initiate a breakthrough in the way the reader perceives nature and to enhance the awareness of "signs" of God (*āyāt*) in nature. In the final chapter, we shall turn to a contemporary Muslim interpreter, Said Nursi, who extends and clarifies these implications of Ghazali's approach for a modern context. For now, however, we shall consider a famous opponent of Ghazali, Ibn Rushd, who struggled with Ghazali's interpretation of natural causality and offered almost an opposite take on miracles. While Ibn Rushd misses the significance of Ghazali's approach, his views are also worthy of attention. Indeed, Ibn Rushd will help us explore what crucial insights lurk behind resistance to a literal reading of Qur'anic miracle stories.

A CAUTIOUS APPROACH TO MIRACLE STORIES: IBN RUSHD'S CASE FOR RATIONALISM AND DIVINE WISDOM

It was He [God] who spread out the earth for you and traced routes in it. He sent down water from the sky. With that water We [God] bring forth every kind of plant, so eat, and graze your cattle. There are truly signs in all this for people of understanding.

—Qurʾan 20:53–54

Do they not see the sky above them—how We have built and adorned it, with no rifts in it; how We spread out the earth and put solid mountains on it, and caused every kind of joyous plant to grow in it, as a lesson and reminder for every servant who turns to God; and how We send blessed water down from the sky and grow with it gardens, the harvest grain. . . .

—Qurʾan 50:6–9

Abu al-Walīd Muḥammad Ibn Rushd (d. 1198), also known in the Latin West as Averroes, was one of the major thinkers of medieval Islam. In addition to writing on philosophy, he composed works on Islamic juris-prudence and on medicine. Moreover, he served as a judge in the Islamic courts of Spain and as a physician for the caliphs. Among his various con-tributions, his commitment to Aristotelian philosophy and his attempts at reconciling it with the Qurʾan are central. He gave utmost importance to logic and science, which he believed were crystallized in "Master" Aristot-le's works, and interpreted the Qurʾan in a way that coheres with them. Ibn Rushd's approach offers a great example of resisting the absurd and mythi-cal readings of Qurʾanic miracle stories and making an interesting case for rationality and science. Ibn Rushd does this by strongly and explicitly denouncing Ghazali's critique of natural causation on logical and scriptural grounds. However, before we delve into Ibn Rushd's response to Ghazali, a brief biographical sketch is in order.

Ibn Rushd was born in 1126 in Cordova, Spain, a city that was known to be home to philosophic and scientific studies and hospitable to people of different faiths living in relative harmony under Muslim rule.[1] His father was a judge in the Islamic court of Cordova. Ibn Rushd studied Arabic, letters (adab), Islamic jurisprudence, theology, philosophy, and medicine. When he was in his late twenties, there was a change in the political authority and he was called by the new Almohad caliph, ʿAbd al-Muʾmin, to Marrakesh, Morocco, and named advisor to the caliph's great project of building learning institutions throughout the dynastic realm. Ibn Rushd also served the caliph's successor, Abu Yaʿqub, who appointed him as the judge of Seville. Abu Yaʿqub had a personal interest in philosophy and encouraged Ibn Rushd to write commentaries on Aristotle. Thus, during this period (ca. 1169–82), he authored commentaries of various lengths on Aristotle's works.[2] Later, Ibn Rushd also composed treatises on the relationship between religion and philosophy. One of his major texts was Incoherence of the Incoherence (Tahāfut al-tahāfut), a running commentary and critique of Ghazali's Incoherence of the Philosophers.

In Ibn Rushd's final years, the previously supportive royal court turned against him. The reason for this change in the caliph's attitude is unclear. The biographical accounts note that he was charged with being too interested in "the sciences of the Ancients"[3] and that he was also blamed for denying the literal sense of a miracle story.[4] Given that some traditional theologians were exiled along with him to Lucena, a small town near Cordova, during a time of impending war with the Christian neighbors, it is unlikely that his loss of favor was simply due to his philosophical views. Ibn Rushd's exile lasted for two years, after which he was called back to the court in Marrakesh and once again honored by the caliph. Ibn Rushd died shortly thereafter, in 1198.

Unlike Ghazali, Ibn Rushd's works did not find a wide audience in the Muslim world after his death. To be sure, his works on Islamic jurisprudence and medicine continued to be utilized and appreciated in the traditional circles, but his philosophy was only partially engaged and often criticized. His criticism of Ghazali and Ashʿarism was not well received on the whole, and this may be the chief reason why his philosophical views did not gain as much attention. In the Latin West and among Jewish thinkers, on the other hand, his exposition of Aristotle was highly admired, and he became regarded as *the* commentator on Aristotle. Schools of Averroism emerged in the thirteenth century, especially in France and Italy, attracting the criticism of the Catholic Church, which condemned Averroes and his teachings as heretical. Yet even Saint Thomas Aquinas, an adamant opponent of Averroism, could not help but benefit from Averroes in understanding Aristotle and in formulating his proofs for the existence of God. Ibn Rushd's works, variously understood—and misunderstood—by Averroists, also enjoyed a "second life" around the time of the Renaissance, becoming a symbol for rationalism and free society.[5] Finally, his scientific treatises, especially the ones on astronomy with a critique of the geocentric system, became a precursor to Galileo's and Copernicus's revolution in astronomy.

Just as we needed to be careful in navigating Ghazali's corpus, Ibn Rushd's writings require diligence. Aside from the fact that he changed some of his views over time, he wrote in different genres and was also very conscious of the different needs of different audiences. Fortunately, we do have a few clues at hand to justly discern his approach to Qur'anic miracle stories. The first clue comes from his theory of Qur'anic interpretation, which outlines his understanding of layers of meaning within the Qur'anic discourse. The second is from his famous contention with Ghazali over natural causality and miracles. Finally, we will turn to his philosophical discourse aimed more at specialists and note his indirect references to miracles in that context.

Ibn Rushd's Approach to the Qur'an

Ibn Rushd offers his theory of scriptural interpretation (*qānūn al-ta'wīl*) in the *Decisive Treatise*, which is devoted to the relationship between Greek wisdom or philosophy (*ḥikma*) and revelation (*shar*ʿ), as its original title also indicates (*Kitāb Faṣl al-maqāl wa taqrīr mā bayn al-sharīʿa wa al-ḥikma min al-ittiṣāl*).[6] In this work, Ibn Rushd argues for the harmony between the two, opposing those who regard Greek philosophy as antithetical to religion. As he defends the legitimacy of philosophical inquiry on the basis of the Qur'an, he also puts forth his Qur'anic hermeneutics.

Ibn Rushd first defines the aim of philosophy as studying and reflecting on beings as they point to "the Artisan"—that is, God. Obviously, this definition strikes a chord with the major Qur'anic theme on nature. He then notes that since the Qur'an urges reflection on the beings so as to know the Creator, the study of philosophy is essential from a Qur'anic perspective:

That the Law [scripture] calls for consideration of existing things by means of the intellect and pursuing cognizance of them by means of it is clear from various verses of the Book of God (may He be blessed and exalted). There is His statement, may He be exalted, "Consider, you who have sight" [59:2]; this is a text for the obligation of using both intellectual and Law-based syllogistic reasoning. And there is His statement (may He be exalted), "Have they not reflected on the kingdoms of the heavens and the earth, and whatever things God has created?" [7:185]; this is a text urging reflection upon all existing things. And, God, (may He be exalted), has made it known that one of those whom He selected and venerated by means of this knowledge was Abraham, (peace upon him); thus He, (may He be exalted) said, "In this way we made Abraham see the kingdoms of the heavens and the earth, that he might be . . ." [and so on to the end of] the verse [6:75].[7] And He, (may He be exalted), said: "Do they not reflect upon the camels, how they have been created, and upon the heaven, how it has been raised up?" [88:17]. And, He said, "and they ponder the creation of the heavens and the earth" [3:191]—and so on in innumerable other verses.[8]

That the Qurʾan calls for using one's reason and reflecting how things in nature point to God would be fairly obvious to most readers of Ibn Rushd, but what Ibn Rushd needs to establish is that a particular literature—namely, Greek philosophy—is necessary for such a reflection. He insists that in order to effectively carry out this Qurʾanic commandment to reflect on nature, one must be equipped with the proper tools; only through the study of logic and philosophy can one do justice to the Qurʾanic call, and one should not shun learning from the "ancients" (i.e., Greeks) who mastered these tools.[9] Ibn Rushd concedes that these tools of the ancients were misused by some, who thought that they disproved religion on the basis of philosophy. He insists, however, that this misuse is accidental to philosophy and not essential to it. One should not suspect all philosophical inquiry simply because of the mistakes of some philosophers.[10] Instead, the truth is that the study of philosophy is either an obligation or commendable from a Qurʾanic perspective.[11]

Ibn Rushd adds a disclaimer, so to speak, to his argument that expertise in philosophy is required by the Qurʾan. He notes that *not* all addressees of the Qurʾan are obliged to engage in philosophical study. Here, Ibn Rushd introduces his crucial distinction between revelation and philosophy: revelation addresses all humanity, while philosophy is suitable only for certain people.

Different Classes of Interpreters

Following three types of reasoning in Aristotelian logic, Ibn Rushd notes that there are three ways of delivering a message: rhetorically (*khitābī*), dialectically (*jadalī*), and demonstratively (*burhānī*). Each believer assents to faith in a manner that is appropriate to his nature. Common people are usually convinced by the rhetorical aspect, while theologians need dialectical methods and philosophers respond to demonstration. In other words, not all people need to engage in philosophical reflection to recognize the truth; only some need and are capable of comprehending a demonstrative approach to scripture. Ibn Rushd argues that in this comprehensiveness lies the universal appeal of Islam: it offers something for everyone.[12]

In *Uncovering Methods of Proof (Al-Kashf ʿan manāhij al-adilla)*, a methodological work devoted to explaining theological issues in a "demonstrative" way, Ibn Rushd offers an example of how the same end can be attained in two different ways, which need not cancel out or disparage each other. His example is how one comes to believe in God. Again highlighting the Qurʾanic discourse on nature, Ibn Rushd notes that the Qurʾan provides two types of arguments for the existence of the Creator: the argument from providence (*dalīl al-ʿināyah*) and the argument from invention (*dalīl al-ikhtiraʿ*), such as the creation of life out of inanimate substances. These two arguments, as formulated by Ibn Rushd, have been widely acclaimed and utilized in Islamic theology. According to him, different classes of people appreciate them differently:

The two ways [the argument from providence and the argument from invention] are exactly the ways of the extraordinary [i.e., the elect], (and I mean by the extraordinary the scientists) and the ways of the common people. And the difference between the two ways lies in the details. . . . The example of the common people in knowing the existent beings is similar to those who view things without having any knowledge of *the way* they are made. All they know of them is only that they are made and that they have a maker. And the example of the scientists is similar to those who view things knowing how they were made and the wisdom employed in making them.[13]

In other words, while the scholars have a more profound grasp of these evidences in nature, both the elite and the common people have some insight into truth. This is one of the various examples with which Ibn Rushd tries to show that there *are* different ways of understanding the Qur'an and that each way is adequate and suited to its audience.

It is worth keeping in mind that Ibn Rushd considers philosophers to have insight into the *wisdom of the way* natural things are made. As we shall note later, it is the philosophers' understanding of the natural processes that allows them to approach the Qur'anic miracle stories differently than the common people. It is also important to note that through this defense of philosophy and the disclaimer that its study is meant only for some, Ibn Rushd protects both the *legitimacy* and the *privacy* of philosophy. Common believers should both *respect* the philosophical endeavor and *leave* it to its experts. Indeed, philosophers, given their expertise, have a deeper grasp of the Qur'an and are allowed a more metaphorical approach to the Qur'an than the common people.

Ibn Rushd's Theory of Scriptural Interpretation

As will be recalled from the earlier discussion of Ghazali, in the mainstream Islamic discourse, diversion from the literal sense of the text was already permitted, albeit under certain conditions.[14] Therefore, Ibn Rushd did not have to argue for the permissibility of metaphorical interpretation of the Qur'an, but he did have to argue for the extent of it. Unlike Ghazali, Ibn Rushd places less stringent conditions on the boundaries of a metaphorical reading that supersedes the literal one. Rather, he thinks that if one can reasonably judge that the text becomes more meaningful when it is interpreted metaphorically, then the literal sense can be easily abandoned for a metaphorical reading. It seems that "in only one case does Averroes *demand* an argument founded on reason in order to justify a proposed interpretation: that is, if a verse in the revelation is to be read metaphorically and this understanding is inferior to the wording of the Qur'an."[15]

While Ibn Rushd is more inclined to metaphorical readings, it is not easy to delineate the difference between Ghazali's and Ibn Rushd's approaches in theory. Both agree that scriptural text conforms to reason, and both are willing to prefer a metaphorical reading over a literal reading if the former seems to be more insightful. The fairly obvious difference is, of course, their disagreement over what constitutes reasonable and insightful. Indeed, unlike Ghazali's more open approach to the text, Ibn Rushd has a fairly specific and limited notion of what best represents rationality and insight: the Aristotelian philosophy.

Ibn Rushd's leniency toward metaphorical readings is framed with the warning that not everyone can do justice to metaphorical interpretation. Not surprisingly, different classes of interpreters also differ in the extent to which they can diverge from the literal sense of a given verse. According to Ibn Rushd, the Qur'an contains three types of passages, which can be summarized as follows:

(1) Passages that should be taken literally by all three classes—rhetorical, dialectical, and demonstrative.

(2) Passages that should be taken literally by people receptive to rhetorical and dialectical methods, but not by the demonstrative class. These passages *must* only be interpreted allegorically by the demonstrative class. As an example, Ibn Rushd gives the case of a woman whose faith in God Muhammad confirmed when she told him that God is in heaven. The statement was acceptable for that illiterate woman as her statement of faith, but for a member of the demonstrative class, such a statement is not permissible except when it is spoken metaphorically. This is because the demonstrative class must know that God is beyond residing in any location.

(3) Passages whose classification in the above two categories is uncertain. Those in the demonstrative class are excused if they err in interpreting these passages. Just as a doctor is excused when he makes a mistake in his diagnosis or a judge is excused when he errs in his judgment of a case, a member of the demonstrative class is excused when he mistakenly takes a literally intended passage metaphorically.[16]

In the third case, Ibn Rushd is not simply asking that one indulge unintentional mistakes on the part of philosophers. Rather, he is clarifying who is *permitted* to make mistakes in which cases. A skilled physician can be excused when he makes a mistake in prescribing a medicine, but a false physician can never be excused, for he was initially in the wrong for attempting to judge a matter beyond his capacity. In the same way, while the philosopher is excused when he mistakenly prefers a metaphorical interpretation over a literal one, a common person is not excused for a similar mistake. Needless to say, the excuse is granted to the philosopher only when the text does not clearly fall into the first category, in which case it must be taken literally by all classes.[17]

Ibn Rushd's classifications revolve around the principle of not giving "meat to babes." After all, if the inclinations and capacities of common people and philosophers are different, then care should be taken to avoid confusing the common people. Ibn Rushd is adamant that disclosing allegorical interpretations in public can be very dangerous, for it can cause lasting harm to the nonspecialist. One pertinent example can be drawn from the Qur'anic passages regarding life after death. In the Qur'an, the pleasures and pains of the afterlife are described not only in spiritual terms but also in vivid physical terms. The Qur'an talks about paradise gardens under which rivers flow (e.g., Q. 2:25, 3:15), raised couches on which the people of paradise recline (e.g., Q. 18:31), and drinks served in crystal cups (e.g., Q. 75:5–6). Alternatively, it warns of the terrible fire and boiling water in hell, shackles and bitter fruits, and so forth (e.g., Q. 44:43–46, 76:4). According to Ibn Rushd, these texts on the afterlife fall into the first category insofar as the existence of an afterlife is a nonnegotiable aspect of faith; all classes, including the philosophers, must take the existence of the afterlife noted in the Qur'an literally. In contrast, the question of whether the descriptions of the afterlife should also be taken literally is a matter open to discussion among the demonstrative class—that is, the philosophers—and hence such descriptions fall into the third category. If some philosophers interpret these passages of punishment and reward allegorically and affirm only that there are spiritual consequences in the afterlife, they cannot be accused of heresy. They may well be mistaken, but they are not rejecting anything that is essential to Islamic faith, nor are they swerving from the path of the truth. At the same time, such a harmless (if uncertain) metaphorical interpretation must be kept secret from the common person who is not skilled at demonstration, for he will not comprehend what necessitates allegorical interpretation in the case of bodily resurrection.[18] It seems that, according to Ibn Rushd, if the demonstrative perspective is disclosed to the common person, he will not only have no use for it but also risk losing his own rhetorically driven understanding of the Qur'an. The incentives that common people derive from the Qur'an by taking the corporeal accounts of punishment and reward literally will be lost, and they will thus be discouraged from following divine guidance.

With regard to the issue of the corporeality of the afterlife, Ibn Rushd criticizes Ghazali for simultaneously committing two wrongs. He argues that Ghazali unjustly blamed the philosophers for preferring a nonliteral reading of corporeal descriptions of the afterlife in the Qur'an[19] and that he harmed the faith of the common people by disclosing his critique of the philosophers to the public. Ibn Rushd rebukes Ghazali in very strong terms:

> For anyone whose duty it is to believe in the apparent meaning, allegorical interpretation is unbelief, because it leads to unbelief. Anyone of the interpretative class who discloses such [an interpretation] to him is summoning him to unbelief, and he who summons to unbelief is an unbeliever.
>
> Therefore allegorical interpretations ought to be set down only in demonstrative books, because if they are in demonstrative books they are encountered by no one but men of the demonstrative class. But if they are set down in other than demonstrative books and one deals with them by poetical, rhetorical or dialectical methods, as Abu Hamid [Ghazali] does, then he commits an offence against the Law and against philosophy, even though the fellow intended nothing but good. For by this procedure he wanted to increase the number of learned men, but in fact he increased the number of the corrupted not of the learned! As a result, one group came to slander philosophy, another to slander religion, and another to reconcile the [first] two [groups].[20]

According to Ibn Rushd, a believing philosopher cannot be asked to defer to anything but essential faith. The rest should be left to the discourse among philosophers, which is unique in its capacity to make allegorical interpretations.[21]

In sum, Ibn Rushd has a clear sense of different groups of interpreters of the Qur'an and insists that the boundaries between them be preserved and respected. Not surprisingly, these hermeneutical principles shape the way in which he interprets the Qur'anic miracle stories. As seen in his position on passages about the afterlife, Ibn Rushd himself seems to prefer a nonliteral reading of miracles, but he exhorts the demonstrative class to keep philosophical interpretation private, allowing other classes to develop different readings of these texts. And he is troubled by Ghazali's "public" contention with philosophers over the literal sense of miracle stories.

Ibn Rushd's Interpretation of Miracle Stories

While Ibn Rushd does not discuss the Qurʾanic miracle passages extensively, his rejection of Ghazali's approach to causality gives us a glimpse
into how he would *not* approach Qurʾanic miracles. Ibn Rushd's *Incoherence of the Incoherence* is devoted to critically engaging with Ghazali's *Incoherence of the Philosophers*. There, Ibn Rushd first quotes Ghazali and then
critiques his interpretation of Muslim philosophers as well as the philosophers' understanding of Aristotle, pointing out the shortcomings that he
sees in both. *Incoherence of the Incoherence* is thus remarkable for the dia-
logic layers and self-consciousness it displays.[22] In the seventeenth section
of the book, entitled "About the Natural Sciences," Ibn Rushd begins by
quoting Ghazali's argument that Muslim philosophers unjustly rejected
the plain sense of miracle stories because of their mistaken commitment
to the necessity of the current natural order. Next, he replies by arguing that
natural causality is indeed logically necessary, and such necessity is actually
confirmed in the Qurʾanic text.

For Ibn Rushd, Ghazali's critique of Aristotelian notions of causality and
logical necessity was yet another blunder, for it is almost self-evident that
things in nature interact, and this must be because things have distinct
natures and inherent powers: "It is self-evident [*innahu min al-maʿrūf bin-
afsihi*] that things have essences and attributes which determine the special functions of each thing and through which the essences and names
of things are differentiated."[23] In other words, natural objects have both
certain capacities with which they consistently act upon one another and
a receptivity through which they are vulnerable to the influence of other
things. Once one admits this "self-evident fact," it is impossible not to posit
an irreversible link between a natural cause and its effect. Barry Kogan
explains Ibn Rushd's understanding of natural causality well: "To assert
that there are necessary connections between causes and their effects is to
claim that once an efficient cause exists, all things being equal, its characteristic effect *must* occur. This means not only that the effect does occur as
a matter of fact, but *that it cannot fail to do so*, because it is necessitated or
compelled to occur."[24]

As we have seen, Ghazali rejected precisely this notion of natural causality. He argued that there is no rational basis on which to assert the necessity
of natural causation, and that the hitherto observed consistency of natural
events does not negate the conceivability of a different set of occurrences

in the future, or miracles. Ibn Rushd, well aware of Ghazali's critique, first defends the necessity of natural causation philosophically on Aristotelian grounds and then on the basis of the Qurʾanic emphasis on signs of God in nature.[25]

Establishing Necessary Causation on Aristotelian Grounds

According to Ibn Rushd, the existence of necessary causation in nature is a demonstrative truth for several reasons. First, it is based on empirical evidence. It is before our very eyes that things affect, cause, produce, and influence other things. As will be recalled, Ghazali had claimed that we do not actually observe causal connections between things, but only observe that certain things go together, such as fire and burning. He admitted that we witness fire and burning occurring together but insisted that we never actually observe fire *producing* burning. According to Ibn Rushd, this distinction is mere sophistry; any reasonable person would admit that she does observe causal connections in nature: "To deny the existence of efficient causes which are observed in sensible things [*inkār wujūd al-asbāb al-fāʿila allatī tushāhid fiʾl maḥsusāt*] is sophistry, and he who defends this doctrine either denies with his tongue what is present in his mind or is carried away by a sophistical doubt which occurs to him concerning this question. . . . The man who reasons like the theologians does not distinguish between what is self-evident and what is unknown, and everything Ghazali says in this passage is sophistical."[26]

Ibn Rushd may sound naive in asserting that we do directly observe causal relations in nature. Indeed, it may seem that he fails to distinguish between sense-data statements and physical-object statements. The former are self-evident, but the latter are not, and thus the "necessary" causal connections are not as obvious as Ibn Rushd presents them to be. Yet one may suggest that Ibn Rushd is perhaps making a more basic and justified claim than that of a naive realist. By saying that things have efficient powers, he may mean that for us to have any impressions at all, we must be acted upon by something. As Kogan explains, "If ordinarily observable entities were *totally* inert and inefficacious, whether at the level of physical objects or of sense data, we would not even so much as apprehend them."[27] Indeed, Ibn Rushd argues that necessary causation is the basis on which one can differentiate between things and talk about their existence. How could one even name things if there were no inherent qualities of things influencing others?

> If a thing had not its specific nature, it would not have a special name nor a definition, and all things would be one—indeed, not even one; for it might be asked whether this one has one special act or one special passivity or not, and if it had a special act, then there would indeed exist special acts proceeding from special natures, but if it had no single special act, then the one would not be one. But if the nature of oneness is denied, the nature of being is denied, and the consequence of the denial of being is *nothingness*.[28]

According to Ibn Rushd, therefore, the very fact that we talk about things and not nothingness means that there is causation and interaction occurring in the world.

Ibn Rushd makes a very valid point here; our inference of causal agency in nature cannot simply be an illusion. Our mind must be responding to some reality "out there," and, as we shall discuss later, it is important to acknowledge a genuine link between our mind and reality for any scientific inquiry to be possible. Such an insight, however, does not obviate the need to distinguish between our observations and logical necessity. Thus, for instance, it is self-evident from our experience that there must be a cause (or causes) producing our sensations, but it is not self-evident what that cause is. On the basis of our experience, to say that our perceptions must be produced is justified and confirms the causal maxim as a logical principle, but it does not necessarily prove that there is genuine causal agency *of* natural objects themselves.[29] Indeed, as Immanuel Kant (d. 1804) was to demonstrate centuries after Ibn Rushd, our observation does confirm the general principle of causality but does not demonstrate the necessity of a *particular* causal connection in nature.[30] Ibn Rushd seems to fail to distinguish between the concept of causality, which Kant would call "synthetic a priori," and the particular causal connections we infer from nature, which are a posteriori statements. Therefore, unlike Ghazali, Ibn Rushd appears to confuse the rejection of the necessity of natural causation with the rejection of the self-evident principle that "every act must have an agent."[31] In fact, he concludes that since "*logic* implies the existence of causes and effects,"[32] to question the necessity of connections between objects in nature poses a threat to human knowledge and reasoning: "Denial of cause implies the denial of knowledge, and denial of knowledge implies that nothing in this world can be really known, and that what is supposed to be known is nothing but opinion, that neither proof nor definition exist, and that the essential attributes which compose definitions are void."[33]

As will be recalled, Ghazali anticipated criticisms about the possibility of human knowledge and insisted that recognizing the inherent vulnerability of natural order has nothing to do with giving up certainty or science. A key concept in Ghazali's scheme that explained the stability in natural order and our confidence in making predictions about the future was the concept of *habit*. Ibn Rushd finds this concept as meaningless as the rejection of the necessity of natural order. As we have seen, Ghazali employs the term "habit" in two senses. His first use refers to our expectation of the continuing natural order. This expectation of ours is a mental "habit" rather than a logically necessary inference. His second use of "habit" is in the concept of *ijrāʾ al-ʿāda*, according to which the course of nature proceeds according to a stable pattern, a habit that is chosen and executed by the Creator. Ibn Rushd does not approve of either usage; he believes that the use of either one will definitely strip human knowledge of all certainty.

In his critique of Ghazali's use of the term "habit" in the context of natural causation, Ibn Rushd first notes that the philosophers do not deny that there is uncertain knowledge that deserves to be called "habit": "As to those who admit that there exists, *besides necessary knowledge*, knowledge which is not necessary, about which the soul forms a judgment on slight evidence and imagines it to be necessary, whereas it is not necessary, the philosophers do not deny this. And if they call such a fact 'habit' this may be granted."[34] To be sure, Ibn Rushd is aware that Ghazali is *not* simply saying that there is uncertain knowledge *in addition to* the necessary knowledge of natural causation. Rather, Ibn Rushd is simply unwilling to let the knowledge of natural causation be relegated to the level of habit, which he deems close to wishful thinking. Thus, after having noted the possibility of fallible knowledge, Ibn Rushd questions the very term "habit" in Ghazali's argument:

> But otherwise I do not know what they understand by the term "habit"—whether they mean that it is the habit of the agent, the habit of the existing things, or our habit to form a judgment about such things? It is, however, impossible that God should have a habit. . . . *If they mean a habit in existing things, habit can only exist in the animated;*

if it exists in something else, it is really a nature, and it is not possible that a thing should have a nature which determined it either necessarily or in most cases. If they mean our habit of forming judgments about things, such a habit is nothing but *an act of the soul which is determined by its nature* and through which the intellect becomes intellect.[35]

In other words, the use of the term "habit" in reference to God is inappropriate, for it is too fallible a term to be applied to God.[36] As for its use with regard to natural things, "habit" is again too loose a term to refer to the consistent behavior of things,[37] for in Arabic "habit" refers to something that is performed often but *not* always. Throughout this argument, Ibn Rushd seems to have in mind Aristotle's distinction between habit and nature, according to which the former is frequent and changeable, while the latter occurs always and is therefore deemed necessary, given the statistical view of modalities.[38] He seems to miss that, in using the term "habit," Ghazali was talking not about the *degree* of regularity in nature but about the *nature* of regularity in the world. For Ghazali, the natural order is not necessary in itself but is a result of God's *choice* or habit to sustain the world in a particular way.

Finally, Ibn Rushd does not object to the use of the term "habit" to denote a mental tendency, which infers certain connections in nature. According to him, an inescapable mental habit can only mean a logical principle in the mind that is instantiated in reality.[39] Here, Ibn Rushd overlooks Ghazali's point again: habitual thinking is *not* itself logically necessary, even if one cannot control whether one has it. Besides, Ghazali accepts logical axioms as necessary but distinguishes them from the habit of the human mind to expect things to occur in a manner consistent with past experience. Not surprisingly, Ibn Rushd concludes his discussion by rejecting the use of the term altogether because he deems it irreconcilable with the possibility of *real* knowledge: "'Habit' is an ambiguous term, and if it is analyzed it means only a hypothetical act; as when we say 'So-and-so has the habit of acting in such-and-such a way,' meaning that he will act in that way most of the time. If this were true, everything would be the case only by supposition."[40]

Obviously, as Leor Halevi also suggested, Ibn Rushd fails to appreciate the core of Ghazali's contention because of the limitations of Aristotelian conceptions of causality. Ibn Rushd thought that "matter acts according to its essence, not according to physical laws. Given such causal explanations, it is unfortunate that Averroes dismissed Ghazali's attack as mere soph-istry."[41] Indeed, our modern scientific theories are built more on the con-cept of natural laws than on theories of essences of matter. By insisting, for instance, that it is the nature of fire that necessitates burning, Ibn Rushd prematurely precluded the possibility that the connection between fire and burning may well be the result of an outside determinant, such as a mani-festation of a particular natural law that connects the two, rather than a necessary quality of the fire itself. As Taneli Kukkonen aptly explains, Ibn Rushd misses Ghazali's groundbreaking distinction between sense percep-tion and logical judgments, and between experienced reality and logical necessity, because he is operating within a framework where reality and intelligibility are merged:

> Averroes offers his traditional worldview in which the limits of pos-sibility are effectively secured and well-defined by a range of natural capacities and incapacities. Here, the mind can come to recognize these by the same process by which it distills the correct nature of the universals from the particularities of sense data. The benefits reaped from an unproblematized isomorphism of the orders of reality, ratio-nality and intelligibility so impress Averroes that he cannot imagine any other arrangement that might secure the possibility of knowledge and order in the universe.[42]

Within the confines of such a system, Ghazali's *breakthrough* can only mean a *breakdown*—the destruction of the certainty of all knowledge. While Ghazali is replacing the statistical view of modality with synchronic alter-natives, Ibn Rushd is trying to make Ghazali's remarks fit into the former. No wonder Ibn Rushd blames Ghazali for creating chaos in epistemology.

Although Ibn Rushd dismisses Ghazali's contention about the natural order too quickly and fails to recognize the philosophical breakthrough, his stance is still important in further disclosing the dynamics of scriptural interpretation. The case of Ibn Rushd demonstrates how when a sensible believer perceives the *implications* of a particular reading of the sacred text to be absurd, he will resist such a reading at all costs. While Ibn Rushd is a bit too confident in reading Aristotelian logic into the Qurʾan, it is out of his commitment to the scripture that he simply cannot allow what he con-siders to be a nonsensical implication. In fact, Ibn Rushd also puts forth theological reasons to resist Ghazali's view of contingency of the natural order. According to him, it is the notion of the effectiveness and necessity of natural causes that leads one to discover the very existence and wisdom of God.

Theological Defense of Necessary Causation in Nature

In his discussion of the necessity of natural causality, Ibn Rushd's main interlocutor is not just Ghazali personally but a theologian figure who makes illogical jumps in his haste to establish God's omnipotence. This figure—whom Ibn Rushd refers to at times as "the Ashʿarite theologian" or "the theologian," while at other times more pointedly naming "Abu Ḥamid" (Ghazali)—presents a problematic case.[43] Unlike the common man who knows his limits, this theologian does not even realize what he does and does not know, and as a result often produces sophistry, confusing dialectic with demonstration. Thus, such a figure does a disservice to faith by rejecting the existence of necessary connections between objects in nature, because he thereby blocks the path to inferring God's existence and his wisdom from nature.

Starting with the proof of God's existence, Ibn Rushd notes that the existence of God is proved on the basis of natural causation. He asks, if one rejects the efficacy of visible causes, how can he then infer the efficacy of an invisible agent? Is it not natural causation, which we observe, that gives us the idea of an invisible maker? Indeed, the basis for inferring divine agency is the agency of natural things: "Those who deny the causes in the visible world do not have any means of proving the existence of an efficient cause in the invisible world, because judgment regarding the invisible world is reached by analogy with the visible world. . . . It is from the existence of the agent [in the visible world], that we infer the existence of the agent in the invisible world."[44] It is tempting to say that Ibn Rushd once again missed a crucial distinction between the causal maxim and apparent causal connections within nature. Such temptation, however, is worth resisting for a moment—not because he is ultimately justified but because he is making a noteworthy case for taking seriously our tendency to identify agency within nature. There is something very counterintuitive—or, in Ibn Rushd's words, "very alien to human nature [gharib jiddan ʿan tibaʿ al-nās]"[45]—in dismissing natural causes as completely inert, a point we shall return to in the last chapter on Said Nursi's reconciliation of Ibn Rushd and Ghazali.

Ibn Rushd insists that the current setup of the world must be taken seriously, especially by a believer. Here, he focuses on the Qurʾanic passages that refer to natural phenomena as pointing to God. He notes that the Qurʾan describes things in nature as well suited for human needs, which provides evidence for divine providence. If one sees natural causes as having no necessity, then such an arrangement would not disclose any wisdom in creation or invite gratitude:

We hold that, *but for the powers that inhere in the bodies of animals and plants, and for the forces diffused throughout the universe due to the movements of the heavenly bodies*, [existing things] could not have lasted for a single moment. How marvelous is God the Subtle and the Well-informed! God has drawn attention to this in more than one verse in His Book saying: "And He subjected to you the night and the day, the sun and the moon," [16:12] and in His saying, "Say: 'Have you considered, what if God had made the night to last, for you, continuously till the Day of Resurrection?'" [28:71] There is also His saying: "It was out of His mercy, that He created the day and the night, so that you may rest in it and to seek some of His bounty, [that perchance you may give thanks]" [28:73]. . . . There are many other verses of this kind. *If these things did not influence what exists here on earth*, there would not have been any wisdom in their existence, with which He has favored us, or reckoned as one of the gifts for which we should be thankful.[46]

Indeed, if, for instance, fire is not necessary (*ḍarūrī*) for cooking, then why should you be thankful for its creation? If a certain number of fingers is not necessary for enabling human action, why should you call God wise for creating the hand in that way? Ibn Rushd reasons, "Were this the case, then there would be no difference whether a man is endowed with a hand, a hoof or any other organ pertaining to any animal, provided it is suited to its action."[47] In fact,

For them [the theologians] it is possible for man to be of a different shape and a different constitution, and still act like a human being! It is also possible, in their view, that he may be part of another world entirely different from this world in definition and detail, in which case there would be no grace for which man should be thankful. *For that which is not necessary or is not the most fitting for man's existence, man can certainly dispense with, and that which man can dispense with does not count as a grace he is favored with.*[48]

Moreover, the undermining of wisdom in creation opens the door to the chance argument, to the idea that things in the world happen by chance: "For if the shape of the human hand and the number of fingers [or their magnitude], for instance, were not necessary or for the sake of the best in point of gripping, which is its action, or holding various things with different shapes or being useful for holding the tools of all the crafts, then the actions of the hand due to its shape, the number of the fingers, and their magnitude would be by chance [or coincidence, *ittifāq*]."[49] This chance argument clashes not only with our experience of regularity in nature but also with the very core of the Qur'an, which "the theologian" claims to follow. Thus, it is clear to Ibn Rushd that the theologian, in his haste to help the religious cause, ends up endorsing the rival view, which attributes events in the world to mere chance, void of wisdom, stability, and blessing. Again, given the limits of the Aristotelian view of modalities, we will have to excuse Ibn Rushd's failure to entertain a third possibility—that the connection between natural events lies somewhere other than in the things themselves.

Nonetheless, Ibn Rushd's argument about wisdom again sounds compelling from a religious point of view: How can one talk about wisdom in the design of the world without recognizing the necessity of certain natures? Moreover, if our understanding of agency within nature is merely a mistake, is it not unfortunate that we are made in such a way that we fall into this understanding so easily and at most times? At the same time, it again seems that Ibn Rushd is too worried about establishing *logical necessity* here. Indeed, Ghazali could also grant the need to appreciate the current order of things and talk about the wisdom of X being placed in relation to Y within a particular plan, without, however, declaring X's function to be necessary and irreversible in itself. More important, Ibn Rushd's insistence on the *necessity* of natural order also complicates his reference to the Qur'an as supporting his view. One may wonder, for instance, whether Ibn Rushd can really make sense of the verse that he has quoted as a proof: "Say: 'Have you considered, what if God had made the night to last, for you, continuously till the Day of Resurrection?'" (Q. 28:71). After all, given Ibn Rushd's scheme of necessary natural causality, it is not possible to entertain that night could have lasted beyond its natural duration; hence the verse's reference to divine choice or agency is puzzling.

Perhaps the most perplexing aspect of Ibn Rushd's theological arguments for the necessity of causal connections in nature comes in his passing statements. For instance, "You should also know that whoever denies that the *causes affect their effects, with God's leave* [*muaththira biidhnillah*], simply repudiates wisdom and knowledge."[50] By adding the clause "with God's leave," Ibn Rushd almost closes the gap between himself and Ghazali. For Ghazali does not deny that things are happening with God's leave or that natural causes may be deemed efficacious *if* we add God's will and power into the equation. More important, the addition of such a clause also shifts the burden of proof to Ibn Rushd: What is it about the efficacy of natural events that leads us to refer to God as the decisive factor in *each* causal relation? For, unlike Ghazali, Ibn Rushd claims to infer from observation that things have their own agency through which they act and create other things.

Ultimately, there is a clash between Ibn Rushd's positions: on the one hand he would like to declare causes to be efficacious and necessary, but on the other hand he wants to affirm that the causes are effective only through God's permission. Yet, as Yamine B. Mermer and Redha Ameur put it aptly, "If causes produce the effects naturally, necessarily, and immutably, how then are things in the world to lead us to witness to the reality and 'Life' of their Creator?"[51] Ibn Rushd is not unaware of this tension, and though he does not give up his preference for the necessity of natural causation, he leaves the decision to the reader:

> The theologians affirm that the soul of man can inhere in earth without the intermediaries known by experience, whereas the philosophers deny this and say that, if this were possible, wisdom would consist in the creation of man without such intermediaries, and a creator who created in such a way would be the best and most powerful of creators; both parties claim that what they say is self-evident, and neither has any proof for its theory. And you, reader, consult your heart; it is your duty to believe what it announces, and this is what God—who may make us and you into men of truth and evidence— has ordained for you.[52]

Aside from Ibn Rushd's ultimately unsatisfactory stance, it is important to note that both Ghazali and Ibn Rushd refer to gratitude—a central concept in the Qurʾan—in the course of their interpretations of natural causality. For Ghazali, it is the realization of the ultimate contingency of natural order that enables the believer to turn to God in gratitude, while for Ibn Rushd it is the very necessity of natural order that enables people to appreciate God's wisdom and be grateful. Their divergent points of emphasis can be reconciled if one takes the analysis of natural causality in light of the Qur'an more as a *process* than as a static and complete judgment about the world that is rendered once and for all. If we understand natural causality to be a dynamic process, then each of the two views has its proper place in the human journey to God. As I shall demonstrate in the final chapter of the book, Nursi offers such an insightful reconciliation of Ghazali's and Ibn Rushd's approaches to nature, gratitude, and divine wisdom in light of his reading of the Qur'an.

Given Ibn Rushd's understanding that an interruption in natural causality is inconceivable from a philosophical perspective, it is clear that he would *not* opt for a literal reading of Qur'anic miracles that allows genuine interruptions in the natural order. Nevertheless, given his hermeneutical principles, Ibn Rushd can allow a range of meanings for the common person.

Ibn Rushd on Miracles and the Demonstrative Class Versus the Common Person

Ibn Rushd notes that a philosopher should never publicly question miracle stories.[53] Clearly, our thinker does not want to disturb the common person, who is admonished by the miracle stories, just as he cautioned against questioning the physical punishments and pleasures in life after death. This concern is not surprising if we recall his role as a judge and his concern for the public good, as well as his understanding of the different groups of the Qur'anic audience. Though Ibn Rushd does not explicitly state it, it seems that the literal sense of the miracle stories impresses the common people and causes them to trust the prophetic message. It encourages them to follow this message, which will enable them to attain the virtues necessary for happiness in this world and in the afterlife. Since the philosopher is a supporter of virtue, he should support its attainment through belief in miracles and should not publicly display a critical or questioning attitude toward the miracles.[54]

A related reason for Ibn Rushd's dropping miracle stories from philosophical discussion is the fact that he does not deem them crucial for

verifying the truthfulness of a messenger of God. As discussed in the previous chapter, Muslim theologians often used the analogy of a king's envoy
to illustrate the evidentiary power of miracles. They argued that if a man
were to rise before the king and speak to people with the claim that he was
the king's envoy, requesting that the king change one of his protocols as a
sign of approval, and as a result the king did it, this would surely indicate
the veracity of the envoy. Ibn Rushd notes that this is a sufficient argument
for the common man, but it is not good enough to be a demonstrative
explanation because the premises assumed in the king analogy are not self-
evident.[55] More specifically, Ibn Rushd finds it inconsistent that one would
first recognize a certain unusual event as a miracle and then accept the
person who brought that miracle as a messenger of God. In order to accept
that the miracle proves the person's prophetic claim, one has to utilize the
following reasoning:

(1) A miracle has taken place at the hands of a given person.
(2) Only the prophets can have miracles.

Therefore, this person must be a prophet of God.

Ascertaining the first premise is not easy, for one must make sure that
what he is seeing is not magic or deception. The second premise assumes a
belief in God and the prophets in the first place.[56] Thus, Ibn Rushd argues
that a wondrous event is only an indication given to a prophet; it is in no
way a proof of prophecy. Rather, the real proof of prophecy is the message
he brings. In his praise of the distinctiveness of the last prophet's miracle—
the revelation of the Qurʾan—Ibn Rushd emphasizes the prophet's message over the wonders he is said to have performed. Prophet Muhammad's
greatest miracle, as attested by tradition, was the message he brought from
God. Only this kind of miracle may count as evidence: "The clearest of
miracles is the Venerable Book of Allah [the Qurʾan], the existence of which
is not an interruption of the course of nature assumed by tradition, like the
changing of a rod into a serpent, but its miraculous nature is established
by way of perception and consideration for every man who has been or who
will be till the day of resurrection. And so this miracle is far superior to all
others."[57]

Thus, only by considering the wisdom and truthfulness of the message
or scripture (sharʿ) can one confirm the veracity of the messenger. Reminiscent of Ghazali, Ibn Rushd says that if two people claim to be physicians,

and one tries to prove it by treating the sick while the other tries to prove it by walking on water, the former's proof is much stronger than the latter's.[58] Indeed, as we saw in the previous chapter, similar concerns about the evidentiary value of miracles have been raised in the mainstream theological discourse, and Ibn Rushd's position is not very different from them or from Ghazali in this regard.

Ibn Rushd further notes that the question of establishing the veracity of a prophet is a historical question rather than a philosophical one. Philosophically, one only affirms the possibility of a class of people who have been chosen by God to communicate guidance to human beings. For him, this possibility of the existence of a messenger is agreed upon by philosophers, with the exception of materialists or naturalists (*dahriyya*). Indeed, Ibn Rushd finds it sufficiently clear that "there exists in fact a class of people who receive revelation [from God], intended to communicate to mankind certain forms of knowledge and virtuous actions, which are conducive to their well-being, while deterring them from partaking certain false beliefs and vicious actions. This, in fact, is the function of the prophets."[59] The exact identities of these people can be ascertained by looking at the historical reports, and thus there is no need to try to discuss them theoretically. Ibn Rushd hopes that "this suffice[s] for the man who is not satisfied with passing this problem over in silence."[60] In sum, a miracle story is not something that Ibn Rushd finds crucial for his purposes of believing in the prophet; neither does he want to undo the edifying effect of miracle stories on the common person. Hence, he is satisfied to skip a detailed discussion of miracles by saying that there are divine things beyond human understanding (*huwa amr al-ilāhiy muʿjaz ʿan idrak al-ʿuqūl al-insāniyya*). Indeed, he finds it significant that "we do not find that any of the ancient philosophers discusses miracles, although they were known and had appeared all over the world."[61]

We may concede that Ibn Rushd had good reasons for not delving into the interpretation of miracle stories and yet still wonder how he ultimately interprets miracle stories for the demonstrative class. After all, according to Ibn Rushd's Qurʾanic hermeneutics, the Qurʾan has something to offer to everyone. Since he avoids discussing the issue in his texts intended for the general public, we will have to look for our answer by turning to his more philosophical works.

One reading Ibn Rushd could have suggested for the philosophers is the metaphorical interpretation of the Qurʾanic miracle stories. Thus, for instance, the staff of Moses that became a snake and swallowed the sorcerers' rods could be interpreted as a metaphor for the victory of Moses's argument in support of belief in God over the sorcerers' disbelief.[62] However, Ibn Rushd does not seem to mention this reading, even though he was accused of such by some of his detractors. On the contrary, in his debate with Ghazali, he insists that those who assert that the extraordinary events mentioned in the scripture could not have taken place are "heretics."[63] This may well be his exhortation for general people, whereas, as was the case in passages on the afterlife, he may be taking these passages metaphorically in his more private discourse directed to the demonstrative class. Yet we do not find such reference to metaphorical readings of miracles in his philosophical works. And, by not referring to any metaphorical readings, perhaps he does mean to suggest the historicity of miraculous events for the philosophers as well. That is, he might be genuinely indicating that miraculous events are extraordinary yet still natural.

Such a view would coincide with the view of some other Muslim philosophers, such as Avicenna, according to whom miracles were unusual yet natural events that were performed by prophets who had special skills.[64] These philosophers offered two types of causal arguments for the occurrence of miraculous events: one is from the Stoic notion of "sympathy," and the other is from the "emanationist" account. According to the notion of sympathy, the human soul, which has control over the body, can exert influence over events outside the body under certain circumstances, such as bringing thunderstorms and rain. This capacity of the human soul to affect natural events is considered unusual but perfectly within natural causation; it is an extension of natural human capacity that is realized by the prophets. According to the emanationist account, the prophets are very intelligent human beings who can receive the "overflow" from the universal Active Intellect and be inspired in ways that normal human beings are not. These two paths are not trodden by most human beings but are still part of natural causation. Thus, these Muslim thinkers could affirm the performance of unusual events by the prophets without having to accept any break in natural causation.[65] Yet Ibn Rushd does not seem to support these explanations. In his *Incoherence of the Incoherence*, he is skeptical that these natural explanations are really possible and states that that which is possible in theory for human beings may still be impossible in practice. He does not seem to make an exception for the prophets in this regard.[66] If Ibn Rushd is neither taking the miracle stories metaphorically nor subscribing to an Avicennan view of the natural powers of a prophet, how does he really make sense of them for the intellectual class?

Barry Kogan pursued this question beyond Ibn Rushd's theological treatises directed to the public, perusing his commentaries on Aristotle to find
clues. He suggests that Ibn Rushd regards the miracle stories as reports of
spontaneous coincidences:

> It appears that miracles, insofar as their existence can be verified,
> are purely spontaneous natural events in the sense which Aristotle
> describes in Book II of the *Physics*. From all that Averroes has said
> regarding such occurrences, it is clear he thinks that (1) they are logi-
> cally possible; (2) they are physically possible, but disruptive of nature;
> (3) they are impossible for men to perform (even, we may add, men
> who are prophets); (4) they are caused; (5) their causes are unknown
> to us, although a philosopher could conceivably discover them; (6)
> they may serve particular ends insofar as they are principles of the
> laws, e.g. enabling men, through their belief in the law, to achieve
> virtue. These same features are matched virtually point for point with
> the Stagirite's account of spontaneous events.[67]

In other words, Ibn Rushd seems to hold that miracles are extraordinary
spontaneous events brought about by a peculiar intersection of natural
causes. That is, even though these extraordinary events cannot be caused
by human agency or be explained by known causal links, they are still the
result of natural causality. Hence, Ibn Rushd can concede that the miraculous events mentioned in the Qurʾan did take place, without conceding
what he regards as impossible—that is, that natural causation can be interrupted for a special purpose.[68]

Majid Fakhry, despite his puzzling appreciation of Ibn Rushd's perseverance on the necessity of natural causation, regrets that Ibn Rushd did
not do justice to miracle stories. Fakhry argues that Ibn Rushd left us with
"nothing but an extraordinary phenomenon which is . . . without special
theological significance."[69] Kogan disagrees with Fakhry's disappointment,
arguing that the idea that these events are the result of natural coincidences
need not cancel their edifying value.[70] Indeed, Aristotle explained how certain things can happen by chance and still serve a purpose. For instance, it
is possible that a man who is fundraising for a cause goes to a town for a
different reason, but while he is there he also happens to collect money for
his cause. His unrelated visit inadvertently serves his purpose of fundraising.[71] Similarly, following his master Aristotle, Ibn Rushd might maintain
that these unusual coincidental events can serve to strengthen the common

person's incentive to believe in revelation and follow the right path. Kogan says that by conceding this edifying effect of miracles, Ibn Rushd is giving theological significance to miracle stories, albeit a philosophically explained significance.[72]

If this is indeed Ibn Rushd's position—a conclusion that needs to be taken with a grain of salt since it is partly based on indirect evidence and Ibn Rushd's silence rather than his explicit statements—the challenge will be that Ibn Rushd does not *philosophically* address the issue of how miracles, when defined as accidents or spontaneous constellations of natural causality, happen to endorse genuine prophets and not anyone else. If his theology is "philosophical," as Kogan has suggested, then Ibn Rushd needs to provide a philosophical account of how these coincidences could coincide with a prophetic claim and hence have theological value. To be sure, it is unfair to expect from Ibn Rushd an *exact* explanation of how innumerable natural causes could become enmeshed in a certain moment to bring about an extraordinary event at the perfect time for a prophetic mission. Yet his theory does not seem to provide any general explanations either, such as the suggestion that these events may have been pre-planned at the very unfolding of the universe.[73] The problem is that if they are not intended for the moment of prophetic mission, their theological value evaporates: the common person's encouragement comes from an illusion that a spontaneous event is actually intentionally placed as a sign by the one who has sent the prophet. And a question arises: Why would the "Venerable Book of God" that Ibn Rushd praises so highly present these accidents as if they were intended to strengthen the prophet's mission?

The result of our inquiry into the significance of miracle stories for the intellectual class, unfortunately, brings us back in a circle. It seems that Ibn Rushd can offer ample space for the common person to take a lesson from the miracle stories: he is willing to be silent when she takes them literally as genuine breaks in natural causality, and he is also prepared to confirm that such extraordinary events could have taken place. He does not, however, seem to make sense of them for the demonstrative class, leaving us wondering how the Qurʾan really speaks to *all* classes at all times, as he claimed.

While Ibn Rushd's explanation of miracles and their meaning for the demonstrative class remains elusive, if not dissatisfactory, it is important that we do not overlook his insights delivered through the medium of *negation*. Ibn Rushd is clear that miracle stories cannot be read as destroying common sense and undermining science. He sees genuine dangers in pressing the plain sense of these stories to their ultimate logical conclusion:

the contingency of natural order. While he did miss some major points of Ghazali's criticism, Ibn Rushd made an insightful case against a mythical reading of miracle stories. He justly rejected what he saw as an irrational universe unworthy of being attributed to a wise creator. He rightly resisted what he thought of as "the theologian's" picture of the universe: a universe that is disconnected and fragmented, in which wisdom and stability are destroyed, and which, in Kogan's words, consists of a "mere parade of discontinuous phenomena, unfolding in regular conjunctions by fiat or by chance, yet beyond our capacity to comprehend."[74] While it is unfair to attribute this picture to Ghazali, miracle stories can indeed be naively read in such a way as to produce this absurd image, and Ibn Rushd rightly does not want to have anything to do with such a reading.

Moreover, Ibn Rushd's attitude toward Qur'anic miracle stories was informed by his response to the Qur'anic passages on nature as well as the passages that criticize the demands for miracles. While he does not try to reconcile these aspects of Qur'anic discourse with the miracle stories in the Qur'an, he clearly showed that the natural order must be taken seriously if one is to talk about deciphering the Qur'anic reference to "signs" in nature as pointing to the *wisdom* of the Creator.[75] We shall return to these insights of Ibn Rushd when we discuss Nursi's contemporary reception of Qur'anic miracle stories.

In the next section of the book, we shall take a detour into early and late modern Western thought and pursue the question of miracle stories and the status of natural causality in these contexts. As we hear the echoes of both Ghazali and Ibn Rushd in these contexts, we will gain a clearer vocabulary that will allow us to make sense of the potential implications of miracle stories for a modern audience. We shall first turn to Hume, who very interestingly incarnates both sides of the classical Muslim debate: he pushes for the epistemological breakthrough that Ghazali had achieved through attending to miracle stories, while simultaneously holding back from miracle stories and worrying about securing science, as Ibn Rushd did.

PART 2

REFRAMING THE DEBATE ON MIRACLES IN MODERN TERMS

3

DAVID HUME ON EMPIRICISM,
COMMON SENSE, AND MIRACLES

David Hume (1711–1776) was a Western thinker whose views on epistemology as well as philosophy of religion have left a crucial mark on modern thought. Known more as a historian than as a philosopher during his
lifetime, Hume's fame grew immensely after his death. He is regarded as
the final major British empiricist, after John Locke (d. 1704) and Bishop
George Berkeley (d. 1753). Hume's commitment to the empirical method
and science was coupled with an incisive critique of rationalism, a critique
that had a significant effect on Western philosophy and made him "the first
post-sceptical philosopher of the early modern period."[1] Hume's critique
of Aristotelian and Cartesian rationalism and natural causation is very
reminiscent of Ghazali's approach, while his commitment to Newtonian
science is as passionate as Ibn Rushd's fascination with science and Aristotelian natural philosophy. Hence, Hume will serve for us as an early modern representative, so to speak, of both Ghazali's and Ibn Rushd's insights
regarding miracle stories. And we shall observe how Hume prepares the
ground for crucial shifts in epistemology and scientific inquiry in an early
modern context.

Hume undertook his first study of philosophy after he left his "half-
hearted" study of law at Edinburgh University at the age of eighteen. He
writes that he underwent a crisis of skepticism during this period, which
calls to mind Ghazali's first crisis. After trying to distract himself with a
brief employment as a clerk for a trade company, Hume moved to France,

where he spent three years studying where Descartes had studied a century earlier, and where Averroism had had its second wave during the Renaissance two centuries earlier.[2] Hume's philosophical studies would eventually culminate in his writing of *A Treatise of Human Nature* (three volumes, 1739–40), in which he pursues a way of studying human nature that is empirically grounded.[3] It was this attempt to create "a science of man," parallel to a science of nature, that earned him the title of "Newtonian philosopher" in some circles.[4] When, to Hume's dismay, his anonymously published *Treatise* did not receive much attention, he reworked certain parts of it and published them separately under his own name as *Philosophical Essays Concerning Human Understanding* (later called *An Enquiry Concerning Human Understanding*) and *An Enquiry Concerning the Principles of Morals*. In the former, he puts forth his famous critique of rationalism, which we shall look at in detail below.

As is well known, Hume is also famous for his criticism of religion. His works such as *The Natural History of Religion*, *Dialogues Concerning Natural Religion*, and parts of his *Enquiry Concerning Human Understanding*, including the essay "Of Miracles," rendered him a controversial person during his lifetime and left crucial legacy for modern philosophy of religion. Hume also penned *Essays, Moral, Political, and Literary*, a collection of approximately forty essays; the six-volume *History of England*, spanning from Roman times to 1688; and a brief autobiography entitled *My Own Life*. While all of these works cover a wide spectrum, they share one major characteristic: "their author's commitment to the experimental method, or to a form of empiricism that sees both the advantages and the necessity of relying on experience and observation to provide the answer to intellectual questions of all kinds."[5]

In what follows, we shall see how Hume's empiricism shakes old epistemological grounds and prepares for significant shifts in modern epistemology. We shall attend to the way he is "translating," so to speak, Ghazali's and Ibn Rushd's insights on miracles to early modern engagements with science and religion. Analyzing Hume's thought will allow us to see intellectual connections between classical Muslim debates about Qur'anic miracles and the early modern debates over epistemology and science. Such connections will be invaluable for understanding the ways in which miracle stories can be meaningfully read in the modern age.

In our study of Hume, we shall encounter interesting twists and noteworthy tensions, not unlike the ones we have seen in the previous two chapters. Let us start with Hume's critique of rationalism, which is similar to that of Ghazali, before we turn to his commitment to science, which echoes that of Ibn Rushd.

Hume's Critique of Rationalism and the "Problem of Induction"

Drawing on his predecessors Locke and Berkeley, Hume offered a compelling criticism of rationalist claims to knowledge that constituted a turning point for modern thought. By putting forth several principles, Hume argued that the most important source of knowledge is not a priori reasoning but experience.

Indeed, Hume's incisive critique of rationalism exposed "the problem of induction" inherent in all human attempts at knowledge beyond immediate experience. At the heart of this critique was his deconstruction of causal reasoning. To be sure, Hume's critique of causal inferences was not new even within the context of Western thought (let alone within the earlier context of classical Islamic thought). Nicholas of Autrecourt (d. ca. 1369), who is called the "medieval Hume" by some scholars, and Nicholas Malebranche (d. 1715) had offered similar critiques of causality. What makes Hume famous is not so much the originality of his ideas but rather his rearticulation of the critique of the demonstrability of natural causation in a compelling and cogent manner.

In *An Enquiry Concerning Human Understanding*, Hume explains that there are two kinds of propositions: (1) propositions based on the relations between ideas, as in geometry, algebra, and mathematics, and (2) propositions based on matters of fact, as received from experience. The crucial difference between the two is that while the relations deciphered by mathematics and geometry are certain and unchangeable, matters of fact are not so. For example, while we cannot conceive of a variation in the sum of the angles of a triangle or in the equation 1+1=2, we can conceive of variation in matters of fact: "The contrary of every matter of fact is still possible; because it can never imply a contradiction, and is conceived by the mind with the same facility and distinctness, as if ever so conformable to reality. That the sun will not rise to-morrow is no less intelligible a proposition, and implies no more contradiction, than the affirmation, that it will rise. We should in vain, therefore, attempt to demonstrate its falsehood. Were it demonstratively false, it would imply a contradiction, and could never be distinctly conceived by the mind."[6] Hume's point here echoes Ghazali's contention with Muslim philosophers that there is a clear distinction between ontological and logical relations.

Hume also notes three principles according to which the *association* of ideas takes place. It is only through the association of ideas that the human mind is able to think beyond that which is immediately perceived by the senses. According to Hume, the three ways in which one idea can call to mind another idea are resemblance, contiguity, and causal inference. The last of these, causal inference, is the most significant mode of mental association, for it opens horizons beyond one's immediate perception: "By means of that relation alone we can go beyond the evidence of our memory and senses." For instance, Hume notes that we can infer from "the hearing of an articulate voice and rational discourse in the dark" that there is a person there. This conclusion is possible because of our causal thinking: we think that voice and rational discourse "are the *effects* of the human make and fabric, and closely connected with it."[7]

Few would disagree that causal inference is extremely important for reasoning. What makes Hume's views a turning point in Western thought is his clear insistence on exposing the source of such inference: this important principle of causality is not a self-evident relation between ideas, nor does it originate directly from our sense perception. Just like Ghazali, then, Hume offers a critique of natural causation on both a priori and a posteriori grounds.

Natural Causation Is Not Rationally Demonstrable

According to Hume, causal relation is the most significant mental association that carries us beyond our current perception, but it is not based on a priori reasoning. Hume offers an insightful way of testing whether our judgments about natural causality are a priori: If we were given the impression of a cause and asked to infer its effect, could we do it merely on the basis of reasoning, without any experience whatsoever? Hume notes, "*The mind can never possibly find the effect in the supposed cause*, by the most accurate scrutiny and examination. *For the effect is totally different from the cause, and consequently can never be discovered in it.* . . . A stone or piece of metal raised into the air, and left without any support, immediately falls: But to consider the matter a priori, is there any thing we discover in this situation, which can beget the idea of a downward, rather than an upward, or any other motion, in the stone or metal?"[8] Our belief that a stone, when left unsupported, will surely fall down is not based on any logical inference, for there is nothing inherent in the idea of the stone that would compel us to link it with the idea of a downward, as opposed to upward, movement. It is because of the absence of any "demonstrative link" between these two matters of fact that reason can never anticipate the effect by reflecting on its cause. Hume offers other striking examples to establish this point:

> Let an object be presented to a man of ever so strong natural reason and abilities; if that object be entirely new to him, he will not be able, by the most accurate examination of its sensible qualities, to discover any of its causes or effects. Adam, though his rational faculties be supposed, at the very first, entirely perfect, could not have inferred from the fluidity, and transparency of water, that it would suffocate him, or from the light and warmth of fire, that it would consume him. No object ever discovers, by the qualities which appear to the senses, either the causes which produced it, or the effects which will arise from it; nor can our reason, unassisted by experience, ever draw any inference concerning real existence and matter of fact.[9]

In his explanation of how causal inferences are not logically necessary, Hume also argues that whatever can be separated in the mind can also be separated in reality. He points out the fact that in the mind the idea of a cause can be separated easily from the idea of an effect.[10] Hume's argument is again reminiscent of Ghazali, who argued that the affirmation of a cause along with the negation of its "habitual" effect does not involve any logical contradiction. Similar to Ghazali, Hume highlights the distinction between actuality and possibility; that which is never observed in reality does not cease to be possible in terms of logic.

According to Hume, if we perpetually find ourselves positing causal relations between things or events, it is *not* because we are *rationally* more capable than Adam in Hume's example.[11] Our only difference is experience: it is only after experiencing the same pattern repeatedly that we start talking of causal relations between different events or objects. This does not mean, however, that our causal judgments are *justified* by our experience. Lest such an association between causal thinking and experience be misunderstood, Hume turns to argue that our causal inferences are not based on a posteriori reasoning, either.

Natural Causation Is Not Proven by A Posteriori Reasoning

Again in a manner reminiscent of Ghazali, Hume argues that even though our ideas of causality follow from experience, they are not demonstrated by it: "Even after we have experience of the operations of cause and effect, our conclusions from that experience are *not* founded on reasoning, or any process of the understanding."[12] Indeed, when Hume searches for the empirical basis of the idea of causation, he does not find any "impressions" serving as its origin.[13] Having failed to find a sense perception corresponding to the idea of causation, he breaks the idea of causation down into its component ideas and finds that it consists of three ideas—namely, "contiguity," "priority in time," and "necessary connection."[14] This is to say, our idea of a causal relation between cause and effect includes the propositions that (1) causes and effects are close to each other in proximity, (2) causes appear immediately prior to effects in time, and (3) causes and effects are necessarily connected to each other. Hume finds the last component—the idea of "necessary connection"—to be the most crucial relation in the idea of causation. Only the assumption of necessary connection can provide the "basis of an *inference* from the perceived to the unperceived," while "spatio-temporal relations [i.e., contiguity and priority] cannot serve this purpose, because they are given *within* experience as the manner in which indivisible perceptibles are disposed to one another."[15] Hume posits that the idea of a necessary connection between cause and effect is related to our sense perception of a "constant conjunction" between a specific cause and its effect.[16]

Not surprisingly, Hume soon realizes that even the impression or sense data of a constant conjunction between two things cannot account for our assumption of a necessary connection between them. Even if a constant conjunction is experienced an infinite number of times, it will not originate a new idea. In other words, our experience only attests that we have so far observed certain events repeatedly occur in a certain sequence, and our memory merely notes that a similar sequence has been observed before. We do not find any "necessity" implied in this perception that will *require* the same sequence to repeat in the future.[17]

As his final recourse in his search for the sensory origin of the idea of necessary connection, Hume turns to inductive inference: "Perhaps it will appear in the end, that the necessary connection depends on the inference, instead of the inference's depending on the necessary connection."[18] Not surprisingly, the analysis of inductive inference reveals to Hume that it does not serve as the origin of the idea of necessary connection because our inductive inference already assumes such a necessary connection between two events:

> Should it be said, that, from a number of uniform experiments, we *infer* a connexion between the sensible qualities and the secret powers; this, I must confess, seems the same difficulty, couched in different terms. The question still recurs; on what process of argument this *inference* is founded? . . . You must confess that the inference is not intuitive; neither is it demonstrative: Of what nature is it then? *To say it is experimental, is begging the question. For all inferences from experience suppose, as their foundation, that the future will resemble the past*, and that similar powers will be conjoined with similar sensible qualities.[19]

This, then, is Hume's lucid articulation of the problem of induction. Past experience, no matter how consistent and regular it has been, does not itself necessitate that such order be maintained in the future. Hume's ease at exposing such a crucial distinction about induction is admirable and worth observing in yet another quote:

> These two propositions are far from being the same, *I have found that such an object has always been attended with such an effect*, and *I foresee, that other objects, which are, in appearance, similar, will be attended with similar effects*. I shall allow, if you please, that the one proposition may justly be inferred from the other: I know in fact, that it always is inferred. *But if you insist, that the inference is made by a chain of reasoning, I desire you to produce that reasoning. The connexion between these propositions is not intuitive.*[20]

The question is, then, whence comes the assumption of a necessary connection between what we consider a cause and its effect? Why do we assume that the future events will resemble the past events? Why do we believe that we observe certain things necessarily entailing other things? Hume's answer to these questions is again reminiscent of Ghazali's; he refers to the concept of habit or custom:

> Custom, then, is the great guide of human life. It is that principle alone, which renders our experience useful to us, and makes us expect, for the future, a similar train of events with those which have

appeared in the past. Without the influence of custom, we should be entirely ignorant of every matter of fact, beyond what is immediately present to the memory and senses. We should never know how to adjust means to ends, or to employ our natural powers in the production of any effect. There would be an end at once of all action, as well as of the chief part of speculation.[21]

In other words, the human mind simply out of *habit* makes a jump from the observation of constant conjunction to positing necessary connections between things. It is an uncontrollable propensity of the human mind: even though the conclusion that there are invariable causal links among objects is not based on any kind of reasoning, we are nevertheless compelled to posit them.[22]

To be sure, this realization that we have no rational justification for our most useful inferences was not an idea original to Hume. Rather, he was simply the one who rearticulated it so strikingly in the early modern era. It was Hume's articulation that woke Immanuel Kant from his "dogmatic slumber" and inspired him to diligently search for a new system that would be immune from the fallacies of reason, which Hume had rightly exposed. Thus, Kant's Copernican Revolution in Western philosophy, which introduced important shifts in epistemology, metaphysics, and philosophy of science, was a response to Hume. On the basis of Hume's critique, Kant acknowledged the decisive role of our own mental makeup in perceiving the world, which "radically and irreversibly transformed the nature of Western thought." After Kant, "no one could ever again think of either science or morality as a matter of the passive reception of entirely external truth or reality. In reflection upon the methods of science, as well as in many particular areas of science itself, the recognition of our own input into the world we claim to know has become inescapable."[23]

Just as Ghazali's similar accomplishment was perceived by Ibn Rushd as an attack on human knowledge, Hume's insistence on making a distinction between logical relations and our mental habits appeared to many to be a breakdown. It came as a shock that there is neither a priori nor a posteriori reasoning on the basis of which we can justify causal inferences, a cornerstone of our thinking. The urgent question thus became: If our causal judgments are, as Kant famously put it, "bastards of the imagination impregnated by experience," on what basis can we be justified in making them? If natural order is not based on any objectively necessary connection between objects, on what basis can we trust that the order will remain stable in the future? In what follows, we shall look more closely at whether Hume's exposition of the problem of induction can escape the crisis of skepticism.

Escaping Absurdity: Hume Between Skepticism and Naturalism

In his *Walking the Tightrope of Reason: The Precarious Life of a Rational Animal*, the contemporary Hume scholar Robert Fogelin neatly summarizes Hume's critique: "When we turn our critical faculties loose on the supposed sources of our knowledge, the fated result is an extreme version of skepticism."[24] Indeed, Hume's critique of the rational basis of causal inferences and induction—as well as his critique, on the same basis, of the existence of body and enduring self—may bring one to the brink of insanity.[25] The most basic inferences seem to be founded on plays of imagination rather than reasoning, and there seems to be no basis on which one can build security. Hume seems to have personally tasted the horrors of such a crisis of certainty. As he notes at the end of book 1 of his *Treatise*, he fell into skepticism following his critical analysis: "When I look abroad, I foresee on every side dispute, contradiction, anger, calumny, and detraction. When I turn my eye inward, I find nothing but doubt and ignorance. . . . *Every step I take is with hesitation, and every new reflection makes me dread an error and absurdity in my reasoning.*"[26]

To mitigate such skepticism, Hume prescribes distraction from rational analysis, which come naturally in daily life once one leaves the study desk.[27] That is, even though our belief in the causal relations between objects and our other natural beliefs are not logically justified and may have no correspondence to reality, we should not take this analysis to mean that we cannot trust our common sense–based assumptions. For we are *compelled* by nature to assume causal relations between objects: "If we believe that fire warms, or water refreshes, it is only because it costs us too much pains to think otherwise."[28] In fact, Hume suggests that to insist that we need rational justification in order to trust our most basic habits goes against the wisdom of nature: "It is more conformable to the *ordinary wisdom of nature* to secure so necessary an act of the mind [i.e., causal inference], by some instinct or mechanical tendency, which may be infallible in its operations, may discover itself at the first appearance of life and thought, and may be independent of all the laboured deductions of the understanding."[29]

Jamie Ferreira insightfully suggests that Hume does not *escape* his skeptical conclusions by appealing to practical needs for human survival.

Rather, he *rejects* the skeptical demand that one must have reasons in order to continue to hold one's natural beliefs: "If the sceptic's thesis is that there is no *argument* justifying those beliefs, then Hume surely accepts that thesis. But such a thesis is not necessarily a sceptical one. *What is skepti-cal about a sceptic's challenge is the claim that* because *there is no argument, something essential is lacking—something which should be there, isn't there. . . .* To refuse to see the 'lack' of argument as a lack is to fail to accept what is distinctively sceptical about the sceptic's thesis."[30] That is to say, while Hume accepts that skepticism cannot be refuted by arguments, this is not a serious concession to skepticism, for the skeptical suspension of belief is no more warranted than continuing to hold that belief. Hume says, "If I must be a fool, as all those who reason or believe anything *certainly* are, my follies shall at least be natural and agreeable."[31] Here, Hume not only concedes to the skeptical argument that our most basic beliefs are *arational*, but he also resists total skepticism by refusing to confuse *arationality* and *irrationality*.[32] In this sense, Hume's solution to the problem of skepticism is analogous to Ghazali's insistence that not all *possible* doubt is *reasonable* doubt.

Hume seems to suggest, then, that we find ourselves making causal inferences and assuming necessary connections all the time. We should submit to this natural flow and admit that it was wisely implanted in us by nature. This naturalist solution, agreeable and smooth as it may seem on the surface, has crucial problems lurking underneath. To start with, what is "naturally striking" may not be the passive and neutral process assumed by Hume.[33] Indeed, while Hume justly defers to common sense as an anti-dote to the crisis of uncertainty and makes a distinction between hypo-thetical and reasonable doubt, his account of how this happens and to what it applies is ambiguous. For instance, Christopher Hookway grants that Hume's reference to human nature can be effective in mitigating skepti-cism about the existence of an external world, but not in mitigating skepti-cism that concerns induction.[34]

What makes Hume's naturalism most difficult to absorb is that he does not ever explain what he means by nature, nor does he employ the term consistently. At times, Hume talks about nature in the way one would talk about a wise and compassionate deity, referring to its wisdom and care for our well being, as Ghazali talked about God. For instance, he says, "Nature has not left this [the existence of body] to his choice, and has doubtless esteemed it an affair of too great importance to be trusted to our uncertain reasonings and speculations."[35] Similarly, nature has wisely implemented causal inferences in us as an instinct rather than a rational inference, just "as nature has taught us the use of our limbs, without giving us the knowledge of the muscles and nerves."[36] Such references to nature's wisdom could well be an anchoring point for Hume's naturalism, if only he consistently used the term "nature" in this sense of a wise and merciful deity. Yet, in other passages, Hume refers to nature as blind and merciless: "The whole presents nothing but the idea of a blind Nature, impregnated by a great vivifying principle, and pouring forth from her lap, without discernment or parental care, her maimed and abortive children!" As I. M. Fowlie rightly noted, it is very difficult to "demythologize" the concept of nature within Hume's writings or reconcile his contradictory references to it.[37]

In contrast, as will be recalled, Ghazali answers the question of certainty by referring to the habit of an unseen eternal maker. The current order shows that there must be a wise maker who has maintained the stability hitherto seen in nature, and it is this wise maker who will also guarantee its stability in the future. According to this view, even in cases where the familiar order is not maintained, as in the case of miracles or during the end of time, the inherent qualities of God—such as wisdom, power, mercy, and justice—remain stable, guaranteeing security and reliability for his creatures. Thus, Ghazali justified his trust in order and hope for consistency by acknowledging the wisdom and mercy of an eternal maker, while Hume does not offer such a stabilizing anchor, so to speak, for his naturalism.

Moreover, unlike Ghazali, who acknowledges a difference between the concept of causality and our judgments about natural causality, Hume goes on to challenge the logical necessity of the "causal maxim," or the "causal principle."[38] Hume claims that we *can* conceive of coming into existence without referring to *any* cause at all.[39] Such a claim further weakens Hume's solution to skepticism. For Hume, it is perfectly logical to say that "the effect, (the 'beginning of existence') may exist without need of *any* cause."[40] Moreover, Hume claims that contrary to the causal maxim, it is possible "for an effect to have perfections that its cause lacks."[41] It will be recalled that all of these rejections exemplify what Ibn Rushd accused Ghazali of doing, and what Ghazali actually avoided.

Of course, as stated earlier, Hume's rejection of the causal maxim is a fallacious overstatement in that our inability to rationally justify natural causality need not mean that the very concept of causality itself is not intuitive.[42] Since Hume goes on to reject the intuitiveness of the causal maxim—unlike Ghazali, whose critique of "habitual" or natural causes leads him to search for the "real cause" of the effects in nature—Hume proclaims our "profound ignorance" of all causal inferences.[43] In fact, for Hume, any explanation of the natural is simply beyond human reach. Hume believes that "we cannot go beyond experience" to offer any explanation of our sense perception or of the world we live in.[44] Thus, by rejecting the concept of causality altogether, Hume confirms Ibn Rushd's fears about the impossibility of human grasp of reality. The baby is thrown out with the bathwater: starting with the critical assessment of natural causation, Hume goes far to retire from all analysis and explanation. The world around us, and our existence, must be treated "as a basic brute fact" that simply cannot be understood.[45]

Such criticisms should be taken as a demand for further explanation rather than as a wholesale rejection of Hume's conclusions about the role of habits in human thinking. Hume is right in that we have no way of proving that the natural order in itself is necessary, and he is also right in that we can still accept many of our natural instincts. He just fails to tell us the path from one to the other, or to give us a critical method for sifting through our common sense. And by rejecting the causal maxim prematurely, he at times takes us too far into the abyss of unknowing. Such shortcomings aside, Hume's writings do foreshadow an early modern articulation of an enduring shift in modern epistemology. By attending to the sources of our ideas and discovering that however instinctive and strong certain ideas may be, they cannot be taken to be *necessarily* instantiated in reality, Hume effectively blocked the way to naive realism and dogmatic rationalism. As David Norton rightly notes, "Hume was satisfied that the battle to establish reliable links between thought and reality had been fought and *lost* and hence he made his contributions to philosophy from a post-sceptical perspective that incorporates and builds on the sceptical results of his predecessors."[46] Hume was a "post-skeptical philosopher" because he was willing to give up the vain attempt to ground all of our beliefs rationally. In addition to such a concession, he strongly felt, though he could not quite consistently articulate, that this was not a real defeat of human knowledge and certainty.[47]

Hume's conclusions about causality, therefore, call us to appreciate the role of deep-seated mental habits when interacting with the world, and to value experience over a priori thinking when talking about it. Thus, Hume's critique of so-called necessary causation sets a different, if not completely new, tone in modern philosophical discourse, confirming, in effect, the breakthrough made by Ghazali's defense of reading miracle stories in their plain sense.[48] However, we are yet to observe Hume's treatment of miracle testimonies, which stands in stark contrast to Ghazali's.

Hume on Miracles

Hume's essay "Of Miracles," which forms part 10 of his *Enquiry Concerning Human Understanding*, has been a topic of intense philosophical discussion up to the present day. This short treatise has been praised by some as a brilliant refutation of the reliability of miracle testimonies, while others have criticized its arguments as subtly circular, as inconsistent, and even as an "abject failure."[49] "Of Miracles" is significant not only for the debates about miracles that it provoked, but also for illustrating the connection between the attitude toward miracles and discussions on modern epistemology and science. Let us take a closer look at this treatise on miracles.

Hume's Argument Against Miracle Reports

Hume's "Of Miracles" consists of two parts. The first is around five pages, and the second is around twelve pages. In the first part, he offers a formula according to which a reasonable person should weigh any testimony. The more an event has been repeated in the past, the more its observer will be justified in anticipating future occurrences of the event. In the case of mixed past experience, the most reasonable thing to do would be to weigh the two possibilities and side with the possibility that has been encountered more frequently: "A hundred instances or experiments on one side, and fifty on another, afford a doubtful expectation of any event; though a hundred uniform experiments, with only one that is contradictory, reasonably beget a pretty strong degree of assurance. In all cases, we must balance the opposite experiments, where they are opposite, and deduct the smaller number from the greater, in order to know the exact force of the superior evidence."[50]

After establishing this "wise rule" of weighing past experience, Hume proceeds to apply it to the evaluation of testimony. The more unusual a narrated event is, the more suspicious we should be in accepting a witness's testimony. That this rule itself is not demonstrated by experience, and that it conveniently glosses over the problem of induction, is strikingly puzzling, but let us bear with his argument here. On the basis of this rule of probability, Hume concludes that if a reported event claims that a totally unprecedented event has occurred, it is only reasonable that we should resist the validity of the testimony, like an Indian prince who refused to believe that water becomes solid ice in cold climates. Hence, "it naturally required very strong testimony to engage his [the prince's] assent to facts that arose from a state of nature, with which he was unacquainted, and which bore so little analogy to those events, of which he had had constant and uniform experience."[51]

Now, so far, Hume's argument does not seem to take issue with miracles. After all, one may caution against the rejection of miracles by noting that the response of the Indian prince, natural as it may be, was nevertheless a mistaken refusal. Yet Hume introduces a definition of "miracle" that sets it apart from unusual events: "A miracle is a violation of the laws of nature."[52] Such a definition tacitly assumes that the laws of nature are absolute, an assumption that the philosopher-scientist Charles S. Peirce will question, as we shall see in the next chapter. For now, let us observe that Hume claims that unlike an unusual event, which is "not conformable" to one's previous experience, a miracle is "contrary" to it and hence must be rejected.[53] It seems that the former represents a new, unusual circumstance, while the latter represents a contradiction. Thus, an unusual event may be believed on the account of strong testimony, whereas a miracle can rarely, if ever, be established by any kind of testimony: "There must, therefore, be a uniform experience against every miraculous event, otherwise the event would not merit that appellation. And as a uniform experience amounts to a proof, there is here a direct and full *proof*, from the nature of the fact, against the existence of any miracle; nor can such a proof be destroyed, or the miracle rendered credible, but by an opposite proof, which is superior."[54] In other words, miracle testimonies, *by definition*, cannot ever be acceptable. Right after defining a miracle as a violation of the laws of nature, Hume, in a footnote, adds a religious qualification to his definition: "A miracle may be accurately defined, *a transgression of a law of nature by a particular volition of the Deity, or by the interposition of some invisible agent.*" Even if an event is deemed to be otherwise natural, such as falling rain, if it is preceded by a claim of a divine mission, then the event is a miracle, "because nothing can be more contrary to nature than that the voice or command of a man should have such an influence" as bringing down rain or healing the sick.[55] To this religious connotation of "miracle" we shall return shortly.

Hume ends part I of "Of Miracles" by noting his "general maxim." Here he explains that the report of a miracle can be reasonably accepted only when "the testimony [is] of such a kind, that its falsehood would be more miraculous, than the fact, which it endeavors to establish: And even in that case there is a mutual destruction of arguments, and the superior only gives us an assurance suitable to that degree of force, which remains, after deducting the inferior."[56]

In part 2 of his essay, Hume applies his general maxim to miracle reports with which he is familiar, showing that there is no single case where the rejection of testimony is more overwhelming than the miracle story itself. It is easier to explain the falsehood of the testimony by referring to ambiguities in human nature than to accept that a regular pattern in nature has been suspended on a certain occasion. After all, Hume believes that typical human tendencies—such as the love of exaggeration, the wish to exalt oneself, vanity, ignorance, barbarism, and so forth—can naturally account for the fabrication and transmission of any miracle story.[57] Furthermore, Hume diagnoses religious enthusiasm as one of the basic motivations for fabricating superstitions. Therefore, one must be especially resistant to miracles that are cited in support of a religious cause: "As the violations of truth are more common in the testimony concerning religious miracles than in that concerning any other matter of fact; this must diminish very much the authority of the former testimony, and make us form a general resolution, *never* to lend any attention to it, with whatever specious pretence it may be covered."[58]

At the very end of his essay, Hume refers to the miracles in the Old Testament and asks the reader to judge for himself whether it is easier to believe in the validity of the miracle stories or to believe that the stories were fabricated:

It [the Pentateuch] gives an account of a state of the world and of human nature entirely different from the present: Of our fall from that state: Of the age of man, extended to near a thousand years: Of the destruction of the world by a deluge: Of the arbitrary choice of one people, as the favorites of heaven; and that people the countrymen of the author: Of their deliverance from bondage by prodigies the most astonishing imaginable: I desire any one to lay his hand upon his heart, and after a serious consideration declare, whether he thinks that the falsehood of such a book, supported by such a testimony, would be more extraordinary and miraculous than all the miracles it relates; which is, however, necessary to make it be received, according to the measures of probability above established.[59]

Thus, Hume's general maxim for evaluating miracle reports yields a hermeneutics of suspicion: miracle stories in the Hebrew/Christian scriptures must be read as absurd fabrications that deserve rejection as the best reasonable response. This conclusion is not surprising given Hume's well-known suspicion of religious matters in general. We must, however, also attend to the crucial contradiction present throughout this essay.

A Puzzling Tension: Hume's Critique of Necessary Causality
Versus His Argument Against Miracles

Hume's treatise has been rightly criticized for unjustifiably rejecting all miracle reports preemptively. Since miracles are, by definition, departures from a hitherto observed regularity in nature, to weigh their occurrences against the regularity of our past experience is not fair, unless we believe that natural order is absolute and cannot admit exception. The treatise calls, in effect, for a categorical rejection of miracles, and such a rejection is especially perplexing given the fact that Hume, through his statement of the problem of induction, recognizes not only that change in the natural order is conceivable but also that the accumulation of past experience does *not* logically decrease the *possibility* of a contrary event happening in the future.[60]

In defense of Hume, some scholars have suggested that he nowhere argues the impossibility of miracles on a priori grounds. According to Fogelin, for instance, Hume concludes that it is inadvisable to take miracle stories seriously only after he provides an analysis of miracle accounts based on his general maxim. Fogelin repeatedly mentions that Hume's example of eight days of darkness shows that Hume did concede, albeit hypothetically, the possibility of proving the truth of a miracle story.[61] It is worth citing the relevant passage so as to follow Fogelin's defense. Hume says,

> I beg the limitations here made may be remarked, when I say, that *a miracle can never be proved, so as to be the foundation of a system of religion*. For I own, that *otherwise, there may possibly be miracles*, or violations of the usual course of nature, of such a kind as to admit of proof from human testimony; though, perhaps, it will be impossible to find any such in all the records of history. Thus, suppose, all authors, in all languages, agree, that, from the first of January 1600, there was a total darkness over the whole earth for eight days: Suppose that the tradition of this extraordinary event is still strong and lively among the people: That all travelers, who return from foreign countries, bring us accounts of the same tradition, without the least variation or contradiction: *It is evident, that our present philosophers, instead of doubting the fact, ought to receive it as certain, and ought to search for the*

causes whence it might be derived. The decay, corruption, and dissolution of nature, is an event rendered probable by so many analogies, that any phenomenon, which seems to have a tendency towards that catastrophe, comes within the reach of human testimony, *if that testimony be very extensive and uniform.*[62]

Fogelin argues that in this example Hume accepts the possibility that a miracle story could be reliable on the basis of outstanding testimony. Hence, Hume cannot be criticized for offering an a priori argument against miracles and thereby contradicting his own rejection of the a priori status of the natural order.

Fogelin's explanation, however, overlooks two problems in Hume's argument. First, Hume eventually disowns the miraculous aspect of his eight days of darkness example by claiming that it is not quite a departure from our previous experience. After all, as quoted above, "the decay, corruption, and dissolution of nature, is an event rendered probable by so many analogies." Indeed, Hume encourages philosophers to accept the testimony about eight days of darkness as a curious *natural* event that is explainable in reference to natural causes, and says that they "ought to search for the causes whence it might be derived." His next example in the treatise, that of a person being resurrected after his death, also reinforces Hume's disallowance of miracles. Unlike the eight days of darkness example, Hume does not think that such a report on resurrection is admissible even on the basis of outstanding testimony.[63] Thus, it is difficult to see how Hume, even in theory, allows for the possibility of miracles.

The second odd aspect of Hume's examples of acceptable miracle reports is his insistence that a clear and overwhelming testimony might be reasonably acceptable if it is *not* associated with a religious claim. Hume's caution against religious fervor is understandable to a considerable extent, given all the proclivities associated with different religious traditions. Yet such proclivities also take place in mundane contexts, and to single out religious reference as a disqualifier in itself is not justified, unless one already shares Hume's belief that religion is purely a result of human wishful thinking. Suppose, for instance, that eight days of darkness were preceded by a prophet's claim that God would darken the earth for eight days as a confirmation of his prophethood. In this case, should we reject the well-attested testimony simply because of this reported religious reference?

One may argue that Hume is not hostile to the element of religion in the miracle report per se, but he is suspicious of the idea that even the strongest miracle testimonies are able to prove the existence of God.[64] As we have seen in the Muslim context, Hume would find that many theologians agree with him on this. Yet the fact that a miracle cannot be foundational evidence need not mean it can never act as *supporting* evidence for any religious belief. Hume's contention that we need to reject miracle reports if they are connected with a religious claim is therefore overstated. Moreover, if the "foundation" of a system of religion could be taken in a broader sense, then the miracles would have, for some, a foundational value. That is, if a deist decides to become a theist on the basis of his perception that a miracle has been performed by someone who claims to be a messenger from the creator of the world, then such a miracle would be, in a way, "foundational" for him. In sum, Hume's dismissal of the religious context of miracle reports is at best overstated, if not simply prejudiced.

While there are other exegetical issues as well as critiques and defenses of Hume's essay on miracles,[65] it is obvious that a crucial tension is present between the two strands in Hume's thought:

(1) Hume's contention that a change in the course of nature *is* conceivable, even after witnessing the same order innumerable times (as expressed in his analysis of causality in the *Treatise* and *Enquiry*).

(2) Hume's contention that based on past experience we should reject *all* testimonies about events that report on an exception to the usual course of nature.

Indeed, it is very odd that Hume, who considers a causal lifting of one's finger to be as extraordinary as moving the mountains with a secret wish, would reject the possibility of miracles so adamantly on the pretext that they are contrary to nature.[66] If, unlike rationalists, Hume clearly sees that the immutability of natural order is not proven by reason, why is he, then, so insistent that miracle reports, especially the ones with religious connections, must be dismissed?

One explanation given for this contradiction in Hume's approach is his dislike for Christianity and organized religion in general.[67] Since Hume believed religious belief to be superstitious and dangerous, after having removed skeptical doubts about commonsense beliefs, he refused to allow religious beliefs to be considered as a type of natural belief.[68] Other scholars, who see that there is much more to religious belief than superstition and conflict, rightly criticize Hume's approach as tainted with a "double standard."[69] While Hume's position here is inconsistent, one can also take some helpful cues from this stark contradiction for the hermeneutics of miracle stories in Qur'anic—and biblical—texts.

To begin with, let us recall that Hume's transition from radical skepticism to his acceptance of naturalism and common sense did not occur on the basis of any arguments but rather as a result of acknowledging the power of natural instincts over reason. Hence, Hume suggested that, while remaining aware of the ultimate contingency of our habits of thinking, we should still cultivate them, and we should continue to consider our predictions beyond reasonable doubt when something has been repeatedly experienced in a particular way. Hume was trying to establish a delicate balance: he wanted to admit the problem of induction and also to trust our natural instincts, despite the fact that he could not explain which of our natural instincts must be trusted in the long run and why. In this effort to resist the crisis of skepticism, Hume might have been concerned that miracle stories, once admitted, will create an opening for the return of the incurable skeptical state of mind.[70] Just as Hume's move from skepticism to empiricism was not warranted on the basis of arguments, his rejection of miracle stories is not warranted by his arguments. In other words, perhaps Hume is so strongly opposed to miracle stories, especially the religious ones, *precisely because* he is aware that there is nothing irrational about them.

In this regard, Hume's views on miracles can be usefully compared with his views on free will. As Fogelin pointed out, Hume opts for determinism so as to be able to produce a "science of man," which would enable him to make predictions about human behavior. If free will is admitted into the scheme, it will make predictions of human action impossible, for it is not possible to add such an indeterminate factor into the equation and still predict human behavior clearly. As with human freedom, Hume felt compelled to leave out miracles, so as to protect the stability of empirical science.[71] As William James aptly highlighted, there is a notable similarity between the issue of miracles and the issue of human freedom: "The wrath of science against miracles, of certain philosophers against the doctrine of free-will, has precisely the same root,—dislike to admit any ultimate factor in things which may rout our prevision or upset the stability of our outlook."[72] Hence, the disregard for miracles or free will in a scientific context is not due to logical reasons, but is for the sake of simplifying the prediction process.

Thus, while Hume's *argument* against miracles does not succeed, there is something valuable in his attempt. Since Hume understands miracle reports as breeding unreasonable doubt and as undoing the natural tendencies that allow us to live our lives, he perceives the need to disqualify them with utmost urgency. Given such an interpretation of miracle stories, such fervor to reject them is not surprising at all. In fact, Hume's resistance to religious miracle stories in *this* sense is reminiscent of Ghazali's dismay at certain theologians who undermined daily trust in the uniformity of nature by giving the pretext that miracles are possible at any time. Both Hume and Ghazali oppose rationalists, positing that the current natural order is not inviolable, and yet they also try to protect common sense and science. In fact, as noted earlier, similar to Hume, who sometimes uses the word "proof" for inductive claims, Ghazali uses the word "demonstration" when he speaks of scientific causal statements. They both admit this kind of usage as shorthand, even though they are aware that natural causality is not rationally demonstrable. Hume's reluctance to acknowledge miracles thus might be compared to Ghazali's reluctance to anticipate breaks in the course of nature, despite his defense of their conceivability.

Indeed, Hume, Ghazali, and Ibn Rushd are all uncomfortable with a view of miracles that undermines science. A major difference between them is on the issue of whether miracle stories may have a different implication than an assault on science and common sense. While for Ghazali the answer is a clear yes, Ibn Rushd seems to agree only with regard to the common people, and Hume fails to see any meaningful reading of miracle stories. To be sure, Ibn Rushd's reservations about miracle stories seem relatively more comparable to Hume's adamant attitude against miracles in his treatise than to Ghazali's viewpoint. The fact that Hume's concern for common sense and science is couched in a rejection of miracle reports reminds us of Ibn Rushd's severe criticism of Ghazali's approach. Just as Hume was concerned about the possibility of the empirical method, Ibn Rushd wanted to protect the possibility of science and human certainty. Hume's stance on miracles and Ibn Rushd's dismay at Ghazali's deconstruction of necessary causality are ultimately not justifiable, but they are valuable in that they highlight the need to make room for certainty within a non-necessitarian epistemology.

Hume's stance on miracles also raises a crucial question about the use of his critical analysis of causality. For Ghazali, such a critique allowed the possibility of miracles, which in turn called for an existential awareness and appreciation of the natural order and its maker. In contrast, Hume criticizes the demonstrability of causality and then proceeds with a complete disregard of that criticism. His critique, when placed within the broader framework of his thought, looks like lightning on a rainy day: the lightning strikes with immense illumination, and then the rain and clouds continue as if nothing has taken place. Hume's critique shed light on the role of experience and habits in epistemology but then seems to have shrunk back to the limits of Newtonian science, without making much difference. Yet the lightning did strike in places, and Hume's writings did become a precursor for important shifts in Western epistemology. In order to see the repercussions of Hume's critique of natural causality, we need to look at the transformations that took place after him. His successors, such as Kant and Peirce, developed Hume's critical assessment in a way that delineates its implications for epistemology and scientific inquiry.

If, after Ghazali's breakthrough, Hume's exposition of the problem of induction, and Kant's Copernican Revolution, there is no going back to naive realism or rationalism, then we need to investigate the promises of a "fallible epistemology." Hume has confirmed the dawn of a post-skeptical worldview without, however, working out its implications. As we shall see in the next chapter, Peirce fills in the gaps for us, standing as an example of a late modern thinker engaging fruitfully with the critical transformations Hume has initiated. Indeed, Peirce furthers Hume's critique of causality and emphasizes the importance of identifying our habits of thinking as more effective than rational demonstration. He also offers a crucial correction to Hume's stance on miracles, reconciling it with a fallible epistemology. In fact, Peirce sees value in miracle narratives for the purposes of scientific inquiry. Peirce will thus uncover for us in a late modern context the scientific and existential implications that miracle stories might have.

4

CHARLES S. PEIRCE ON PRAGMATISM, SCIENCE, AND MIRACLES

"Stones do not fall from heaven," said Laplace, although they had been falling upon inhabited ground every day from the earliest times.

—Charles S. Peirce, *Collected Papers*

It is a great thing for the field of philosophy when a well-trained scientist becomes devoted to its study. Charles Sanders Peirce (1839–1913), arguably the best American philosopher to date, represents such an immense gain: with an advanced degree in chemistry from Harvard, years of scientific practice at the U.S. Coast Survey, and an early kindled interest in philosophy and logic, Peirce contributed to contemporary philosophy in various fruitful ways. Hookway aptly sums up Peirce's rich intellectual legacy:

> [Peirce] is best known to the wider philosophical community for his writings about the nature of truth and for the papers in which he formulated and defended his "pragmatist principle." He also wrote on probability and the foundations of statistical reasoning and constructed a complex account of meaning and representation which he called "semiotic" or "semeiotic." Mindful of the Kantian roots of his thought, he relied upon an original theory of categories, one which, from the late 1890s, was grounded in a kind of phenomenological investigation. He also worked on ethics and aesthetics, on the foundations of mathematics, on the nature of mind, and on the construction of an ambitious system of evolutionary metaphysics. This list merely samples his philosophical interests and does not touch on his mathematical and scientific work.[1]

As an important thinker in his own right, Peirce is significant for our purposes of engaging with the Qurʾanic miracle stories for a number of reasons. First, as a major philosopher *and* an accomplished scientist, he offers an invaluable perspective on modern epistemology and scientific method. Moreover, he fills two major gaps that were present in Hume's tantalizing analysis of natural causality. First, he works out its implications for scientific inquiry, and second, he provides a metaphysical support for Hume's escape from the skeptical results of such critique. Peirce stabilizes Hume's fallible epistemology by anchoring it in his own "scientific metaphysics." It is therefore within the context of a broader framework of scientific epistemology and metaphysics that we shall look at Peirce's approach to miracle stories and see how he reads them as relevant to the modern mind and scientific praxis. In what follows, we shall start by observing how Peirce develops Hume's post-skeptical stance, in effect translating into modern terms Ghazali's medieval breakthrough from rationalism.

Pragmatism, Scientific Method, and Natural Order

Peirce structured key aspects of his pragmatist thought as a response to rationalism. He saw major problems in the Cartesian tradition inaugurated by the rationalist thinker Descartes (1596–1650), who is considered the first modern philosopher. As a solution to such problems, and as an expression of the inspiration he gained from long years of practicing and reflecting on the method of science, Peirce offered his pragmatist philosophy. Even though Peirce's criticism of Cartesianism was somewhat modified over the years—and he himself may not have heeded his own criticism early on[2]—it stayed at the center of his thought as he tried to work out his alternative to Cartesianism in the forms of pragmatism and "critical commonsensism." In what follows, we shall attend more closely to the problems he found to be inherent in a rationalist approach, a dominant disposition before the inauguration of the post-skeptical era in Western philosophy.

In his early papers, written around 1868–69, Peirce notes that Descartes's philosophy marks a departure from scholasticism.[3] In this sense, Descartes is the father of modern philosophy (5.264, 1868).[4] Peirce thinks that the "father" was right to depart from scholasticism in certain respects, but what he replaced it with, namely Cartesianism, was not good enough. Peirce identifies four major problems with Cartesianism. To start with, scholastic thought revered authority and saw logic as a primarily analytic affair in which one learned how to break down a given proposition in order to see its coherence with the voice of authority (5.359, 1877). Cartesianism rejected this approach, and rightly so. But then it asserted that philosophy must start with universal doubt, not taking anything for granted. Peirce notes that this move was misguided, for it is simply not possible to doubt everything: "We cannot begin with complete doubt. We must begin with all the prejudices which we actually have when we enter upon the study of philosophy. These prejudices are not to be dispelled by a maxim, for they are things which it does not occur to us can be questioned. Hence this initial skepticism will be a mere self-deception, and not real doubt; and no one who follows the Cartesian method will ever be satisfied until he has formally recovered all those beliefs which in form he has given up" (5.264, 1868). By insisting on this impossible method of questioning everything, Cartesianism had deluded itself with a pretension.[5]

In a piece written decades later, in 1905, Peirce explains his rejection of "paper doubt" as follows:

> In truth, there is but one state of mind from which you can "set out," namely, the very state of mind in which you actually find yourself at the time you do "set out,"—a state in which you are laden with an immense mass of cognition already formed, of which you cannot divest yourself if you would; and who knows whether, if you could, you would not have made all knowledge impossible to yourself? Do you call it *doubting* to write down on a piece of paper that you doubt? If so, doubt has nothing to do with any serious business. (5. 416, 1905)

Peirce's criticism of paper doubt does not imply that any assumptions one happens to have at a given time should never be doubted. Rather, he means that (1) not all beliefs can be doubted at the same time, and (2) instinctive or commonsense beliefs are to be trusted until we find a reason *not* to do so. In Peirce's epistemology, "an inquirer has a fallible background of 'common sense' belief which is not in fact in doubt. Only against such a background can a belief be put into doubt and a new, better belief be adopted. All our beliefs are fallible but they do not come into doubt all at once."[6] Hence, Peirce admits that a person may come across a reason that will make him doubt what he initially took for granted and, in such a case, the person will experience doubt because she or he has a positive reason for it, not because she or he has artificially decided to doubt everything as a matter of principle. Peirce's advice is, therefore, "let us not pretend to doubt in philosophy what we do not doubt in our hearts" (5.264, 1868).

Peirce's rejection of universal doubt is not only an optimistic move but also a humbling one. By rejecting the claim that at a given time *all* of our beliefs could be wrong, Peirce not only values common sense but also limits the scope of certainty of our knowledge. Since we cannot start with universal doubt, we cannot end in universal certainty, either: "There are three things to which we can never hope to attain by reasoning, namely, absolute certainty, absolute exactitude, absolute universality" (1.141, ca. 1897). Peirce's epistemology transforms Hume's—and Ghazali's—skeptical crisis into discernment about the possibility and horizons of human knowledge.

Peirce also affirms Hume's demonstration that reason on its own never suffices, and that instincts and habits play an indispensable role in acquiring knowledge. To him, Hume's skeptical conclusions show "the intensely ridiculous way in which a man winds himself up in silly paper doubts if he undertakes to throw common sense, *i.e.* instinct, overboard and be perfectly rational," and they thus confirm pragmatism's principle that "reason is a mere succedaneum to be used where instinct is wanting" (6.500, 1906).[7]

The second problem Peirce diagnoses in Descartes's thought is that when Cartesianism rejected reference to authority, it put individual certainty in its place. The hallmark of Cartesianism thus boils down to the idea that "whatever I am clearly convinced of is true" (5.265, 1868), which amounts to establishing private certainty in place of public certainty.[8] And yet "to make the individual the judge of truth" is very problematic, as "the result is that metaphysicians will all agree that metaphysics has reached a pitch of certainty far beyond that of the physical sciences;—only they can agree upon nothing else" (5.265, 1868). Thus, Peirce emphasizes that the search for truth is a community task. Moreover, as we shall see, Peirce insists that truth is not attained simply through clear thinking but needs to be constrained and guided by our collective experiences in the world.

According to Peirce, a third problem in Cartesianism is that it rejected the scholastic way of argumentation in favor of "a single thread of inference depending often upon inconspicuous premises [*sic*]" (5.264, 1868). Peirce claimed that this was also wrong, because successful reasoning proceeds not in one single syllogistic thread but through the accumulation of different links between the premise and the conclusion: "Reasoning [of philosophy] should not form a chain which is no stronger than its weakest link, but a cable whose fibers may be ever so slender, provided they are sufficiently numerous and intimately connected" (5.265, 1868).[9]

Finally, Cartesianism rendered certain facts as "absolutely inexplicable" by saying that "God made them so" (5.265, 1868). To be sure, Peirce is aware that scholasticism also had its mysteries of faith, but Cartesianism seems worse on this score. Having started with the pretense that it will explain all things, Cartesianism is inconsistent in concluding that certain things are inexplicable. Pragmatism, on the other hand, does not claim that it will explain everything and is willing to allow concepts to be interpreted in reference to their consequences and implications, rather than explained theoretically.[10]

Peirce suggests that his pragmatist theory of meaning and truth can escape all of these Cartesian problems. Pragmatism "corrects rather than negates Cartesian foundationalism: transforming Cartesian anxiety into pragmatic critique and Descartes' clear-and-distinct, self-legitimating intuitions into irremediably vague, indubitable beliefs."[11] In what follows, we shall discuss how Peirce's pragmatism affirms the insights of rationalism while remedying its shortcomings.

Pragmatism as an Alternative to Cartesianism

Peirce is considered the founder of pragmatism. Before we discuss what that is, a disclaimer will be of use: the term "pragmatism" does not mean pragmatism in the popular utilitarian sense. In fact, when this term began to quickly gain popularity, mainly through Peirce's friend William James (d. 1910), an original thinker, physiologist, and psychologist, Peirce felt the need to distinguish his understanding of pragmatism from other popular understandings of the term. Thus, he coined a new term, "pragmaticism." Since, in this book, I will mostly talk about Peirce's understanding of the term, I shall continue to refer to his version, "pragmaticism," simply as "pragmatism," with the awareness that it is different from the more popular use of the term.

In his 1901 article "What Pragmatism Is," Peirce notes that he first coined the term as a man of science who had been reflecting on the task of philosophy: "[As a "man of laboratory," I] framed the theory that a *conception*, that is, the rational purport of a word or other expression, lies *exclusively in its conceivable bearing upon the conduct of life*; so that, since obviously nothing that might not result from experiment can have any direct bearing upon conduct, if one can define accurately all the conceivable experimental phenomena which the affirmation or denial of a concept could imply, one will have therein a complete definition of the concept, and *there is absolutely nothing more in it*" (5.412, 1905).[12] In other words, Peirce's pragmatism defines a concept exclusively in terms of its actual and potential consequences. According to this "pragmatic maxim," if a concept has no experimental consequence whatsoever, then it is meaningless. For any concept or proposition to have any meaning, it should be translatable into a certain attitude or action that can be experienced by us: "Pragmatism is the principle that every theoretical judgment expressible in a sentence in the *indicative mood* is a confused form of thought whose only *meaning, if it has any*, lies in its tendency to enforce a corresponding practical maxim expressible as a conditional sentence having its apodosis in the *imperative mood*" (5.18, 1907, italics added).

Peirce's famous example is the proposition that a diamond is hard. The indicative mood in such a proposition is actually a summation of a range of possible conditionals such as: if you press it, it will resist; if you try to scratch it, it will not easily scratch. To say that the hardness of the diamond means something that is not expressible in any form of conditional or imperative does not make sense, "just as it is entirely without meaning to say that virtue or any other abstraction is hard" (7.340, ca. 1873). To be sure, Peirce does not claim that each concept or proposition should have a handful of imperative moods attached to it. On the contrary, a concept may have many different consequences in different contexts and most probably has certain consequences that are discoverable only in the long run. Indeed, one cannot define a concept once and for all.[13]

One major benefit of pragmatism is that the definition of a concept only in terms of its experimental results precludes many meaningless discussions on ontology and metaphysics.[14] An interesting example in this regard is the thorny issue of free will versus determinism. If the issue is phrased in terms of the consequences of an action, what is at stake becomes much clearer and unnecessary disagreements can be dropped: "The question of free-will and fate in its simplest form, stripped of verbiage, is something like this: I have done something of which I am ashamed; could I, by an effort of the will, have resisted the temptation, and done otherwise?" Once the pragmatic significance of the issue is thus defined, it is easier to see that "this is not a question of fact, but only of the arrangement of facts."

Arranging them so as to exhibit what is particularly pertinent to my question—namely, that I ought to blame myself for having done wrong—it is perfectly true to say that, if I had willed to do otherwise than I did, I should have done otherwise. On the other hand, arranging the facts so as to exhibit another important consideration, it is equally true that, when a temptation has once been allowed to work, it will, if it has a certain force, produce its effect, let me struggle how I may. There is no objection to a contradiction in what would result from a false supposition. (5.403, 1878)

Thus, the pragmatic implication of the belief in free will is that when I am tempted to do wrong, I can and should tap into my strength to resist it. And the pragmatic meaning of the belief in determinism is that if I would like to avoid doing wrong, I should not place myself in the path of temptation, for once temptation is allowed to work, the consequences are almost inevitable. In both cases, the doctrine at hand has direct relevance for my choices. In contrast, when the pragmatic questions are ignored, one may debate the issue forever, without any real import being brought to the fore.

Peirce's emphasis on the consequences of a concept and his claim to expose the "meaningless gibberish" (5.423, 1905) in metaphysics may remind us of positivism. In fact, Peirce concedes that pragmatism may be a precursor to it; pragmatism is "a species of prope-positivism." Yet it is distinguished from other brands of prope-positivism in three regards. First, pragmatism does not limit rational discourse to mere "brute facts" and "tangible phenomena"; rather, it leaves room for a "properly executed metaphysics." Second, it affirms the "main body of our instinctive beliefs." And third, it insists on realism (5.423, 1905).[15] Indeed, as Robert Corrington noted, Peirce's pragmatism "never degenerates into an unrestricted use of Ockham's razor, always honoring complexity and continuity where it obtains, but it does provide a means for weeding out some of the less useful concepts within both science and philosophy."[16]

Two more clarifications about the pragmatic maxim are in order. First, by insisting on the consequences, Peirce does not mean to reduce all conception to action—he does not mean to "make Doing the Be-all and the End-all of human life." In fact, according to him, "to say that we live merely for the sake of action, as action, regardless of the thought it carries out, would be to say that there is no such thing as rational purport" (5.429, 1905).[17] Second, it should be noted that with his emphasis on experiment, Peirce does not simply mean the experience of an isolated event; rather, he means experimentation as part of a larger project of discerning a *general pattern* in the world through manipulating and modifying given conditions.[18] Indeed, "no agglomeration of actual happenings can ever completely fill up the meaning of a 'would-be'" (5.467, ca. 1906). Peirce's emphasis on action and experimentation, therefore, should be understood at the background of his regard for generals and overall tendencies. Hence, in a letter to William James, Peirce feels the need to bring to attention the significance of *generalization* for his pragmatism: "That everything is to be tested by its practical results was the great text of my early papers. . . . In my later papers, I have seen more thoroughly than I used to do that it is *not mere action as brute exercise of strength* that is the purpose of all, but say *generalization, such action as tends toward regularization, and the actualization of the thought* which without action remains unthought" (8.250, 1897, italics added).

In sum, Peirce's pragmatism defines the meaning of a concept in terms of (1) its practical and conceivable *consequences*, and (2) the ways in which these consequences instantiate *general* tendencies. And, by leaving room for metaphysics and appreciating the complexity of human experience, it departs from both positivism and the popular sense of pragmatism. Before we analyze how such an approach relates to the conceptions of natural order and miracles, we shall further highlight two key notions of Peirce's pragmatism: habit and the triadic nature of signs.

After having discussed Ghazali's and Hume's critiques of rationalism, it is not surprising to find "habit" accompanying Peirce's critique of rationalism, too. Peirce's understanding of habit not only converges with but also broadens and enriches the concept of habit that we have seen thus far. "Habit" is Peirce's more specific term for "tendency toward regularization," and he uses it especially (but not exclusively) in the context of human behavior. A habit is our tendency "actually to behave in a similar way under similar circumstances in the future" (5.487, 1891); it is our "readiness to act in a certain way under given circumstances and when actuated by a given motive" (5.480, 1893). Similar to James, Peirce recognizes the biological basis of habit, which means that habit is not merely a mental state but also part of *how nature operates* (6.259–62, 1891).[19]

A crucial aspect of Peirce's understanding of human habit is the notion that each person exercises some control over the modification of his habits.[20] Indeed, habit is distinct from natural dispositions in that the latter are formed through "multiple reiterated behavior of the same kind."[21] It is this ability to form and revise our habits or dispositions that lies at the heart of Peirce's pragmatism; what gives meaning to a concept is the potential to

influence our habits of thinking and acting. In order to have a better grasp
of the significance of habit for pragmatism, let us briefly venture into one
of Peirce's areas of expertise: his semiotics or sign theory.

Semiotics and Habit

When we think of signs, we often think of them in dyadic terms: there
is the sign, such as a word or an utterance, and there is the object that
it represents, such as an apple or a situation. In the same way, the word
"apple" represents the object apple, and the utterance "I am surprised"
represents my state of mind. This dyadic picture of signification, essential
to the view of Ferdinand de Saussure (who is considered the founder of
semiotics, along with Peirce), is simply insufficient for Peirce. It overlooks
the fact that "the expression or thought has the content that it does only
because it is (or can be) understood or interpreted in that way."[22] By adding
a third element, the "interpretant," to the dualistic (sign-object) account of
Saussurean semiotics, Peirce emphasizes the contextual and consequential
aspect of signification (5.484, ca. 1906).

The "interpretant" of a sign may be mental, but it may also be non-
mental. A sign can be interpreted in the way we "use it as a premise in
inference, form expectations about the future run of experience, show surprise when experience clashes with it, and so on."[23] Hence, an "emotional
interpretant" denotes the feelings accompanying the sign, while an "energetic interpretant" is the resultant effort (physical or mental) of the sign.
There is also the "logical interpretant" that could occur as a thought, which
is another mental sign and will in turn have its own logical interpretant. For
Peirce, the *ultimate* logical interpretant of a sign, which is not a mental sign
in itself (though it could be a sign in another respect), is *habit-change*. It is a
change in one's predisposition to act, "a modification of a person's tendencies toward action, resulting from previous experiences or from previous
exertions of his will or acts, or from a complexus of both kinds of cause"
(5.477, ca. 1906). This habit-change includes changes in habits of thinking
(mental associations and dissociations) as well.

It is noteworthy that, according to Peirce, action, which is the "energetic
interpretant" of a sign, is *not* the ultimate logical interpretant of a concept.
This is because action is specific and individual, and thus it lacks *general-
ity*. Instead, it is *habit*, with its future orientation—the posture of "if such
conditions occur, I shall do/assume X"—that has the potential to go beyond

individual instances. Therefore, "the deliberately formed, self-analyzing habit—self-analyzing because it is formed by the aid of analysis of the exercises that nourished it—is *the living definition, the veritable and final logical interpretant*" of a sign (5.491, ca. 1906, italics added).[24]

From a pragmatic perspective, therefore, the best description of a concept will be offered through an account of how a concept is calculated to bring about a change in a *habit* (5.491, ca. 1906). Similarly, "to predicate any such concept of a real or imaginary object is equivalent to declaring that a certain operation, corresponding to the concept, if performed upon that object, *would* (certainly, or probably, or possibly, according to the mode of predication), be followed by a result of a definite *general* description" (5.483, ca. 1906, italics added). What makes scientific descriptions so precious is not that they describe "any particular event that did happen to somebody in the dead past" but that they indicate "what *surely will* happen to everybody in the living future who shall fulfill certain conditions" (5.425, 1905). In sum, pragmatism must be future oriented and attentive to consequences and overall tendencies.

Peirce's repeated references to the future not only distinguish his pragmatism from a particularistic vision but also highlight, once again, the importance of the consequences of a concept. When one becomes aware of a fact or a situation, if such awareness cannot yield any recommendation *whatsoever* for the future, if it cannot induce *any* change in one's habits, then such awareness is simply meaningless. Here, the link between anticipating the future and genuine knowledge becomes apparent once again—recall Hume's point that induction is the most important mental association precisely because it connects past experience to predictions about the future. Now, the crux of the matter is this: How does Peirce address the problem of induction? Does pragmatism assume natural determinism, according to which natural order is necessary and absolute and our past experience guarantees what will happen in the future? In order to answer these questions, let us now turn to Peirce's reflections on scientific method.

Peirce on Scientific Method and Laws of Nature

Peirce's reflection on scientific method, among other things, offers two major innovations. First is his concept of "abduction," which highlights the creative element in scientific inquiry, and second is his evaluation of the use of commonsensical assumptions for science, including the idea of the uniformity of natural order. His analysis gives nuance to Hume's walking of the tightrope between skepticism and empiricism, and clarifies the implications of a post-skeptical epistemology for modern science.

According to Peirce, there are three kinds of reasoning in scientific inquiry as well as in philosophical reflection. We are all familiar with these different types in daily life, but only two are typically named in most logic books: deduction and induction. Deduction is "the *only necessary* reasoning. It is the reasoning of mathematics. It starts from a hypothesis, the truth or falsity of which has nothing to do with the reasoning; and of course its conclusions are equally ideal" (5.145, 1903, italics added). Induction, on the other hand, starts out with a theory to be tested, with the hope that as the testing proceeds, there will emerge a more or less correct representation of facts. Even though their starting point and conclusions are different, both deduction and induction share a common limitation: neither of them can offer new ideas. It is only the third type of reasoning, "abduction," that brings a new element into any scientific inquiry.

Peirce defines abduction as "an act of insight" (5.180, 1903). It represents a moment of pause and creative thinking in response to a surprising event or unknown object. It is the light bulb that goes on in our head, offering a hypothesis for explaining the puzzling situation: "Could it be this? Could it be that? Could it be the result of such and such?" Our daily life is saturated with this kind of reasoning. To give an example, when my bus, which is always on time, does not arrive on a weekday, it may occur to me: "Is today a public holiday?" Then I can take out my calendar to see if the day is indeed marked as a holiday, and the result may be that I confirm that indeed it is. In Peirce's terms, I first had an abductive insight in response to a puzzling situation and then formed a deduction from it—"If it is a public holiday, then it should be marked on my calendar"—and proceeded to test it.[25] In fact, abduction is present in the very act of perception, although it is so quick and unconscious that it is often not noticed.[26] Indeed, Peirce was aware, in a Kantian fashion, that there are no "brute givens," that each act of perception is an act of interpreting present immediacies.[27] In other words, abductive reasoning is always at the background of our reasoning, even when we are not aware of it (6.469, ca. 1908).

To be sure, abductive reasoning is not infallible. In the case of our example, it may be that I missed the bus because I was not aware of the change in daylight savings time. Yet abduction is still very important, for it is the only type of reasoning that *can* promise the discovery of something new. Indeed, "all the ideas of science come to it by the way of abduction" (5.145, 1903). Referring to abduction as "retroduction"—because it speculates from the consequence to its antecedent—Peirce notes, "Observe that neither Deduction nor Induction contributes the smallest positive item to the final conclusion of the inquiry. They render the indefinite definite; Deduction Explicates; Induction evaluates: that is all. . . . Yet every plank of [human] advance is first laid by Retroduction alone, that is to say, by the *spontaneous conjectures* of *instinctive* reason; and neither Deduction nor Induction contributes a single new concept to the structure" (6.475, 1908, italics added).

If abduction lies at the heart of scientific discovery, its key lies in the hand of our human instincts. In the process of our reasoning about how to explain an unusual phenomenon, what we need is not *any* hypothesis but rather a hypothesis whose testing is likely to lead us to the solution, or whose testing will at least advance our path to the solution by narrowing down the number of explanatory hypotheses. Otherwise, the capacity of the human mind to generate abductions would be of little use: theoretically, the number of possible hypotheses is endless, and if we were not gifted the capacity to guess correctly more quickly, testing them out would take forever and we would not be able to discover any laws or arrive at any scientific theories. While acknowledging the intuitiveness of the causal maxim, Peirce recognizes that there is no logical connection between a particular natural cause and its consequent—hence the importance of our instincts: "Though there exists a cause for every event, and that of a kind which is capable of being discovered, yet if there be nothing to guide us to the discovery; if we have to hunt among all the events in the world without any scent; if, for instance, the sex of a child might equally be supposed to depend on the configuration of the planets, on what was going on at the antipodes, or on anything else—then the discovery would have no chance of ever getting made" (6.415, 1877). And yet we *have been* able to decipher many patterns in nature and advance in scientific knowledge. Thus, the "very bedrock of logical truth" is that "man's mind must have been attuned to the truth of things in order to discover what he has discovered" (6.476, 1908). Indeed, for Peirce, while it is impossible to assume that our inductions are ever complete and infallible, "there are certain of our inductions which present an approach to universality so extraordinary that, even if we are to suppose that they are not strictly universal truths, *we cannot possibly think that they have been reached merely by accident*" (6.416, 1878, italics added).

In other words, the relatively successful interaction of the human mind with the world shows that "the mind of man is strongly adapted to the comprehension of the world; at least, so far as this goes, that certain conceptions, highly important for such a comprehension, *naturally arise* in his mind; and, without such a tendency, the mind could never have had any development at all" (6.417, 1878, italics added). Hence, Peirce's understanding of scientific inquiry both acknowledges a correspondence between our mental apparatus and the world around us, and admits that our empirical conclusions are never absolute—an approach that makes the best of both Ghazali's and Ibn Rushd's insights articulated through their responses to miracle stories. In what follows, we shall look more deeply into how Peirce explains the parameters of such a fallible epistemology guiding scientific inquiry.

Critical Commonsensism

In his later years, as he was seeking to explain the reasonability of his pragmatist principle, Peirce increasingly put more emphasis on the role of common sense.[28] Pragmatism, he argued, presupposes "critical commonsensism," which is, in Peter Ochs's words, "the belief that there are certain habits of mind which we are ordinarily incapable of doubting." Peirce calls these habits "indubitable beliefs."[29] As we have noted earlier, Peirce has no patience for paper doubts and assumes that our "instinctive beliefs are innocent until proven guilty."[30] Peirce's "critical commonsensism" shares much with the famous British thinker Thomas Reid's defense of common sense, in that it recognizes that certain beliefs do not need grounding. It is, however, different from Reid's commonsensism in that Peirce calls attention to the *vagueness* and *fallibility* of common sense. Thus, like Reid, Peirce thinks that common sense is a matter of instinct and is agreed upon by both "the learned and the vulgar."[31] But, unlike Reid, he also recognizes that "the original beliefs only remain indubitable in their applications to affairs that resemble those of a primitive mode of life" (5.445, 1905). To give an example, to assume that the motion of electrons is three-dimensional is an instinctual move, and while we can proceed with it, we must be willing to modify it if contrary evidence is encountered (5.445, 1905).[32] Our "vague" instincts are thus fallible, may come out to be wrong if they are called to support precise contexts, and are to be trusted and assumed "indubitable" until such a context arises.

Peirce's appreciation of vagueness is an exceptional move on the part of a logician, for in many logical systems there is "an almost imperial sense that all vague structures must be overcome so that clear antecedents and clear consequents can emerge to guide inferences." Peirce's contribution is that he realized that "if these beliefs were anything *but* vague, they would make it difficult for the self to function in a variety of situations, each with its complex variables."[33] As an example of the "vagueness" of our instinctual assumptions, Peirce gives the belief that "fire burns"—a nice coincidence indeed, given that Ghazali also engages with the same statement in reference to the Qur'anic story of Abraham's miraculous survival in the fire. (We shall later apply Peirce's insights more specifically to our case of Qur'anic interpretation.) The statement is vague in that it "leaves open which things fire burns and under what circumstances. While we know what kind of experience would falsify 'fire burns all kinds of dry wood at normal temperatures,' and can therefore test it empirically, almost any experience can be rendered compatible with the vague statement 'Fire burns.'"[34] The statement is very vague, but not "perfectly so": if fire never burned anything, then this proposition would be false (5.498, 1905).

The fire example is also good for demonstrating how a vague, indubitable belief can become misleading if taken out of its primary context and forced to be more precise than it is. The vague belief that "fire burns" is crucial for averting the lethal consequences of fire for human life, but this still leaves the possibility that in a new context it may not apply. For instance, we may want to develop a vest for a firefighter that fire will not burn, and in that context we will be looking to invent a situation in which this indubitable belief is not applicable. This concept of a "vague and indubitable belief" is ingenious in that it expresses how certain axioms can be both certain and contingent at the same time. The statement is contingent because our human conditions may have been different so as not to need or have such a vague belief, and yet it is necessary because, given our current human circumstances and that we are who we are, it *is* an indubitable belief, albeit a vague one.

Peirce notes that our belief in the stability of natural order, or the "uniformity of nature," is also a commonsense belief. In what follows, we shall observe how Peirce's critical engagement with this "vague and indubitable belief" soothes the tensions between Hume's skeptical and empirical moments, as well as between Ghazali's and Ibn Rushd's understandings of natural order.

Uniformity of Nature, Necessitarianism, and Nominalism

According to Peirce, the fact that we note consistent patterns in nature would not mean anything at all if we did not have an instinctual tendency to predict future events on the basis of our past experience. Peirce insists that this commonsense tendency must have a connection to reality in the form of real laws operating in nature (1.26, 1903). In other words, the only way to explain the possibility of our predictions is to refer to some laws, some *real* correlations between things in nature. Otherwise, mere observation of uniformity in nature cannot account for our capacity to make predictions: "If a pair of dice turns up sixes five times running, that is a mere uniformity. The dice might happen fortuitously to turn up sixes a thousand times running. But *that would not afford the slightest security* for a prediction that they would turn up sixes the next time. *If the prediction has a tendency to be fulfilled, it must be that future events have a tendency to conform to a general rule*" (1.26, 1903, italics added). In other words, *if* we are to talk about prediction at all, it is not possible to confine the regularities in nature to mere mental associations.[35]

Nominalism about general rules is therefore deeply mistaken, Peirce says: "'Oh,' but say the nominalists, 'this general rule is nothing but a mere word or couple of words!' I reply, 'Nobody ever dreamed of denying that what is general is of the nature of a general sign; but the question is whether future events will conform to it or not. If they will, your adjective "mere" seems to be ill-placed'" (1.26, 1903). That is, just because the human mind identifies certain tendencies in nature does not necessarily mean that they are *only* present in the mind, with no correlation in nature. To note that the content of an idea is mental does not prove that it is a creation of human fancy; after all, is there any idea that is *not* mental (8.145, 1901)? In this regard, it is useful to note that Ghazali was not a nominalist in his criticism of the necessity of natural causation. He did agree that there was a genuine order reflected in nature; he only suggested that the source of order did not lie in nature itself but in the will of its wise maker, in God's "habit" of creating consistently in a particular way.[36] In Ibn Rushd's strong disagreement with Ghazali, we now more clearly discern what was at stake: Ibn Rushd must have been worried about nominalism. And, even though he was wrong in his interpretation of Ghazali's stance, Ibn Rushd was right in insisting that our mental habits are not mere projections onto reality and that our minds and nature are relatively attuned to each other.

According to Peirce, while nominalism disregards the operation of real generals on which our capacity of prediction is based, "necessitarianism" goes to the other extreme and claims that these general laws operating in nature are without exception, are exact, and leave no room for spontaneity (6.592, 1893). In this sense, necessitarianism takes a true and vague commonsense belief beyond its realm of application to a more precise context than it was intended for. And, just as nominalism fails to account for our relative success in predicting many events, so does "necessitarianism" fail to account for the variety and diversity in the world. In fact, the moment the instinctual assumption of regularity in nature is turned into an assumption of a precise and rigid regularity—into a deterministic worldview—it simply fails the test of experience:[37] "Those observations which are generally adduced in favor of mechanical causation simply prove that there *is* an element of regularity in nature, and have no bearing whatever upon the question of *whether such regularity is exact and universal or not*. Nay, in regard to this exactitude, all observation is directly opposed to it. Try to verify any law of nature, and you will find that the more precise your observations, the more certain they will be to show irregular departures from the law" (6.46, 1892, italics added). While resisting nominalism, therefore, Peirce also resists the temptation to fall into necessitarianism, unlike Ibn Rushd and Hume did.

According to Peirce, five kinds of interpretation have been offered to explain the elements of variety and the uniformity in nature, only one of them being the most appropriate. Different versions of necessitarianism make up three of these views, each of which asserts that uniformity in nature is "exact and inflexible." Another view, which is the opposite of necessitarianism, asserts that imminent breaks in the regular course of nature should be expected. Finally, there is the point halfway between these two extremes, which Peirce considers to be the most agreeable interpretation of variety and uniformity of nature. In what follows, as we discuss these different conceptions of natural order, we shall also make connections between these positions and various responses to miracle stories. Peirce's analysis will thereby act as a prism, as it were, through which we can identify more clearly the epistemological implications of various stances on miracles.

According to Peirce, the three most common versions of necessitarianism are as follows:

(1) Version *A* deems that every feature of the universe is fully determined and conforms to a law, including all the relations. It posits that

everything is precisely calculated and governed by Providence (6.89, 1903).

(2) Version B states that natural laws fully determine all facts, but not all relations. If someone happens to cough in China at the same moment that someone else is eating candy in America, we need not interpret this coincidence as part of a bigger uniformity or law (6.90, 1903). That is, while two such events are fully determined by exact laws, their relation is not always determined (6.92, 1903).

(3) Version C states that not all phenomena are law-bound, but the ones that are under a law's jurisdictions are perfectly determined by it. For instance, the arrangement of stars seems random, though other things are very uniform and must be under a precise and absolute law (6. 89, 1903).

Peirce maps these three common forms of necessitarianism on a spectrum, from the least flexible to the more flexible: "A holds that every feature of all facts conforms to some law. B holds that the law fully determines every fact, but thinks that some relations of facts are accidental. C holds that uniformity within its jurisdiction is perfect, but confines its application to certain elements of phenomena" (6.91, 1903). Obviously, all these forms of necessitarianism correlate with the rejection of miracles, insofar as miracles imply interruption of regularities in the universe.[38]

In opposition to these forms of necessitarianism, version E states that the regularities in nature are not stable; rather, they are subject to real freaks and violations. Peirce notes that this position interprets miracles "not simply as manifestations of superhuman power but as downright violations of the laws of nature, absolutely abnormal" (6.92, 1903). As I noted earlier, Hume's strong and conflicted position on miracles suggests that he reads miracle stories as supporting such a counterintuitive approach to nature. Similarly, Ibn Rushd's critique of Ghazali reflects concern about an understanding of miracles that implies an unstable natural order, as in Version E.

Peirce presents his interpretation of uniformity and diversity as the middle-of-the-road approach. He insists that laws are real and quite stable, but he also insists that "uniformities are never absolutely exact" (6.91, 1903). Indeed, Peirce does not find any version of necessitarianism as capable of explaining the growth, diversity, consciousness, and even regularity observable in the world: "Mechanical law . . . can never produce diversification. That is a mathematical truth—a proposition of analytical mechanics; and anybody can see without any algebraical apparatus that mechanical law out of like antecedents can only produce like consequents" (1.174, ca. 1897). Similarly, it cannot account for growth in nature, because growth is an irreversible process (6.72, 1898). Besides, existence of the mind and free will cannot be accommodated by a rigid determinism (6.61, 1892), as we partially observed in the case of Hume.[39] Peirce claims that even regularity itself cannot be explained in a rigid, deterministic framework. By declaring the natural laws to be exceptionless and exact, necessitarianism in effect denies that the laws can have an explanation for their very production:

> [I ask a necessitarian] how he would explain the uniformity and regularity of the universe, whereupon he tells me that *the laws of nature are immutable and ultimate facts*, and no account is to be given of them. . . . That single events should be hard and unintelligible, logic will permit without difficulty: we do not expect to make the shock of a personally experienced earthquake appear natural and reasonable by any amount of cogitation. But *logic does expect things general to be understandable*. To say that there is a universal law, and that it is a hard, ultimate, unintelligible fact, the why and wherefore of which can never be inquired into, at this a sound logic will revolt, and will pass over at once to a method of philosophizing which *does not thus barricade the road of discovery*. (6.60, 1892, italics added)

In other words, interpreting the natural laws as unchangeable amounts to positing innumerable inexplicables (7.509, 1898), replicating Descartes's conundrum. Yet recent scientific findings reveal that there are "very remarkable relations . . . between the different laws of nature," and these relations call for explanation, *not* a necessitarianist insistence that the natural laws are inexplicable and are simply what they are. Peirce gives some examples of striking similarities between the laws of nature. For instance, the formula that expresses the relation between body mass and distance (in the law of gravity) and the formula that calculates the ratio of distance to intensity of light (in the law of illumination) are the same. Similar proportion obtains in the movement of electrical current (7.509, 1898). As Peter Turley puts it, for Peirce, "it is rather ironic, therefore, that the very element of nature [i.e., regularity] which he [the determinist or the necessitarian] takes such pains to extol proves troublesome to the determinist."[40]

It is noteworthy that Peirce's arguments against necessitarianism countered strong deterministic views at the time, which originated from eighteenth-century Enlightenment thought. By appealing to "the evidence of the actual phenomena in laboratories and fields," Peirce showed that there was "not the slightest scientific evidence for determinism and that in fact there was considerable scientific evidence against it."[41] Peirce's critique of necessitarianism and determinism provoked the anger of many, for it "hit upon the most vulnerable spot of the contemporary scientism."[42]

In sum, resisting a common tendency in his time, Peirce sought, as a scientist and pragmatist thinker, to cleanse scientific inquiry from the unjustified dogmas of scientism, such as the belief in absoluteness and exactitude of natural laws. In place of such unjustified assumptions, Peirce develops in his later writings a metaphysical framework to explain the very possibility of scientific inquiry.

Peirce's Scientific Metaphysics

According to Peirce, the variety, regularity, and growth in nature, as well as the existence of consciousness, for which necessitarianism provides no "pigeon-hole," call for "another agency" (1.174, ca. 1897). The needed "pigeon-hole," Peirce suggests, is provided only by the assumptions that the natural laws are not absolute and that there is a real element of spontaneity in nature. Peirce increasingly became convinced that a thinker faithful to experience must admit that there is a degree of genuine indeterminacy in nature.[43] Peirce calls this the principle of tychism: that there is an element of "chance" or freedom in nature that makes room for growth and variety as well as spontaneity of feeling (6.64, 1892). In a sense, "the laws of nature are being constantly breached by purely chance occurrences," events that Peirce relates to direct divine agency. This breach is not breaking into the universe; rather, it is a regular part of the fabric of the universe.[44]

It is important to highlight that tychism is needed *not* because we are ignorant of the inner workings of nature, but because there *is* a small but real "swerving" of things away from the regular path they usually follow. The necessitarian position assumes that "possibilities are merely intrapsychic products that disappear whenever a future event becomes actualized. The future is held to be as determined as the past and thus not open to real possibilities." In contrast, for critical commonsensism the possibilities are genuine, and "to speak of possibility is not to speak of human subjective ignorance, which assumes that we only speak of possibilities whenever we have insufficient data as to the laws governing a region of the world and its future prospects."[45]

Peirce combines his tychism with his theory of "agapistic evolution." He speculates that regularities in nature have evolved from an initial moment of freedom and spontaneity, with a guiding *telos* of love and effort. Thus, starting from pure potential and the tendency to adopt certain habits, the universe unfolded, and gradually certain regular patterns emerged, thus decreasing the realm of spontaneity but never extinguishing it.[46] By "evolution" of the universe, Peirce does not mean a blind, random mechanism based on the struggle for existence (6.293, 1893). Rather, Peirce's "agapistic evolution" refers to a process that implies the growth, spontaneity, and habit-forming tendencies in nature. It is a process that displays traces of love and a striving to flourish rather than a brutal and blind struggle for survival.[47]

Against necessitarians, Peirce also offers a penetrating analysis of the concept of natural law. Having affirmed that natural laws or regularities in nature are *real*, albeit not absolute, Peirce highlights how reference to laws does not obviate the need for a metaphysical context. Natural laws serve as *descriptions* of natural events, *not* as *explanations* of these events: "No law of nature makes a stone fall, or a Leyden jar to discharge, or a steam engine to work." Indeed,

> a law of nature left to itself would be quite analogous to a court without a sheriff. A court in that predicament might probably be able to induce some citizen to act as sheriff; but until it had so provided itself with an officer who, unlike itself, could not discourse authoritatively but who could put forth the strong arm, its law might be the perfection of human reason but would remain mere fireworks, brutum fulmen. Just so, *let a law of nature—say the law of gravitation—remain a mere uniformity—a mere formula establishing a relation between terms—* and *what in the world should induce a stone, which is not a term nor a concept but just a plain thing, to act in conformity to that uniformity?* (5.48, 1903, italics added)

In other words, a law of nature is not an agent "out there" that makes things obey such regularities. Rather, it is a description, "a mere formula," coined by an observer in order to express a particular regularity in nature. In our scientific inquiry, we are justified in searching out these regularities and assume that they will, for the most part, remain stable, but we cannot pretend that we thereby *explain* what makes the events happen. Laws, as descriptions of regularity, cannot make things happen; there needs to be a "cosmic sheriff" putting such laws into effect each moment. Clearly Peirce is here making reference to a transcendent reality, identified either as an infinite God or as his instrument,[48] a view that is very reminiscent of Ghazali's insistence that the natural order is maintained through divine agency, either directly or through the mediation of angels. We shall return to the metaphysical connotations of natural law in the next chapter on Nursi. For now, let us note that behind this dynamic unfolding of the universe, with its regularity, diversity, and openness, lies the agency of a "cosmic sheriff."[49]

Precise details of Peirce's scientific metaphysics need not concern us here; the point is that, taking into account the facts of diversity and uniformity in the world, Peirce postulates a framework that can allow for scientific inquiry—a framework that was missing from Hume's account.[50] Peirce's scientific metaphysics also sheds light on the tension between Ibn Rushd and Ghazali. As may be recalled, Ghazali argued that, since an alternative to the current state of affairs in nature *is* conceivable, we are not justified in calling natural order necessary. Ibn Rushd regarded Ghazali's stance as a threat to realism and as mere sophistry, and he argued that if things were not necessary, then all the current findings of science would be redundant. Within Peirce's framework, these concerns are reconciled; Peirce offers an illuminating example of how one can regard natural laws as non-necessary in themselves (for nature *could* have been conferred different habits over the course of its unfolding or "agapistic evolution") and yet real and dependable, thus accounting for our relative success in predicting the future. Besides, these *real* laws are not absolute and do leave room for spontaneity and new possibilities, including miracles, a point we shall return to in the next section of this chapter.

The contours of Peirce's scientific metaphysics can also be used to reconcile Ibn Rushd's and Ghazali's existential priorities articulated around the interpretation of miracle stories. Ibn Rushd's emphasis on appreciating the *wisdom* in nature finds a home, as Peirce's "properly executed metaphysics" makes room for the idea that the laws according to which the universe is governed are interrelated and wisely proportioned. There is wisdom in the way things happen in the world. There is also room for Ghazali's emphasis on contingency and *gratitude*: since these laws in themselves are not necessary, nor do they have their own agency, a believer can be grateful to the sustainer of the world and be appreciative of every moment, without taking natural events for granted in themselves.

In sum, Peirce offers a fallibilistic and yet optimistic epistemology in line with our experience of the world: commonsensical intuitions are trusted in their vague directional sense, and natural laws are identified with real generals, while it is also conceded that the laws are neither exact nor necessary in themselves. Now, it is time to discuss more specifically what kind of reading of miracles such a framework of scientific inquiry and scientific metaphysics calls for.

Peirce on Miracles

While his approach to natural order gives important clues about how he would approach miracles, Peirce does not comment on miracles at length.[51] Fortunately, he does briefly comment on definitions and interpretations of miracles by others, and he also answers a question about his own personal belief regarding miracles. We shall piece together these brief remarks in order to see how he offers a very interesting reading of miracle stories consistent with his pragmatism, critical commonsensism, and scientific metaphysics. In what follows, we shall first look at Peirce's comments on the rejection of miracle stories as well as his views on their evidentiary value. Next, we shall discuss the implications Peirce draws from miracle stories.

Peirce on the Rejection of Miracle Stories

Peirce's writing on the rejection of miracle stories can be grouped into comments about three types of reasoning against the possibility of miracles. The first kind of reasoning comes from the necessitarian approach mentioned earlier, according to which any change in the laws of nature is inadmissible. The second argument against miracles is the religious endorsement of necessitarianism, according to which it is inappropriate to suggest that God ever interrupts the course of nature. The third argument is the rejection of miracles on the basis of probabilistic reasoning. Peirce makes most of these comments in the context of his evaluation of Hume's essay on miracles.

Peirce notes that the definition of a miracle as a "violation of laws of nature" (6.541, ca. 1901) produces an immediate resistance to the idea of a miracle. Miracles seem unacceptable to the modern mind because of the widespread implicit commitment to a necessitarian view of nature: "The marvelous appealed to the childish mind of the Middle Ages, while the scientific regularity appeals to the modern mind" (6.542, ca. 1901). Needless to say, Peirce finds a necessitarian view of nature to be woefully inadequate in accounting for the facts on the ground.

According to Peirce, another type of reasoning against miracles is a religious brand of the necessitarian approach. Peirce notes that not only scientists but also modern theologians prefer determinism and believe that natural causes and their affects are necessarily and invariably linked. In fact, Peirce speculates that if anyone was persuaded by Hume's argument against miracles, it must be because of this widespread veneration of "obstinacy":

> Of course, formalism was rife among the men of that generation. *There was in many minds such a worship of obstinacy that they would naturally look upon the immutability of a divine decree as an attribute of Deity, regard[less] of the circumstances of any particular case.* The extreme irrationality of many rules of law fostered such sentiments. It may have been, therefore, that as soon as some men of that description were credibly informed that a miracle was a violation of a law of nature, or divine decree, *they would be unable to conceive that such a Deity as they could worship,* the personification of obstinacy, would ever consent to such a thing; and they may perhaps have read that argument into Hume. (6.546, 1901, italics added)

Even if one hesitates to accept such a diagnosis of public opinion in Hume's time, Peirce's comment lucidly exposes a common religious reason for resisting miracles. The idea of a God who does not carry out the same plan regardless of circumstances sounds impious to a religious determinist. Such a sentiment echoes to some extent Ibn Rushd's insistence that the term "habit" is too flexible to be applicable to divine activity. Peirce not only disagrees with necessitarianism in general but also argues that its religious endorsement fails as an argument:

> For if there are any "laws" of nature, they must be supposed to be supremely reasonable. Now the supreme reasonableness of a "law" will consist in its advancing a rational purpose in every particular case. Hence, *if there is really a need of an apparently exceptional phenomenon,* it will not be contrary to real analogies, but on the contrary required by them, that that apparently exceptional phenomenon should occur.

. . . To look upon the order of nature as being of the nature of a "law" is to adopt a view which is really favorable to miracles, rather than the reverse. (6.547, ca. 1901, italics added)

According to Peirce, the third type of reasoning against miracles is the one that Hume employed: reasoning based on probabilistic arguments. As we noted earlier, while Hume is not apparently offering an a priori argument against miracles, his probabilistic reasoning amounts to one: "As close a reasoner as Hume was could easily see that it would not materially affect the force of his argument to admit that miracles do, from time to time, occur; for in regard to any special miracle it would still remain more likely that the miracle had not occurred and that the witnesses had not given exact testimony than that the witnesses had been exact and that the particular miracle in question had occurred" (6.542, 1893). Yet Peirce notes that such probabilistic reasoning in evaluating testimony entirely contradicts the engine of *scientific inquiry*—the principle that a totally new and unprecedented event may deserve attention and that the weight of past experience should not be allowed to crush a new possibility. To be sure, Peirce notes, Hume's method of balancing likelihoods is useful in highly circumscribed circumstances, such as when we are playing dice and want to know the likelihood that certain numbers will turn up. However, this method is highly misleading when applied to human testimony about miracles, for a number of reasons.[52]

First, unlike dice, in the case of human testimony we are not dealing with independent probabilities. The fact that a die turned the same number twice does not affect its probability of occurring the next time, whereas in ancient testimonies narrators are often influenced by one another or by a common source that is now lost to us.[53] Moreover, as Peirce notes, "the method of balancing likelihoods not only supposes that the testimonies are independent but also that each of them is independent of the antecedent probability of the story. . . . But how very remote from the real state of things it is to suppose that the narration of an ancient event is independent of the likelihood of the story told! Roughly speaking, it may be said that all detached stories of Greece and Rome were told chiefly because the writer had something marvelous to recount."[54] That is, there is a link between an event's probability and its transmission in history: the more improbable an event is, the more likely that it will be talked about and narrated. As Catherine Legg aptly put it, "It is wrong to treat the testimonies as a tapestry of events of the kind we ourselves inhabit." Indeed, our daily lives are full of boring events, unusual things happen very rarely, and we are justly inclined to reject the testimony of someone who reports that her life is full of wonders.[55] Yet, when we are reading ancient testimonies, we cannot approach them as if we are listening to a contemporary of ours telling us about her memories, since "the boringly probable events which occurred in ancient times have been lost to history, leaving a Reader's Digest of marvels." Therefore, one cannot be justified in suspecting ancient testimonies on the basis that they report *too many* improbable events, as Hume did.[56]

Finally, for arguments regarding probability to work, we need to have a clearly defined reference class, which is not easy to establish in human testimony. As Legg explains,

> Probability proper, according to Peirce, is a statistical notion, which only makes sense against a clearly defined reference class. Thus, if a scientist attributes to me a 50% chance of dying before the age of seventy, in the background of that claim is a claim that half of all white people will die before the age of seventy, or that half of all philosophers . . . or some other class that includes me. For this claim to be useful to me, the reference class needs to be defined so as to include as many of the salient features of my situation as possible.[57]

As an illustration of how probabilistic method can be misleading when applied to human testimony, Peirce refers to German historicists of the nineteenth century. These scholars evaluated historical testimonies through the method of balancing likelihoods. They rejected many things with the argument that they were too wondrous to be true. Peirce notes that "German 'higher criticism' of history in general and above all of ancient history, is still marked by a strong disposition to discredit all the testimony which alone can give us any information about that history, in favor of *what the modern German conceives to be likely*." Yet later archeological findings confirmed that these dismissed stories were actually reliable.[58] Thus, Peirce concludes that "the maxim of exact logical analysis, that no regard at all, or very little indeed, ought to be paid to *subjective* likelihoods in abduction, has been fully confirmed by inductive tests" (6.536, 1901, italics added). Hence, the reasoning Hume employs in his argument against miracles "has completely mistaken the nature of the true logic of abduction" (6.537, 1901), for the whole point of abduction is to be open to considering an unprecedented phenomenon.[59]

Evidentiary Value of Miracle Stories

Interestingly, Peirce's critique of the reasoning behind the rejection of miracle accounts does not amount to arguing for their evidentiary value. Indeed, right after he notes his disagreement with Hume's position against miracles, Peirce notes that he would not go so far as to claim that miracle stories constitute strong proofs for the truth of Christianity:

> I beg to say that I go no farther than that. I do not assent to the contention of many theologians that the miracles of Jesus can properly convince a modern man of the divinity of Jesus. On the contrary, all the evidence which can now be presented for them is quite insufficient, unless the general divinity of the Christian religion be assumed. *The evidence which may have been overwhelming for eye witnesses and persons near them is of a very different and inferior character to that which may weigh with a modern Christian.* (6.538, 1901, italics added)

It is significant that in his questioning of the evidentiary value of miracles, Peirce points out the difference between a witnessed event and a narrated one: while an event could be impressive to its eyewitnesses, its report may not have the same value for a later generation.

Peirce's position here is interestingly parallel to that of Ghazali, who hesitated over the evidentiary value of miracles, even though, like Peirce, he criticized the reasoning behind the rejection of miracle stories. The question we raised in Ghazali's case can be raised here, too: If miracle stories do not have strong evidentiary value for faith, what is the significance of accepting that they took place? In Peirce's terms, what is the pragmatic value of these stories, if there is any? For an answer to this, we shall turn to Peirce's reply to a theological question, for this is one of the few places where Peirce explains what he personally makes of miracle stories.

The Meaning of Miracles Within a Pragmatic Framework

Peirce was asked explicitly whether he believed "that He [God] ever modifies or changes the laws of nature or interferes with the course of events in individual cases" (6.511, 1906). Peirce responds by first of all issuing a reminder that miracles need not be interpreted as violations in the course of nature to have religious significance:

I call your attention to the circumstance that some of the most respected theologians, such as St. Augustine, and others before him, St. Thomas Aquinas, Bishop Joseph Butler, are decidedly of the opinion that God never interfered with what they call the *cursus naturae,* which is what we call the operations of the laws of nature, "laws of nature" meaning with them the items of the *jus naturae.* . . . Miracles are for them simply what no man can do without special aid from on high, or which at least are signs of some special authority, without being in reality deviations from the regular uniformities of the world. (6.511, 1906)[60]

By noting this first, Peirce seems to distance himself from the interpretation of a miracle story as a freak account, an utterly strange interruption, a *deus ex machine,* as conceived by the early Greeks (and a consequence of the version *E* view of nature, as mentioned above). This means that Peirce opposes an understanding of miracles that would destroy commonsense assumptions of regularity, something both Ibn Rushd and Hume, as well as Ghazali, were concerned about. Next, Peirce notes that his principle of tychism requires a small measure of pure spontaneity in nature, and thus he cannot accept the necessitarian position either (6.511, 1906).

As will be recalled, Peirce's tychism made room for spontaneity and indeterminacy by noting that there are real patterns that the world tends to follow, but that these patterns are not rigid or absolute. Hence, he thinks that there is always some room, however small, for departure from the mechanistic or deterministic course of nature. To accept spontaneity in nature is to accept that there is room for growth, variety, and human freedom in the universe. In this sense, Peirce interprets miracles as signifying the presence of such freedom in nature, as events that are not merely conditioned by any deterministic law. In fact, in the context of his explanation of his theory of agapistic evolution, Peirce identifies miracles with these tychistic moments: "It is the action of this law together with *a ceaseless torrent of miracles,* that is to say, of events absolutely uncaused except by the creative act of God, is all that has brought about and is bringing about the whole universe of mind and matter in all its details."[61]

Here, we should highlight that Peirce is not offering his agapistic evolution as a simple historical narrative. Rather, in line with his pragmatic method, Peirce's scientific metaphysics has implications for anticipating the future and for adopting a new habit of thinking—that is, an epistemology that is more humble and more truthful to our experience. Indeed,

Peirce insists that giving up necessitarianism and adopting fallibilism has important consequences. It removes a crucial block in the way of inquiry: "[A] philosophical obstacle to the advance of knowledge . . . is the holding that this or that law or truth has found its last and perfect formulation—and especially that the ordinary and usual course of nature never can be broken through. . . . But there is no kind of inference which can lend the slightest probability to any such absolute denial of an unusual phenomenon" (1.140, ca. 1899). Within the context of Peirce's pragmatism, therefore, miracle stories signify the presence of indeterminacy in nature, and encourage us to keep the road of inquiry open for new discoveries and possibilities. In the next chapter, we shall turn to a contemporary Muslim exegete who would agree with Peirce's insights about scientific inquiry as well as the key points of his scientific metaphysics, and also extend the existential implications of miracles for a contemporary reader of the Qurʾan.

PART 3

CONTEMPORARY CONNECTIONS

5

SAID NURSI'S CONTEMPORARY READING OF QUR'ANIC MIRACLE STORIES

God has sent him [Prophet Muhammad] as a human messenger so that . . . he will disclose human beings the incredible Divine artistry and agency within ordinary events, which are in fact the miracles of God's power.

—Said Nursi, *Mektubat*

Bediuzzaman Said Nursi (1877–1960) was an important Muslim exegete and thinker whose writings and public engagements reflected a deep concern for interpreting the Qur'an in the modern age. Nursi's lifetime spanned the final decades of the Ottoman Empire, its collapse and dissolution after the First World War, and the first thirty-seven years of the nascent secular Turkish Republic, which constrained religious freedom, especially until the 1950s. Nursi lived in an era during which the global Muslim community, with whom he had a strong sense of solidarity, faced major intellectual and political challenges, including colonization, modern criticisms of religious belief, and the failure of traditional structures.

Given his central concern of making sense of the Qur'an in the modern age, Nursi is a promising case for our purposes of looking at a contemporary Muslim reception of miracles. His interpretations both reflect concerns shared by other Muslim theologians of the time and display a distinctive attempt at understanding the relevance of the Qur'an for everyday life. As I shall demonstrate, Nursi provides rich material for pursuing our question of "what to do" with miracle stories and for making sense of the apparent tension within the Qur'an between the themes of nature and miracles. His case also shares much with Peirce's approach to a fallible epistemology, with its non-necessitarian appreciation of natural order.

Before we turn to Nursi's interpretation of the Qur'anic miracle stories, however, a brief overview of his biography is in order.

Nursi's Life

The Muslim world, from Africa to the Middle East and from the Indian subcontinent to the Far East, went through massive changes in recent history, which reached their peak in the nineteenth century. While internal shifts and decay are no less crucial in explaining these changes, external influences on the Muslim world are often easier to point out. A major external effect on the Muslim world came from the "new Europe," with its military might and colonialism as well as its scientific developments and new philosophical currents, such as materialist positivism, scientism, and secularist humanism. The initial response of the many Muslim bureaucrats and intellectuals to this "new Europe" was awe: "progress" and "new sciences" became the buzzwords throughout the Muslim world. The question that preoccupied Muslim scholars and reformers was how to remedy the so-called backward state of the *umma*, or Muslim community. The task was both to defend against the military might of the Europeans and to catch up with the scientific developments in Europe. There was a strong yearning to retrieve "the golden ages" of medieval times, during which Muslim societies enjoyed political, cultural, and scientific eminence. As European colonialism advanced further into Muslim lands and attacks on religion under the pretext of science and progress increased, many became more critical of the Western model. Nevertheless, throughout the peak colonial era in the Muslim world (1800–1950) and later, the words "reform" and "progress" remained at the forefront of Muslim public discourse.[1]

The Ottoman Empire, where Nursi was born, was one of the major centers of the Muslim world that encountered this new Europe. The empire experienced unexpected military defeats at the hands of European powers and was taken aback by the recent technological developments in Europe. The Ottoman rulers responded to the practical challenges by introducing reforms in education, the military, and political structures. New schools and universities modeled on the European style of education were founded, students were sent to study in Europe, and experts and professors were brought in from Europe to help advance education as well as the army. Moreover, inspired by democratic trends and nationalist movements in

Europe, a new constitution was promulgated and the powers of the sultan were limited through a consultative parliament.

Ottoman society at that time also encountered Europe's major ideological currents, including secularism, materialist positivism, and nationalism. Indeed, "Nursi lived in a time, when some influential figures in Europe, such as Auguste Comte, Sigmund Freud, Emile Durkheim, among others, were claiming that the extinction of religion was only a matter of time."[2] In fact, in the newly established Ottoman engineering and medical schools, not only scientific information but also atheistic ideologies were being passed down. Eventually,

> the Ottoman modernization of the nineteenth century resulted in *intellectual dualism* and an inevitable conflict between reformist and conservative bureaucrats. Long before the foundation of the Turkish Republic, a tiny, but effective, pro-Western Turkish elite emerged in the Ottoman Empire, an elite that was deeply impressed by biological-materialist and Darwinist science, and was occupied with popular materialist literature. . . . Original or translated European works by such scientists and philosophers as Ludwig Buchner, Ernst Heackel, J. William Draper, and Auguste Comte were read by students of newly established Western style schools . . . [whereas] nineteenth-century idealism seems to have been excluded by the Westernized Ottoman thinkers, as it was too abstract and speculative for their ambition of effecting urgent change.[3]

Thus, Nursi's efforts to revitalize faith were taking place in the midst of tensions between the secularized educated class of the Ottoman Empire, which enthusiastically adopted the materialist positivism of nineteenth-century Europe, and some of the traditional 'ulamā or religious scholars, who were deeply suspicious of all intellectual interactions with Europe.[4] Nursi belonged to neither camp; rather, he was among the religious intellectuals who rejected materialist positivism but appreciated the "new sciences" and conditions flourishing in Europe, and who wanted to show how faith is relevant in the contemporary era.[5]

Reminiscent of Ghazali, Nursi went through an existential crisis and a spiritual transformation in his mid-forties. Considering this experience to be a turning point, Nursi divided his life into two major periods: "Old Said" and "New Said." I shall accordingly narrate Nursi's biography in these two stages.[6] In the Old Said period (1890–1922), Nursi was a public intellectual as well as a scholar who wrote and taught about Qurʾanic interpretation, Islamic theology, and ethics. He also briefly served as an expert scholar in Daruʾl Hikmet-il Islamiye, the highest religious institution in the Ottoman Empire at the time, which was founded to create solutions for contemporary intellectual and social issues.[7] During this period, in addition to engaging with theological questions, Nursi commented on the major social changes occurring in his society, such as the introduction of a representative government that limited the powers of the sultan, and on social problems across the Muslim world. Some of the important books that Nursi wrote during his Old Said period are *Reasonings (Muḥakamāt)*, on Qurʾanic hermeneutics; *Discussions (Munaḥarāt)*, on religious justification for new social reforms; and his celebrated partial Qurʾanic commentary penned in Arabic, *Signs of Eloquence (Ishārat al-iʿjāz)*. He also wrote two texts on logic in Arabic, *Taʿliqāt* and *Qizil iʾjaz*.[8]

Old Said was also enthusiastic about modern progress in the sciences and Enlightenment, which he considered to be the end of dogmatism in Europe. As noted earlier, such excitement about the "new sciences" was not unique to him; there was strong optimism about science and progress among many Muslim intellectuals at the time. As Jamal al-din al-Afghani (1838–1897), the famous Islamic scholar and activist who traveled across the Muslim world for the sake of Muslim solidarity and reform, had put it, "There was, is, and will be no ruler in the world but science."[9] Indeed, Afghani's Egyptian students Muhammad ʿAbduh (1849–1905) and Rashid Riḍa (1865–1935), Indian scholars such as S. Ahmad Khan (1817–1898) and Shibli Nuʿmani (1857–1914), and many Ottoman activists and scholars were all excited about scientific developments in Europe. They argued that Islam was compatible with science and progress—even more so, some claimed, than Christianity had been.

Nursi believed that the Muslim world not only needed to learn things from Europe but also needed an internal revival. In the Old Said period, Nursi's primary target for revival was Islamic education. He proposed educational reforms to the Ottoman sultans ʿAbdulhamid II (r. 1876–1909) and Mehmet Reshad (r. 1909–18) aimed at putting the traditional *madrasa* or seminary training, Sufism (*tasawwuf*), and the modern sciences in conversation with one another. Although he eventually received funding for his educational project (Medresetüʾz-Zehra), his endeavors were interrupted by the eruption of the First World War. When Russians invaded Nursi's town, he rose to its defense along with his seminary students. Eventually captured as a prisoner of war, Nursi ended up living in Russia for two years in solitary confinement. When the communist revolution started, he managed to escape the prisoner camp, returning to Istanbul via Petersburg, Warsaw, Berlin, and Vienna.[10]

Several years after Nursi's return to the country, in 1922, when many were celebrating the Turkish nationalist victory over European colonial powers, Nursi wrote a defense against what he considered to be a more serious danger infiltrating the nation: the positivistic attitude, which pretended to explain the world in materialistic terms and rejected the transcendent. It was around this date that Said Nursi seems to have gone through his spiritual transformation, provoked by a deeper reflection on his own finitude and the realization of what he now saw as the real challenges facing the modern person. Thus, the transition of the Old Said to the New Said coincided with the demise of the Ottoman Empire in the aftermath of the First World War and the foundation of the Turkish Republic in 1923.[11]

The New Said devoted much more energy to existential issues facing the contemporary person. Nursi noted that he now wanted to expose the Qur'an's guidance for the individual, stressing that faith in God could not be taken for granted or simply be inherited from generations past. Faith based on imitation (Ar. īmān al-taqlīdī, Tk. taklidi iman) did not have much worth and would not survive, especially in the contemporary era, when there was so much criticism of religious belief. Nursi argued that faith assertions were not a given; rather, they were conclusions to be reached after careful reflection and personal engagement (Ar. īmān al-taḥqīqī, Tk. tahkiki iman). Faith based on imitation had to be transformed into faith based on a conscious and justified choice. Thus, Nursi now focused more on disclosing the *why* and *how* as he wrote on faith and spirituality and on the Qur'an.[12]

The New Said also departed from the Old Said with regard to his writing style. The Old Said's dense scholarly writing was replaced with the New Said's simplified writing style, which aimed to reach a wider audience. This shift further distinguished him from other contemporary Ottoman intellectuals, whose scholarly discourse proved inaccessible to nonspecialists in theology.[13] In addition to reflecting a clear intention to speak to a wider audience, the New Said's writings placed more emphasis on personal transformation in light of the Qur'an.

Another distinctive feature of the New Said was that he turned away from trying to support faith through the use of the new developments in Western philosophy. This was a move that again set him apart from some theologians at the time, such as the Ottoman intellectual İzmirli İsmail

Hakkı (1868–1946), who penned *The New Discipline of Theology* (*Yeni İlm-i Kelam*), and the renowned Indian thinker Muhammad Iqbal (1877–1938), the author of *The Reconstruction of Religious Thought in Islam*. Having given up the attempt to revive Islamic theology through the help of new currents in philosophy, the New Said turned to the task of constructing what can be called a "Qurʾanic theology." He resolved to seriously engage with the Qurʾan to see how it can meet the needs of the heart and questions of the mind.[14]

The New Said also turned away from ideas of political reform. That is not to say that he gave up the idea that Islam provides guidance in all aspects of human existence, including the social and political realms. Rather, he seems to have grasped an urgent need to revive the faith of the individual before anything else. Nursi argued that until human beings were reformed in their hearts and minds, it was not only useless but also harmful to talk about social and political reform in the name of religion. For one would end up using spirituality and religion for political ends.[15] In this new profile, therefore, Nursi gives up the socio-political engagements of the Old Said and also departs from the Muslim reformists of the nineteenth and twentieth century who were occupied primarily with effecting social and political change. Nursi's style thus differed from that of Muslim reformers such as Sayyid Abuʾl ʿAla Mawdudi (1903–1979), Ḥasan al-Banna (1906–1949), and Sayyid Qutb (1906–1966), who often conceived of a "top-down" style of change, according to which a reformed political leadership would then help reform the society and the individual.

Nursi's views on modern science and technology also changed with the advent of the New Said. The Old Said was quite optimistic about the Enlightenment, which he considered to be the "awakening" of Europe from dogmatism and the flourishing of honest inquiry and progress. He was sure that the awakened man would turn to religion with a renewed energy.[16] In contrast, the New Said was disappointed that the changes in the West had taken a direction away from what he saw as an honest, open-minded inquiry and belief in God, and saw, especially after World War I, that technology without proper guidance caused more destruction than service to humanity. The New Said now viewed the Enlightenment not as an awakening but rather as a fall into deeper sleep. All of the real good that had issued from Europe came from the truths of Christianity, and all of Europe's vices were the result of its turning away from God.[17] While disillusionment with European ideals was not unique to Nursi in this period, he was one of the few

Muslim intellectuals who critically engaged with the materialistic connotations of modern science and addressed the challenges of being a believer in the modern age.[18] Thus, while Nursi's trust in human rationality and empirical science did continue into the New Said period, it was now coupled with a much clearer insistence that an existential transformation in the light of divine revelation is essential for genuine progress.[19]

The Old Said lived through the demise of the Ottoman Empire and the horrors of World War I, but life was not easy for the New Said either. As the new Turkish Republic emerged from the ruins of the Ottoman Empire, its founders continued some of the processes of Westernization and secularization that had started in the late Ottoman period. However, they also broke continuities with the past to create a new order, whose most fundamental characteristic was its identity as a "secular" nation-state that sought to control religious interpretation and practice. Thus, in the determination of M. Kemal Ataturk and other founding elites to create a secular state, there was a passionate drive to erase earlier, traditional forms of Islam. These founders enacted a series of radical reforms in different realms, from law to daily life, such as the replacement of Islamic law with Swiss code in state courts, the enforcement of a new dress code, the changing of Arabic script to Latin script, and the closure of Islamic seminaries and Sufi lodges. The founders were also keen on eliminating any resistance to their project of building a secular state and society. Thus, they did not hesitate to punish and even execute many religious scholars as well as common people who disagreed with them or failed to adopt to the reforms. Some of the radical reforms of the early republic were carried to an even further extreme in later decades, as seen in the banning of the call to prayer in Arabic, severe punishments for teaching the recitation of the Qur'an, and the censorship of religious texts. In short, in the Turkish case, a more aggressive form of secularization was carried out than in most other cases in the Muslim world, and it was accompanied by controversies over the state's suppression of religion as well as the state's promotion of its own vision of Islam. As for Nursi, he spent much of his remaining life in prison and in exile (1925–56), persecuted by the state for having invested in faith revival.

It was during this extremely difficult period that Nursi composed his magnum opus, the *Risale-i nur* (Ar. *Risālāt al-nūr*, literally, epistles of light), a six-thousand-page collection seeking to expound the Qur'an and nurture a life infused with belief in and love of God. In the *Risale*, Nursi attempts to interpret the Qur'an in a way that appeals to both the heart and the mind by bringing the traditional legacy of Qurʾanic exegesis, theology, *usūl*, and Sufism into conversation with contemporary issues. While more close studies of Nursi's works are yet needed, various scholars agree that Nursi's *Risale* is to be regarded as part of the classical Ihhaʾ, or revival tradition, as it is an impressive project of reviving Islamic faith in the modern age.[20]

Nursi's *Risale-i nur*, banned by the state, was secretly disseminated and hand-copied by thousands of people, many of whom were also persecuted, imprisoned, and at times tortured. Despite severe state persecution, Nursi's following increased over time as his writings were avidly read in different parts of the country. The ban was finally lifted several years before Nursi's death, with the transition to a multiparty political system in Turkey that favored more civil liberties. Nursi also made it a point to share some of his writings internationally, with Muslims in the Arab world and in Southeast Asia. As a gesture of interfaith collaboration ahead of his time, he even sent them to the Pope, emphasizing the need to collaborate as believers to uphold faith in God in the modern age.[21] When he passed away in 1960, Nursi left behind not only his extensive writings but also various flourishing grassroots movements that sought to internalize the message of the Qurʾan. Today, most of Nursi's works have been translated into various languages, including English, Arabic, and other Asian, African, and European languages.

We shall now turn to a brief summary of Nursi's approach to the Qurʾan before we delve into his interpretation of Qurʾanic miracle stories.

Nursi's Qurʾanic Hermeneutics

In addition to commenting extensively on the Qurʾan, Nursi wrote about how to define and approach it and about the principles of its interpretation.[22] In what follows, I shall identify some of the key rules of his Qurʾanic hermeneutics.

According to Nursi, in addition to the *content* of a text, four factors should be taken into account in the act of interpretation: (1) speaker (*mutakallim*), (2) audience (*mukhātab*), (3) purpose (*maqṣad*), and (4) context (*maqām*).[23] The exact same sentence will have a different meaning depending on who is saying it, to whom, for what purpose, and in what context.[24] Hence, for Nursi, approaching the Qurʾan as *God's* speech to *humanity* for the *purpose of their guidance* directly influences its interpretation.

Not surprisingly, like other Muslim interpreters, Nursi approaches the Qur'an as authored by the maker of the universe, God. Nursi views God as using two kinds of speech. In the first mode, God speaks to his creatures and inspires them all, including animals, common people, saints (Ar. awliyā', Tk. evliya), and angels.[25] In this form of speech, God addresses each individual or species in a special way, inspiring each creature according to his/her particular needs. This kind of speech, which Nursi calls ilhām (inspiration), occurs in varying degrees depending on the particularity and directness of the conversation. According to Nursi, the Creator also speaks in a mode called revelation (wahy), the category into which the Qur'an falls. Using the metaphor of a king, Nursi tries to convey the difference between the two modes of God's speech, inspiration and revelation: "A king has two forms of speech, two forms of address. One is to speak on his private phone with a common subject concerning some minor matter, some private need. The other [is to speak with an envoy or high official under the title of the sublime sovereign, the supreme king, and the universal ruler] for the purpose of making known and promulgating his commands, to make an utterance through an elevated decree proclaiming his majesty."[26]

Hence, according to Nursi, revelation is different from inspiration in that it is intended for a universal audience, not tailored to the personal situation of the recipient. Moreover, unlike inspiration, which gets shaped by the recipient's emotions and subjectivity, revelation is transmitted to the prophet in a pure form. Indeed, it is because of the majesty involved in revelation that it is always transmitted to humanity through an intermediary, a messenger, while inspiration occurs in a more casual manner, such as a particular intuition felt within.[27] With this distinction between the two modes of God's speech in mind, Nursi defines the Qur'an as a revelation from "the Greatest Divine Name and from the greatest level of every Name [of God]. It is God's word in respect of His being the Sustainer of All the Worlds. It is His decree through His title of God of All Beings; an address in regard to His being the Creator of the Heavens and the Earth."[28]

Moreover, according to Nursi, when interpreting the Qur'an, one should keep in mind not only that God is speaking there as the creator of all, but also that he is talking to us, the creatures. That is, the Qur'an is coming from God and, at the same time, it is a discourse specifically tailored to human understanding for the purpose of our guidance.[29] In other words, for Nursi, belief in the transcendental origin of the Qur'an is not a reason for not attempting to make sense of it. The excuse that the divine is too complicated for human beings to understand is unfounded. On the contrary, the revelation is intended for human comprehension.

Hence, in addition to commenting on who is speaking in the Qur'an and in what manner, Nursi comments on the intended audience of the Qur'an. He repeatedly claims that all kinds of people with varying levels of understanding, different backgrounds, and different inclinations are among the Qur'an's intended audience. The all-knowing God's address includes and *intends* numerous meanings at once.[30] Thus, like many other Muslim exegetes, including Ghazali and Ibn Rushd, Nursi highlights the polysemy of the text: as long as one does not violate the rules of Arabic language and the inner consistency of the overall text, the same verse may have many meanings; there is no limit to interpretation.[31] In other words, since the God of all is the author of the text, the text carries many meanings suited to the needs of all.

In clarifying the remaining two factors in interpretation—namely, purpose and context—Nursi offers two key principles (among others). First, he emphasizes the need to read the Qur'an and the universe in light of each other. The Qur'an firmly belongs to the here and now in that it interprets, enlightens, and makes sense of the universe in which human beings live. At the same time, it comes from the beyond, from the all-encompassing perspective of the divine, which is precisely why it is able to speak so well to the human condition and make sense of the world.[32] Thus, Nursi defines the Qur'an as "the pre-eternal translator of the mighty book of the Universe," "the interpreter of the various tongues reciting the verses of creation," "[an eternal commentary on the great book of the universe]," and "the [voice] of the Unseen in the Manifest World [*lisan al-ghayb fi ʿālam al-shahāda*]."[33] There is thus a direct relationship and harmony between the divine word and the world—the former being God's verbal speech and the latter being his speech in action. God creates and speaks simultaneously, just as an artist may explain his art as he is performing the artistic act.[34] Therefore, not only will the Qur'an and the universe not contradict, but they actually shed light on each other.

Indeed, Nursi argues that the meaning of the universe without the light of the Qur'an will remain a mystery. That is, at first it seems as if we can decipher the meaning of existence by closely studying it, but in fact the riddle of existence can only be solved through the cues provided by divine revelation. Hence, while Nursi affirms the widely shared traditional notion that the Qur'anic message is reasonable and that there is nothing irrational or absurd in it, he stresses that the reasonability of revelation should not be confused with its dispensability. Unlike Ibn Rushd, Nursi insists that human reason cannot find Qur'anic truths on its own. Rather, reason needs to encounter Qur'anic guidance first; only then will it have the capacity to confirm the Qur'an's truthful commentary on existence.[35]

According to Nursi, just as the world cannot be deciphered without the Qur'an, reading the Qur'an without referring to the universe will cause it to be incomprehensible. For instance, one simply cannot make sense of God's mercy, discussed in the Qur'an, without paying attention to his mercy manifested in the world. The world is only intelligible because of the Qur'an, and the Qur'an will only make sense if it is read as a manual for looking at the "book" of the universe. (Nursi must have derived this principle of reading the Qur'an and the world in light of each other from the Qur'an's emphasis that the signs [ayāt] of scripture disclose signs [ayāt] in the universe, a notion that was mentioned in chapter 1.)

Another crucial hermeneutical rule that Nursi follows in interpreting Qur'anic passages is to identify the maqāṣid, or overall purposes, of the Qur'an. The idea is that a faithful reading of the Qur'an is only possible by reading its parts in view of these overarching purposes. Traditionally, there have been slightly different views of what these main aims of the Qur'an are. In general, however, it has been agreed upon that the Qur'an is about faith in one God and the establishment of human life in connection to and in response to this God, who is known through his different attributes, such as mercy, power, justice, and wisdom.[36] Similarly, according to Nursi, the Qur'an's very purpose is to guide us in answering core human questions about the meaning of existence and to solve the "riddle" of the universe. More specifically, he argues that the purpose of the Qur'an is to establish four major points: (1) tawḥid, or the oneness of God, that is, the oneness of the source of all the power, beauty, and perfection reflected in the world; (2) prophethood (al-risāla); (3) resurrection (hashr); and (4) justice ('adāla) and worship ('ubūdiyya). According to Nursi, any particular issue mentioned in the Qur'an is discussed not for its own sake but only as a means to teach these major aims.[37]

Indeed, Nursi emphasizes that the Qur'an never talks about things for their own sake but rather for the sake of their signification of God.[38] In other words, from Nursi's perspective Qur'anic purpose is never about giving technical information about history, social norms, or nature, nor about providing literary entertainment (an interesting point that converges with the Qur'an's insistence that it is not "poetry" or "the fables of the ancients"). This means that in anything the Qur'an speaks about—from a woman's complaint about her husband, to a bee making honey, to financial contracts—the aim is to make God better known to the Qur'anic audience.

Nursi claims that all of the *maqāṣid* are implied in every *sūra* or chapter of the Qur'an, including the shortest one, and even in most of its verses. Each bit of the Qur'an is like a hologram, representing the overall purposes of the entire text. The consistency of its central aims gives the Qur'anic discourse, which does not follow a linear organization, a cohesion and consistency. Moreover, Nursi suggests that the apparent free style of the Qur'an frees its verses from being bound to their particular place in the corpus and enhances its intertextual dynamic.[39]

As a corollary to his understanding of these primary purposes of the Qur'anic discourse, Nursi reads Qur'anic stories as containing essential lessons for the reader's edification. Such narratives form the "tips of an iceberg"—that is, "universal principles" and lessons are hidden underneath these stories. Apparently insignificant events, such as the choosing of a cow for slaughter (Q. 2:67–72), actually contain insightful instruction on the oneness of God and other *maqāṣid*.[40] This view that particular Qur'anic stories communicate universal lessons is directly relevant to Nursi's interpretation of miracle stories, which we will discuss below.

Furthermore, consistent with his claim of the compatibility of reason and the Qur'an, Nursi confirms the traditional dictum that if the plain sense of the Qur'an seems to contradict reason, the text needs to be reinterpreted so as to conform to reason. Of course, Nursi adds a disclaimer to this hermeneutical rule: reason on the basis of which the Qur'anic text will be interpreted must be "a reasonable reason" (Tk. *o akıl akıl olsa gerektir*), a reason that is balanced and guided, not distorted or misled.[41] Such a disclaimer is not surprising; it will be recalled that Ibn Rushd and Ghazali also agreed on the principle of reasonability in scripture, though they strongly disagreed on what constitutes rationality in the case of natural causality.

With this introduction to Nursi's hermeneutics, we are now better equipped to analyze his interpretation of miracle stories. Nursi's approach is reminiscent of Ghazali's in that he takes the plain sense of the stories as worthy of serious attention and as providing invaluable cues for interpreting the world around us. He also indirectly addresses Ibn Rushd's concerns by drawing surprising connections to science and technology. Moreover, Nursi's reading extends Peirce's insights about science and its metaphysical underpinnings to a contemporary Islamic context.

Nursi on Miracles: Defining the Miraculous and the Ordinary

According to Nursi, the Qur'an communicates its *maqāṣid*, or main purposes, by re-presenting what is familiar and usual to the reader in a new
and fresh light. Indeed, the key insight that the Qur'anic discourse provides
is an invitation to rethink what seems to be too familiar. Nursi argues that
the Qur'an heals a common ailment of human thought by tearing apart the
"veil of familiarity" or customariness (Ar. *ulfa*, Tk. *ülfet*).[42] Instead of mistak-
ing familiarity for understanding, the reader is called to pause and contem-
plate what she takes for granted: "With its acute expositions, the Qur'an of
Miraculous Exposition [Ar. *Qur'ān al-muʿjiz al-bayān*, Tk. *Kur'an-ı Mucizü'l-
beyan*] rends the veil of familiarity and [draws back the curtain of habit] over
all the beings in the universe, which are known as *ordinary* things but are
[in fact each] extraordinary and a miracle of Divine Power. [It] reveals those
astonishing wonders to conscious beings. It attracts their gazes and opens up
for minds an *inexhaustible treasury of knowledge.*"[43]

Thus, the Qur'anic discourse corrects the common tendency to privilege
"freaks" over ordinary events. Too often, says Nursi, we ignore the formation of innumerable healthy babies as commonplace and only regard an
abnormal baby, such as one born with two heads, as worthy of wonder. In
contrast, the Qur'an constantly brings to attention what is often overlooked
simply because of its familiarity, and it presents the ordinary phenomenon
as "a miracle of God." Time and again, Nursi notes that the mission of
divine revelation is to "decipher" the world and to reveal the "treasures"
in nature—that is, messages embedded in nature about God's beautiful
names or qualities, such as mercy, power, and wisdom. Indeed, for Nursi,
the primary task of divine revelation and its exposition by a messenger of
God is to disclose to people the *miracles* in everyday life.[44]

Thus, Nursi seems to depart from the technical definition of a miracle
in traditional *kalām* texts as he repeatedly uses the Arabic term *muʿjiza*, or
miracle, to refer to the wonderfulness of everyday events that call for the
existence and the qualities of a transcendent being. Natural events, such as
rain, the growth of a plant, and so on, are all referred to as *mucize-i kudret*
(Ar. *muʿjiza al-qudra*), or a "miracle of divine power."[45] By employing the
term "miracle" for natural events, Nursi is in fact provocatively redefining
what is natural and what is miraculous. Since *muʿjiza* literally means "that
which renders weak, that which overwhelms," Nursi regards a miracle as
anything that natural causes are incapable of producing. In other words,
whenever an effect "overwhelms" its natural cause—that is, whenever we

realize that a regular result associated with a natural cause is beyond the capacity of that apparent natural cause—we are justified in calling it a miracle, even if it happens repeatedly and frequently.

Recalling the discussion in the first chapter, this term for miracle used in the classical Islamic theology, *muʿjiza*, does not occur in the Qurʾan. Instead, the Qurʾan frequently uses *āya*, literally meaning "a sign," in reference to miracles; this is the same term it uses for natural phenomena. Hence, Nursi's use of the term "miracle" in reference to natural events subtly mirrors the Qurʾanic combination of the miraculous and the natural in the word *āya*. Nursi's innovative use of the term "miracle" along Qurʾanic lines alleviates some of the apparent tension between the natural and the miraculous in the Qurʾan. That is, when viewed from a perspective that is cleared of the blind spots of familiarity, the normal birth of a baby is no less worthy of wonder than the virgin birth. Both exceed the natural causes associated with them and act as a sign or *āya* of God.

According to Nursi, such interpretation of natural causality is a *central* aim of the Qurʾan, especially reflected in the numerous verses that refer to natural phenomena as signs, as well as in the verses that emphasize the complete dependence of all existence on God. For example, "God is the Creator of all things; He has charge of everything; the keys of the heavens and earth are His" (Q. 39:62–63), and "There is no moving creature which He does not control" (Q. 11:56; see also 15:21, 36:38, etc.).[46] In what follows, we shall first look in some detail at how Nursi substantiates his claim that natural causes fail to account for the results associated with them and that ordinary events *are* in this regard worthy of wonder (and worthy of the term "miracle"). We shall observe how Nursi's account of natural causality both follows and gives nuance to Ghazali's account. Then, I shall offer more specific examples of Nursi's engagement with Qurʾanic miracles and discuss its pragmatic implications.

Nursi on Natural Causality as a Sign of God

According to Nursi, the Qurʾan calls the reader to rethink his causal judgments and to discover the agency of the One behind the flow of the universe. As we shall see, Nursi's approach to nature in light of his reading of the Qurʾan is similar to Ghazali's and to the mainstream Islamic views on natural causality. His presentation, however, improves upon Ghazali's in that it is more explicit in its engagement with Qurʾanic verses and its regard for common sense.

The starting point for Nursi seems to be our commonsensical assumption that every new existent requires a cause. Affirming the causal maxim, Nursi notes that our habit of looking for a cause for any new existent is an intuitive move. If things are happening and previously absent conditions and situations are obtaining, especially in an orderly fashion, there must indeed be a cause for them.[47] On the basis of such intuition we start making causal judgments about events happening around us. Our first instinct is to identify certain events or objects as the causes of other events that follow them. Indeed, upon repeatedly witnessing the conjunction of certain events, we suggest that the antecedent must be the cause of the precedent. To return to the classic example, when we see that burning occurs in the presence of fire and that it stops when the fire is extinguished, we are inclined to say that fire is the cause of burning. It is a commonsensical move, and in a limited sense (which we will discuss below) Nursi grants that this can be regarded as an appropriate initial interpretation of facts. Yet, in a deeper sense, it is a mistaken conclusion. And human beings are called by the Qur'an to dig beneath the surface and reach for a more profound and accurate grasp of the agency behind natural phenomena. Indeed, Nursi suggests, when we take the time to reflect on the cues provided by the Qur'an, we do realize that what we regard as a causal relationship is usually a mere conjunction (*iqtirān*) between natural events pointing to the transcendental agent, or *musabbib al-asbāb* (literally, causer of the causes).[48]

In order to move to a deeper understanding of causation in nature, Nursi, like Ghazali, questions what can be called "the argument from absence"—that is, identifying A as the cause of B simply because of the absence of B in the absence of A. He finds this argument from absence to be unreliable, pointing to the fact that there may be multiple factors preparing the ground for B to exist, while the absence of only one of these factors, such as A, will result in the absence of B. Thus, for instance, the fact that a garden dries up when I do not open the water canal and that it flourishes when I do open the canal is not sufficient evidence for me to conclude that my action *causes* the flourishing of the garden. The garden dries up in the absence of one thing, but it flourishes in the presence of many things, such as air, bacteria in soil, sunlight, minerals, gravity, and so forth. My inaction may be squarely blamed for the absence of the result, but my action alone cannot be taken to have created the result. Thus, in the second step of interpreting natural causality, we can discover that using an argument from absence to identify a cause can be quite misleading. Unfortunately, Nursi regrets, many people never realize the mistake. Instead, they *direct* their *gratitude* to what they identify as causes through the process of an argument from absence.[49] It is noteworthy that for Nursi, as it was for Ghazali, there is a direct link between identifying a cause and offering gratitude.

Nursi's next step is to note that if the argument from absence can be misleading, then the simple fact that a garden *stops* flourishing in the *absence* of a *number of things* is also not sufficient to prove that these natural factors *collectively* produce the garden. Actually, the presence of all these natural factors (such as a certain temperature and pressure level, sunlight, air, soil, water, seeds, bacteria, movements of the earth and sun, and so forth) serve only as a background for the real cause or agent—namely, divine will and power—to produce the result.

How does Nursi transition to this final step, concluding that an unseen maker is the *real* cause and that what we habitually refer to as causes are only apparent causes? To be sure, given the limits of the argument from absence, it is hard, if not impossible, to disprove that there is such a "real agent" responsible for what happens in nature. Yet the crux of the question is this: Why posit a "real" cause at all? Even if it is *possible* that these different factors are only "apparent" and not real causes, why take that possibility seriously? Why not simply say that all of these many different natural factors collectively create the result? Thus, we might ask whether it is an arbitrary choice to opt for one of these two possibilities: either (1) natural causes are collectively producing the effect, or (2) there is a "real agent" behind the scenes who creates the effect through these natural factors.

For Nursi, there is more than personal taste involved in deciding between these options. He is confident that there is clear evidence to decisively tilt the balance toward inferring the activity of a divine will and power behind the scenes. The evidence comes from the mismatch between the attributes of apparent causes and their effects. As Nursi argues, "To attribute a well-ordered and well-balanced being which has unity such as [a living being] to the jumbled hands of innumerable, lifeless, ignorant, aggressive, unconscious, chaotic, blind and deaf natural causes, the blindness and deafness of which increase with their coming together and intermingling among the ways of numberless possibilities, is as unreasonable as accepting innumerable impossibilities all at once."[50] In other words, the attributes of the apparent causes, such as soil, water, and sunlight, fall short of bearing responsibility for a well-ordered and well-balanced unified being, such as a garden or a living being. That is, the apparent causes, even when they are considered as a collective, clearly do not display the knowledge, contrivance, power, mercy, or life displayed by their effects. The natural causes are "lifeless, ignorant, aggressive, unconscious, chaotic, blind and deaf," and they become messier as an "innumerable" quantity of them mix with one another. This gap between the qualities of the natural causes and the qualities of the effects associated with them is the key to realizing that an unseen real cause must be acting through these natural causes. Interestingly, Nursi presents this reasoning as inspired by Qur'anic verses such as "Those you call on beside God could not, even if they combined all their forces, create a fly" (Q. 22:73).[51]

To give another example of how Nursi understands the Qur'an as teaching God's agency behind natural events, let us look at his interpretation of the following verse: "Let man consider the food he eats! We pour down abundant water and cause the soil to split open. We make grain grow, and vines, fresh vegetation, olive trees, date palms, luscious gardens, fruits, and fodder: all *for you and your livestock to enjoy*" (Q. 80:24–32, italics added). Nursi places the emphasis on the final phrase of the verse—*"for you and for your animals to enjoy"*—which indicates purpose. According to him, the verse makes reference to "the *aims* and *fruits* of the effects, so that it may be understood that causes are only an apparent veil." That is, reminiscent of Ibn Rushd's use of the *dalil al-ʿināya*, Nursi argues that such wise and purposeful aims can be attached to natural processes only by someone who is most knowing and wise. The natural causes themselves are "lifeless and without intelligence. [Thus,] by mentioning the aims and results, such verses show that although [natural] causes [are seemingly proximate to and are connected to the effects], in reality there is a great distance [i.e., "gap"] between them." Indeed, even what appear to be the greatest natural causes cannot be responsible for creating the smallest effects.[52]

In a long treatise devoted to justification of belief in God, Nursi summarizes his interpretation of natural causality in light of the Qur'anic discourse:

> We look at things which appear to be causes and effects in the universe and we see that the most elevated cause possesses insufficient power for the most ordinary effect. This means that causes are a veil, and something else makes the effects. To take only a small example out of innumerable creatures let us consider the faculty of memory, which is situated in man's head. . . . We see that it is like a book so comprehensive—indeed, like a library—that within it is written without confusion the entire story of a person's life.

What cause can be shown for this miracle of power? The grey matter of the brain? The simple unconscious particles of its cells? The winds of chance and coincidence? [Rather] that *miracle* of art can only be the work of an All-Wise Maker. . . . Thus, since they are comparable to man's faculty of memory, make an analogy with all eggs, seeds, and grains, and then compare other effects.[53]

That is, while the gray matter of the brain is observed in conjunction with memory, it cannot be regarded as the genuine cause of memory because of the obvious mismatch between the apparent cause and the result. Conjunction and "co-absence" (i.e., absence of the consequent upon the absence of the precedent) are factual: it is observed that (1) one's memory comes into existence with the existence of certain conditions, such as brain cells, and (2) the memory is lost or damaged when any of these factors are absent (e.g., if the cells get damaged). For Nursi, this consistent spatiotemporal conjunction is not sufficient to conclude that these natural conditions collectively produce our memory. In order to designate the proper cause, one has to also consider the alleged cause's attributes. Since the result is very orderly and powerful, indicates purpose, and is interconnected with the rest of the human body as well as a human being's lifelong experience in the world, one has to either declare these natural causes to be wise, knowing, and powerful on their own or posit a real agent who is at work through them—who is, as Nursi puts it metaphorically, behind the "veil" of the causes. In other words, since these causes do not seem to posses the attributes that the effects display—such as knowledge, contrivance, power, and mercy—they cannot be considered the real agents of these effects. Instead, they point to the wisdom, power, planning, mercy, and life-giving attributes of the One. Hence, the very conjunction of apparent causes and effects reveals and praises the One. It is this type of praise that Nursi understands as being the main point in verses such as "The seven heavens and the earth and everyone in them glorify Him. There is not a single thing that does not celebrate His praise, though you do not understand their praise: He is most forbearing, most forgiving" (Q. 17:44).[54] And it is in this sense that Nursi regards natural events, such as the "normal" functioning of the human brain, as a "miracle" of God.

In sum, Nursi suggests that the close proximity of causes and effects is instructive when one pays closer attention to it in the manner outlined in the Qurʾan. The Qurʾan teaches the reader to notice the surprising "gap" between what we habitually call the cause and its effect. To employ Nursi's metaphor, it may at first seem that mountains are joined to the sky, but when one approaches the scene, she sees that there is a huge distance between the two, and it is within this vast distance that "the stars rise and other things are situated." So too, says Nursi, "the distance between causes and effects is such that it may be seen only with the light of the Qur'an [and] through the telescope of belief." And "it is within this long distance between cause and effect that the Divine Names [asmā al-ḥusna, i.e., attributes of God] each rise like stars. The place of their rising is this distance."[55]

In sum, Nursi tries to demonstrate that the Qur'anic view of God's agency in nature is not a dogmatic imposition but a precious *abduction* offered by the Qur'an that is tested out, so to speak, and confirmed by human reason and experience. In addition, Nursi's articulation of natural causality as a *gradual process* softens the counterintuitive edges of Ash'arite occasionalism.[56] Furthermore, his perspective reconciles Ibn Rushd's and Ghazali's differing emphasis on wisdom and contingency. We shall now discuss these reconciliatory implications of Nursi's Qur'anic theology of natural causality before turning to his specific engagement with Qur'anic miracle stories.

The Qur'anic View of Natural Causality and Common Sense

The occasionalist Ash'arite formulation that the universe is being created and re-created every moment down to its smallest atom has been received by many as doing injustice to our feeling of continuity in the world.[57] Even after the modern discoveries in quantum physics that revealed the constant movement and dynamism in the subatomic level of all things, the Ash'arite view remains too abstract for most people. The question is this: How can one cook, eat, build, compose, and so on, and yet know that the tools she uses are not really efficacious in any way? Similarly, if there is no causative link among things and events, is our instinct for evaluating past experience and learning from it entirely misplaced? Indeed, why do we have such a strong tendency to analyze a repeated sequence of events if nothing in the world has any genuine causal efficacy whatsoever? While Nursi ultimately agrees with the Ash'arite view of continuous creation—that the world is constantly and entirely sustained by God at each moment—his approach eases the tension between the occasionalist view and our commonsensical perception in daily life.

As I shall demonstrate below, Nursi seems to be aware that it is neither possible nor desirable to speak without making reference to natural causes.

Rather, he shows how our everyday causal thinking can be a *means* to *gradually* uncover the constant divine agency in the world. Our commonsensical notion of causality is a stepping-stone that is to be employed in reaching for a deeper awareness of the sustainer of the universe.

In other words, our almost instinctual reference to natural causes is not regrettable; it is not unfortunate that we are wired to engage in causal thinking. Rather, it is a blessing that we are able to posit causes and to perceive ourselves and other forces and objects as having agency. It is such causal thinking that becomes a bridge to a deeper understanding of the causer of causes (*musabbib al-asbāb*), who is the source of all power and beauty. In his crucial treatise on the self, Nursi stresses that our habit of talking about causal agency actually starts very close to home: in our own inner selves.[58] We each have a sense of agency, a sense that we know, do, produce, accomplish, will, wish, love, and so on. This sense of agency is a gift, for it enables one to draw an analogy between one's agency and God's agency, and thus to relate to divine attributes. By making analogies such as "As I built this home, God built the world; just as I know what I built, God knows the entire universe," we are able to relate to divine attributes, such as "creator" and "all-knowing." However, it is important to keep moving forward—that is, after the step of analogy, to move on to the step of surrender, admitting that even our power, knowledge, creativity, and very existence are dependent on the One.

According to Nursi, our possession of a sense of agency is an aspect of the momentous "trust" given to human beings, as mentioned in the Qurʾanic verse "We offered the Trust to the heavens, the earth, and the mountains, yet they refused to undertake it and were afraid of it; mankind undertook it" (Q. 33:72). Nursi notes that it is only when one hijacks that "trust" as his own that he starts pretending he has genuine agency independent of his sustainer; he becomes extremely unjust and ignorant, as noted in the rest of the verse: "He [the human being] has always been prone to be most wicked [ẓalūman], most foolish [jahūla]" (Q. 33:72).[59] Indeed, Nursi argues that our capacity to posit ourselves as agents is mirrored in our understanding of natural causality. If one interprets that capacity incorrectly and claims to be independent of God, then she imposes such a vision onto nature as well, claiming that nature acts on its own and natural causes are genuine creators. As a result, Nursi argues, this human being idolizes not only herself but also natural causes: "It is just like a man who steals a brass coin from the public treasury; he can only justify his action by agreeing to take a silver coin for each of his friends who is present. So the man who says: 'I own myself,' must believe and say: 'Everything owns itself.'"[60] In contrast, the more we realize our personal dependence on our creator, the more clearly we shall see the world around us as sustained by God—and vice versa. And just as we must continue to take responsibility for our actions after surrendering to God, we must continue to work within the parameters of natural causality after affirming that God's agency enables everything.[61]

In addition to his appreciation of apparent causality as a crucial step in the process of discovering the Creator, Nursi makes references to the interconnectedness of created beings in his approach to nature, a move that further eases the counterintuitiveness of Ash'arite atomism or occasionalism. For, even if he eventually infers that each particle is in need of the continuous creativity of God, Nursi often takes into account the "panoramic view," so to speak. He is aware of the importance of looking at things in meaningful chunks rather than only as momentary particles, so as to appreciate the overall regular patterns that are displayed across nature.[62] The idea is that things in the world, especially living things, come into existence as related to most, if not all, things in the universe. Nursi notes, for instance, that the eye is in a constant organic exchange with the entire body (including the digestive, respiratory, and urinary systems) as well as with what is outside the body (such as sunlight, visible objects, air pressure, etc.).[63] The world around us, when observed from the perspective of interconnectedness, thus again becomes a sign. If things and events in the universe are interconnected, then what is required for the production of a thing or event is not just some knowledge and power but an *all-encompassing* knowledge and power. That is, Nursi argues, the real maker of my eyes should have power and knowledge of all the universe, since my eyes are interconnected with the entire universe. Indeed, from sunshine, to nourishment from plants, to air pressure and gravity, an eye functions within the entire web of creation. And if one does not grant that an all-powerful and all-knowing transcendent creator must be operating, then he will have to posit that "in every particle working in your eye there would have to be an eye such as could see every limb and part of your body as well as the entire universe, with which you are connected."[64]

In other words, the maker of one part of the universe must have power over all the rest. Nursi takes this notion from his interpretation of the Qur'anic verse "Creating and resurrecting all of you is just like creating or resurrecting a single soul: God is all hearing and all seeing" (Q. 31:28).[65] Nursi's emphasis on the interconnectedness of things leads not only to the discovery of divine activity in the world but also to an appreciation of divine wisdom.

Reconciling Ghazali's and Ibn Rushd's Views on Nature:
Contingency and Wisdom

Indeed, Nursi's emphasis on the *process* of deciphering natural causality on the basis of our own sense of agency, as well as his recognition of the interconnectedness of nature, sets aside the picture of a fragmented and disconnected world attributed to Ash'arite occasionalism. It also puts the disagreement between Ghazali and Ibn Rushd to rest. As will be recalled, for Ghazali the realization of the ultimate contingency of natural order enables the believer to turn to God in gratitude, whereas for Ibn Rushd it is the very necessity of natural order that enables people to appreciate God's wisdom and be grateful. To illustrate their divergences through the example of rain, Ghazali might ask: If it is rain that really grows your crop, why be thankful to God instead of the rain? From the opposite angle, Ibn Rushd could say: If rain is not necessary for harvest, why thank God for creating the rain? Although these two interpretations of natural order seem to contradict, each has a point, and together they highlight the two authentic faces of the same world: its consistency and its contingency.

Nursi's works offer a helpful vocabulary for articulating the reconciliation of these two aspects of the world, presenting them not as alternatives but as complementary interpretations of its complex reality. The first pair of terms he employs, which occurs more frequently in his earlier works, consists of "sphere of faith" (Ar. *dāira al-i'tiqād*, Tk. *daire-i itikad*) and "sphere of [apparent] causes" (Ar. *dāira al-asbāb*, Tk. *daire-i esbab*). Nursi argues that we live in a world of *asbāb*, of apparent causes: the world is structured in such a way that certain apparent causes are *connected* with certain effects by the Creator. Thus, if we wish to obtain a certain result, we need to have recourse to the apparent cause connected with it. Not doing so would be disrespecting the One who organized the world that way; it would be taking the wisdom of the maker of the order lightly. On the other hand, respect goes hand in hand with the recognition that these causes are merely *apparent* causes pointing to the Creator's activity. Such recognition belongs to the sphere of faith. To affirm this sphere of faith is to be keenly aware that an "Absolutely Powerful One is in no need of [powerless] intermediaries to share in His [governance (*rubūbiyya*)] and creation." Rather, objects are ordered in a particular sequence so as to display "His wisdom and the manifestation of His Names."[66] Nursi repeatedly cautions his reader to be mindful of the stations of each sphere, lest one fall into one of the two extremes. Confusing the "sphere of apparent causes" with the "sphere of faith" will bring one to the brink of *shirk*, or idolatry; such a person will end up "worshipping" the apparent causes, taking them to be the real creators of events, putting his trust in them, directing his hopes and gratitude to them. One falls into the other extreme when he uses the "sphere of faith" as an excuse to violate the "sphere of causes"; that person will then make his faith in God an excuse for his laziness. Refusing to work within the sphere of causes, with the excuse that God is the only real cause, he will thus disrespect the protocols set on earth by the Creator. To keep clear of both *shirk* and insult to the order and its maker, one needs to recognize the integrity of each sphere. According to Nursi, in this world the "sphere of apparent causes" predominates over the sphere of faith, the former being more readily perceived than the latter at first sight. In the world to come, the reverse will be true: the causes will be readily transparent for all, not just to the thoughtful. In the hereafter, it will be abundantly clear to everyone that God is in charge, and no apparent cause will veil his agency from anyone.[67]

Another set of terms that Nursi introduces in order to offer a balanced response to our experience of nature refers to two types of divine laws: "the lesser Law" (*sharī'a al-sughra*)—that is, the religious law—and "the greater Law" of God (*sharī'a al-kubra*)—that is, the laws of the universe or creation.[68] Nursi's use of the term *sharia*, by including a reference to the laws of creation, is new, for the term has traditionally been used to refer to religious law—that is, sacred guidelines for human conduct. Nursi's use of *sharia* is thus innovative, although the concept it refers to is not new. After all, classical Islamic theology also talked about God's laws or "habits" in nature by using terms such as *ijrā' al-'āda* (as will be recalled from chapter 2) as well as *sunnatullah* and *'ādatullah*.

Building on this broader conception of the term *sharia*, Nursi intriguingly argues that part of a believer's submission to God is obedience to the natural order God establishes and maintains on earth. To neglect the formalities of the order and demand that God create in a different way than that which He has chosen in this world implies rebellion against God and a rejection of his wisdom.[69] In other words, when a believer waters her plant, it is an act of obedience to God as long as she does it with the awareness that the life-giver has decreed that he shall create life in such conditions. If the believer were to lazily demand that God grow the plant without her watering it, it would be disrespecting God's will and disobeying the greater *sharia*.

Indeed, Nursi notes that just as Prophet Muhammad was exemplary in following the "lesser Law" of God, the sacred law, he was also exemplary in his obedience to the "greater Law" of God, the laws of God manifest in the cosmos.[70] This is the reason why the Prophet was granted a generally normal life, with the exception of occasional miracles he performed. Nursi is highly critical of people who try to embellish the life of the Prophet by exaggerating the frequency of miraculous events in his life. They miss the point that the Prophet's main mission was to teach us to appreciate the normal order as full of signs of God. The Prophet was sent "so that he might disclose to human beings the wonders of Divine art and His [sustaining] power that underlie all occurrences," and to teach that what appears to be ordinary is in fact a "miracle" of God's power.[71] The people who favor the interruption of order over its preservation are disparaging God's creation by failing to recognize the miracles in everyday life. Thus, they miss precisely what lies at the heart of the prophetic teaching.[72]

Through its reference to the concepts of sphere of faith and sphere of apparent causes as well as the greater *sharia* and the lesser one, Nursi's approach can offer a reconciliation of Ghazali's and Ibn Rushd's different views on the question of natural order.[73] To return to the rain example, one could accept that there is wisdom and mercy in God's sending down the rain, given how he chose to govern the world (giving us bodies that are mostly created out of water, making plants grow in the presence of water, etc.). Yet this affirmation that there is a need for rain in a frame sustained by divine wisdom would not mean that rain itself is inherently necessary for God to be able to create life. After all, "lifeless" rain obviously lacks the necessary qualities—such as knowledge, planning, mercy, and power—to account for the life created through it.

Translating Nursi's reconciliation of Ghazali's and Ibn Rushd's main points in their classical debate into Peirce's terminology of scientific metaphysics, one could say that the laws of nature are in fact the result of a contingent process. Since, hypothetically speaking, the universe *could* have followed a different route in its growth and been gifted other "habits," there is neither logical necessity nor ontological necessity involved in the existence of current natural laws. Yet Peirce would grant that the laws are necessary in a different, lighter sense of the word because, given where we are now in terms of the universe's current status, we *have to* act and predict on the basis of these laws; these laws *are* real, not mere products of our imagination.

Nursi's approach to natural causality in light of the Qur'an forms the backbone of his engagement with miracles. Having discussed his approach, as well as its promise for reconciling some of the tensions that emerged in the medieval debates, we shall now turn to specific examples of his interpretation of miracles.

Nursi on Qur'anic Miracle Stories

It seems that, for Nursi, the Qur'anic miracle stories and the Qur'anic discourse on "signs in nature" are both sides of the same coin: both alert the reader to the presence and qualities of the Creator revealed through nature. Thus, according to Nursi, the story of Abraham's miraculous survival in fire (Q. 21:69) suggests that when fire burns, it does so because of God's command. In other words, the miracle story of fire not burning Abraham because of God's command teaches the reader that fire burning in everyday life is not a simple event. Rather, it is an event that requires no less than the agency of an all-powerful One.[74]

Similarly, in his treatise devoted to explaining the Qur'anic phrase *bismillah* (Ar. *bi'smi'llāh*, literally, in the name of God) Nursi interprets the story of Moses's miraculous rod, which split the rock and brought forth water, as interrupting our smug familiarity with the natural order. The story enables us to see the wondrousness of ordinary events around us. For instance, each fragile rootlet of a delicate plant obeys God's command and reaches out for water within the earth, just like the staff that Moses was commanded to "strike the rock with" (Q. 2:60). That is, the usual event of "roots spreading through hard rock and earth and producing fruits as easily as the branches spread through the air and produce fruits" is actually no less wonderful than Moses's miracle. Just as the performance of Moses's staff was miraculous, in the sense that it exceeded the capacity of an ordinary staff, the rootlets of a flower piercing through hard soil and rock is miraculous in the sense that such a feat exceeds the capacity of the apparent causes associated with it. Both miracle stories and natural events declare *bismillah*—that is, they announce that events can take place only "in God's name."[75]

It is worth stressing that, according to Nursi, these ordinary events are "wonders not because the apparent causes have not yet been discovered, but because the apparent causes are insufficient to breach the *transcendental* gap between the apparent causes and their effects. In the case of rootlets piercing through hard soil, for instance, we may know that these delicate leaves release a secretion with which the soil is pierced."[76] Yet our discovery of "this secretion does not obviate the need for an unseen maker. Rather, the production and secretion of such a liquid points again to the wisdom and power of an agent other than the poor, unconscious rootlets."[77] As noted earlier, similar to Ghazali, Nursi's approach does not rest on the denial of empirical data or on ignorance of natural causes; rather, his argument starts by accepting them and recognizing the conjunction of a natural cause and its effect as a sign of divine agency to be deciphered in the light of Qur'anic cues.[78]

In sum, similar to Ghazali, Nursi's approach to miracle stories reconciles the apparent tension between the miraculous and the ordinary in the Qur'an. Rather than contradict each other, the Qur'anic discourse on nature and the miracle narratives actually converge in calling the reader to pause and reflect more deeply on natural order around her. As noted in the previous section, Nursi's approach also reconciles Ghazali's emphasis on the "metaphysics of contingency" and Ibn Rushd's emphasis on the "metaphysics of wisdom."

Now the interpretive field may well be clear from any inherent tension between the natural and miraculous phenomena, but what remains to be answered is our pragmatic question—the question of "So what?" That is, what is the implication of reinterpreting natural causality through miracle narratives? If these stories of the interruption of natural order make us pay more attention to nature and regard it as worthy of wonder, so what? What is the "cash value" of discovering that the natural world is full of "miracles" of divine power—that is, situations that exceed the capacities of the apparent causes and that direct our attention to an all-knowing, wise, and powerful God? To offer a metaphor, if you have to knock on a door to have it opened to you, what difference does it make to add to your act of knocking a disclaimer that it is not your knock but an unseen host that opens the door for you? Does such a disclaimer about not taking the opening of the door for granted, and your belief in an unseen agent, make any difference for your reality? In what follows, I shall interpret Nursi's writings in light of such questions. In other words, I will press Nursi's approach to see whether there is any pragmatic juice, so to speak, in such an approach to the Qur'anic miracles.

Pragmatic Implications of Reinterpreting Natural Causality
in Light of Miracles

To my mind, Nursi's answer to the question of whether the reinterpretation of natural causality in light of the Qurʾan has pragmatic import would
be an emphatic yes. In terms of the metaphor mentioned above, Nursi
would say that to regard the opening of a door as a mysterious but regularly
recurring phenomenon is substantially different from interpreting it as an
expression of a powerful and generous host's response and welcome. Nursi
provides a crucial cue for such a reply to the pragmatic question when he
makes a distinction between receiving an item as a gift and stealing it or
stumbling upon it. Although the person ends up getting the same item—
say, an apple—either way, when it is received as a gift more is gained than
just the item itself. A gift can signify the initiation of a relationship and is
an expression of care and love. And, unlike the item itself, which vanishes
upon consumption, the relationship initiated through the item can hold
promise for the future.[79] Hence, from a pragmatic perspective, trusting a
mysterious natural order is not the same as believing in a wise and merciful
maker of the order.

In fact, in one of his treatises, Nursi emphasizes that belief in God offers
implications for the future. If it weren't for such implications, we could
have done without religion. In a parable, the righteous person addresses
the one who attacks faith in God and life after death, saying, "If you can
kill death, banish separation and finitude from the earth, take away vulnerability and poverty from human race, and close the door of the grave, then
speak and we shall listen! Otherwise shut up!"[80] Of course, none of these
results can be achieved as long as human beings limit themselves with a
belief in finite existence and reject faith in the eternal. Nursi repeatedly
highlights the challenge that finitude presents for each person: not only
does death—by which we will vanish into an apparently dark pit—await
each person, but in every moment of our lives we encounter death. Every
day we are reminded of the "cemetery of the past," which leaves us with
memories of utter transience. We are each surrounded by separation and
death—of loved ones, of familiar ones, of living beings associated with
our lives, of cherished moments. In each case of separation, the heart is
wounded by the reminders of our helplessness before finitude.[81]

Moreover, Nursi repeatedly notes that a human beings are essentially
helpless before a universe over which they have no control.[82] This means

that neither through figuring out natural laws and manipulating aspects of the natural order nor through invoking rational necessity can humanity be genuinely secure. None of these offers us any guarantee that the natural order will remain as is or that the future will turn out as we need it to be, and none answers our needs for eternity, for unending beauty and power. Therefore, discovery of the maker of this world, of ourselves, and of our existential dilemmas is not a frivolous speculation but rather a deep human need, or, to recast it in pragmatic terms, a very meaningful and "useful" move.

According to Nursi, discovering the God "behind" the world sheds light on the here and now; it offers a genuine future in the midst of "waves" of separation, finitude, and alienation.[83] Using colorful imagery, Nursi talks about how belief in God turns "death gallows" into "playful swings."[84] That is, a perspective of belief reveals that while things pass away and come and go, the qualities that they signify and tantalizingly point to—such as wisdom, power, beauty, majesty, and life giving—are stable; they reveal an eternal source.[85] Thus, the continuous flux of the world, instead of becoming painful in its apparently endless reenactments of death, becomes an enjoyable drama, continuously renewing the reflections of the various beautiful qualities of God. By viewing the transient world as a "screen" on which the colorful motifs of asmā al-ḥusna are manifested, one connects to the eternal source who can fulfill her needs for unending beauty and life and finds peace.

Moreover, Nursi repeatedly notes that belief in God familiarizes an otherwise alien world; the beings in nature are all creatures of the same maker and support one another. The world around us is not hostile to us; rather, we are all brothers and sisters sustained by the same One.[86] Thus, Nursi repeatedly points out, the perspective of faith relieves existential anxiety, helps one genuinely enjoy an eternal life journey, and offers hope and strength in the face of the world's challenges.

From this perspective of faith, even the most difficult situation can then be engaged to yield good fruits, since nothing comes without the will of God and nothing fails to bring a message from the divine. And each threat of finitude can be braced for, because our "weakness and finitude," revealed at every turn, become an appetizer in enjoying the bounties of God. Our hunger, for instance, becomes a means for enjoying his bounties, and our vulnerabilities become a means for appreciating his protection and care. Indeed, Nursi claims that profound human neediness becomes an "intercessor" at the divine court of mercy, making us look for and discover "an unending source of mercy," and act in mercy.[87]

In sum, the belief in God disclosed by the Qur'anic approach to nature can make a crucial difference in that it enables the believer to enter into a relationship with the merciful and wise maker. It has direct consequences for a believer's life, provided that the believer renews her awareness of belief and aligns herself with it.[88] Given these pragmatic implications of belief, it is noteworthy that Nursi finishes his discussion on *bismillah* and Qur'anic miracles with advice for the believer's praxis: "Since all things say, 'In the Name of God,' and bearing God's bounties in God's name, give them to us, we too should say: 'In the Name of God.' We should give in the name of God, and take in the name of God."[89] For Nursi, acting in God's name translates into a particular posture in benefiting from the world (enjoying it with gratitude for having been honored as a guest), access to a genuine future (through the initiation of a relationship with the source of all power and mercy), and gracious and generous interactions with others (instead of being arrogant, one can reflect God's mercy when sharing God's blessings with others). It is also worth noting that gratitude to God and compassion toward his creatures are key themes in the *Risale-i nur*.[90] Indeed, according to Nursi, recognizing one's vulnerability and having compassion for others, along with *tafakkur*, or reflective meditation, constitutes the quickest path to God.[91]

Having noted some of the examples of Nursi's interpretation of miracle stories in connection with natural causality, and having pursued some of the pragmatic implications of such an approach, I shall now turn to another example of Nursi's engagement with Qur'anic miracles—the story of the virgin birth.

Nursi on the Virgin Birth Story

The angels said, "Mary, God gives you news of a Word from Him, whose name will be the Messiah, Jesus, son of Mary, who will be held in honor in this world and the next, who will be one of those brought near to God." . . . She said, "My Lord, how can I have a son when no man has touched me?" [The angel] said, "This is how God creates what He will: when He has ordained something, He only says, "Be," and it is.

—Qur'an 3:45–47; cf. 19:16–21

Nursi comments on the Qur'anic story of the virgin birth upon being asked a question about someone's claim that Jesus did have a father. Nursi argues that while the individual who offers such a nonliteral reading of the virgin birth narrative in the Qur'an may mean well, in that he wants to defend the Qur'an in the face of its critics, he is clearly mistaken.[92]

According to Nursi, the obvious plain sense of the Qur'an (ṣarāḥa al-qur'āniyya) can be superseded only if there is a compelling reason, and there is no such compelling reason in the case of virgin birth. After all, the assumption that natural laws, including the "law of reproduction," can never be broken is unfounded: "There is no law at all that has no exceptions and from which [no] individuals are exempt. And there is no universal rule which has not been breached by extraordinary individuals." In fact, the virgin birth story is a reminder that natural laws are not as absolute as we may take them to be. Nursi argues that the very diversity of nature itself confirms the "permeability" of natural laws. In the case of reproduction, for instance, there are many creatures that multiply without having two parents, and in the case of the origin of the species, each species must have started with no parents involved. Nursi's point here is not that the case of virgin birth follows another natural law, though of course such an unexpected switching of laws would be still be an exception and a miracle. Rather, his move is reminiscent of Peirce's criticism of necessitarianism: given the variety in the world, it is unreasonable to deem any natural law as absolute. Nursi argues that what people mistakenly call "natural laws" are actually "universal manifestations" of divine will and command, and they may be "breached" in exceptional situations if divine wisdom sees fit.[93]

Throughout his works, Nursi engages with the modern concept of natural law and cautions against a common misunderstanding of it. Similar to Peirce, Nursi insightfully challenges the notion that natural laws have an agency on their own. What is called a natural law is a *description* of a regularly occurring event, and the description cannot be taken as the *cause* of the event itself. Natural law is an abstract concept that has been mistaken for an external entity because of the consistent way the Creator creates events.[94] To appreciate Nursi's point here, let us think about the case of a homemaker who has a habit of making pancakes every Sunday morning. We cannot talk of a "Sunday pancake rule" independent of her agency; such a rule has no efficacy on its own. Just as it would be nonsensical to suggest that the "Sunday pancake rule" makes the pancakes, it would be absurd to suggest that the reference to natural laws obviates the need for an unseen agent—or, in Peirce's words, to think that a court can do without a "sheriff" who would put the laws into effect.[95]

For Nursi, therefore, the virgin birth story is a provocative reminder that if it were not for the will and power of the Creator such regularities that we call natural laws would not take place. It reminds us that there is no inherent logical necessity that links the natural causes (e.g., the union of both parents) and the consequences (e.g., the creation of a new individual). To be sure, the connections between apparent causes and their consequences are regular and the regularity is *real*, but such regularity is neither logically necessary nor absolute. Such a nuanced appraisal of the concept of natural law sets Nursi apart from some nineteenth- and twentieth-century Muslim theologians who considered natural laws to be absolute.[96]

Moreover, for Nursi, the miracle story highlights that while the regularities in the universe point to God's power and wisdom and make a case against blind chance, there is also genuine variety and irregularity in the world, revealing divine choice and freedom.[97] Indeed, "the All-Powerful and All-Knowing One, the All-Wise Maker, shows His *power* and His *wisdom* and that *chance can in no way interfere in His works*" through the regularity with which he governs the world. Such regularity takes the "form of *laws*" in nature. At the same time, "*through exceptions to the laws, the wonders of His habits* [Ar. *kharq al-ᶜāda*; Tk. *hark-ı adet*, literally, breaking of habit], apparent changes, differences in individual characteristics, and changes in the appearance and descent [of blessings]," God shows "His *volition, will, choice, that He is the agent with choice*, and He is *under no restrictions whatsoever*."[98]

Here, we might again raise the crucial question of pragmatism: Does such inference of God's freedom from the variety and irregularity in the world have any implication for the reader? That is, what difference does it make to recognize that natural laws are neither absolute nor self-operating, and that the "sheriff" who maintains them has freedom and choice, as reflected through the exceptions to the laws? From Nursi's perspective, it seems that one implication of such belief is that in all of the various challenging circumstances of life, one can reject the victim mentality and act with hope. That is, if the universe is not run according to rigid and impersonal natural laws, and if there is room for flexibility, then there is the possibility of customizing these natural laws for the genuine needs of the creatures. A cue for such interpretation comes from Nursi's suggestion that the mercy clause was included in the very blueprint of the universe, so to speak. He suggests that the all-merciful Creator softens the "universal laws and general principles" of creation by allowing for exceptions: "In a special way [God has] sent His Names of Most Merciful and All-Compassionate to the assistance of individuals crying out at the *constraint* of those universal laws. That is to say, *within those universal and general principles He has special favours, special succour, special manifestations, so that everything may seek help from Him and look to Him at all times for every need.*"[99] Hence, the very structure of the universe is such that, instead of being resigned to the ruthless precision or "constraints" of natural laws, one can hope for a special dispensation in unique situations, and act with that hope.

Indeed, for Nursi, what is absolute is not the natural laws per se, but the *asmā al-ḥusna*, the beautiful or perfect attributes of God. In other words, the law of mercy, law of wisdom, law of justice, law of beauty (Tk. *kanun-u rahmet, kanun-u kerem, kanun-u adl, kanun-u cemal*), and so on are absolute. Hence, there are ultimate principles with which the Creator acts, and one can be assured that the source of mercy will never turn into ruthlessness and that the source of justice will never be unjust.[100] In the above quote, Nursi emphasizes the "law of mercy" as taking precedence over any particular law of nature in effect in the universe: "His Names of Most Merciful and All-Compassionate [are sent] to the assistance of individuals crying out at the constraint of those universal laws." Nursi's reference to the "law of mercy" must have been inspired by the Qurʾanic verses that describe God as having "taken it upon Himself to be merciful" (*kataba ʿalā nafsihi al-raḥma*) (Q. 6:12).

Affirming divine freedom thus makes room for human freedom: natural laws are not the only blueprint for events; the Creator also takes into account human will, choice, and needs as he sustains the world in each moment. Belief in a non-necessitarian view of the world is thus a belief in genuine human free will granted by the Creator.[101]

Interestingly, Nursi suggests that when interpreted in this vein, the Qurʾanic miracle stories offer profound implications not only for personal life but also for scientific innovation. Furthering Peirce's hunch about miracle stories and science, Nursi interprets Qurʾanic miracles as encouraging scientific discoveries as well.

Qurʾanic Miracle Stories and Technology: A Contemporary Interpretation

According to Nursi, the Qurʾan speaks to all ages, and to all classes of people. Unlike other writings, it does not become outdated or "old" as time progresses. Rather, the Qur'an is an unending, inexhaustible treasury of guidance, whose treasures are further revealed as time goes on. Indeed, in addition to the crucial message of the Qur'an that is pertinent across all times, each age enjoys a special share from the word of God. A particular time period cannot trespass on the future "share of another which is concealed [for it]."[102] In this sense, for Nursi, miracle stories have a special meaning intended for the contemporary age.

To begin with, Nursi notes that the stories of the prophets narrated in the Qur'an "are not merely historical stories, but [rather] comprise numerous meanings of guidance."[103] In other words, each Qur'anic story contains a lesson and guidance for the reader. One lesson lurking behind miracle stories is "the final limit of man's science and industry," and it encourages the reader to move forward toward that goal. Hence, just as in the Qur'anic narratives the prophets serve humanity "as leaders and vanguards in respect of spiritual and moral progress," they also provide instruction "in regard to humankind's material progress." That is, "just as by speaking of the spiritual and moral perfections of the Prophets, [the Qur'an] is encouraging people to benefit from them, so too in discussing their miracles, it is [encouragingly hinting that we can] attain to similar things and imitate them."[104]

Nursi accordingly offers examples of Qur'anic miracle stories that he interprets as encouragements to discover, in God's name, further wonders in nature. One example is the miracle of Solomon: "And [We subjected] the wind for Solomon. Its outward journey took a month, and its return journey likewise" (Q. 34:12). Nursi understands this verse to mean that Solomon traveled through the air, covering the distance of a two months' journey in a single day. The verse indicates that human beings can also discover speedy means of travel, and, by telling this story, the Qur'an is *indirectly* encouraging the reader to discover those means. Similarly, the Qur'anic reference to the transportation of the Queen of Sheba's throne by one of Solomon's men in the blink of an eye (Q. 27:40) can be interpreted as hinting at the possibility of transporting "either things themselves or their images instantaneously" across a long distance, and that "Almighty God bestowed this ability on Solomon (peace be upon him) in the form of a miracle, to establish his innocence [*sic*] and justice." Through this story, Nursi suggests, the Creator is addressing the reader, saying, "O [human being]! I mounted one of my servants on the air because he gave up the desires of his [ego]. If you too give up [the ego's laziness] and benefit thoroughly from [some] of my laws in the cosmos, you too may mount it."[105] Likewise, Nursi interprets the story of Moses's miraculous staff, with which he brought forth water from a rock (Q. 2:60 and 7:160), as encouragement to find tools to drill the earth in order to reach its resources.

Perhaps the most striking example Nursi gives is that of Jesus's healing miracles in the Qur'an: "[Jesus said] I will heal the blind and the leper, and bring the dead back to life with God's permission" (Q. 3:49). Nursi suggests that Jesus's miracles point to "the horizons" of medicine—that with God's leave, the most difficult diseases can be cured and we can even temporarily reverse death.[106] It is noteworthy that Nursi does not see any tension between his "pro-science" interpretation and the spiritual interpretation of the verse. God has given two gifts to Jesus: "One was the remedy for spiritual ills, and the other the cure for physical sicknesses. Thus, dead hearts were raised to life through the light of guidance. And sick people who were as though dead found health through his breath and cure." Through these miracle stories, God is encouraging the believer both to seek to internalize Jesus's message and to seek further development in the art of healing; that is, the reader may seek and find cures in the "pharmacy" of divine wisdom.[107] Following Nursi's logic, "the virgin birth narrative can also be taken as hinting at the horizons of reproductive technology and helping the reader to entertain the possibility of conception even when sexual intercourse is unsuccessful."[108] Hence, Nursi's understanding of divine freedom and the endless possibilities articulated through miracle stories translates into a hopeful perseverance and initiative to solve problems through scientific study.[109]

Nursi was not unique in suggesting this "pro-science" interpretation of miracle stories. The Indian Muslim scholar Shibli Nu'mani (1857–1914) also insightfully interpreted miracle stories as pointing to future technological development.[110] A crucial difference between Nursi and Nu'mani is that the latter assumed that natural laws are absolute and natural causation is logically necessary, thereby committing a rationalist mistake reminiscent of Ibn Rushd. According to Nu'mani, miracle stories in the Qur'an are accounts of natural events whose possibility was unknown to the prophet's audience at the time. In contrast, for Nursi, it is precisely by challenging our commonsensical assumptions about natural laws and natural causality that these miracle stories point to the horizons of technological development.[111] Moreover, by freeing the reader from a hasty rationalization of the natural order, Nursi's position, like Ghazali's, harvests existential implications from these stories—namely, that the reader can receive the natural order as a divine gift instead of a logical given. It is noteworthy that such "a non-necessitarian" view of nature, to use Peirce's terminology, *still* makes room for science and technology. Nursi's case shows that one need not at all subscribe to the idea of natural laws as immutable in order to embrace scientific development.

As Kelton Cobb rightly pointed out, Nursi's (and, we might add, other Muslim theologians') interpretation of miracle stories in connection with technology may come across as an act of reading *into* the Qur'anic text rather than reading *of* it.[112] Yet such a contemporary reading is not a stretch at all from Nursi's perspective, in that he believed it is truly the all-knowing God who is speaking in the Qur'an and addressing not only seventh-century Arabia but also later centuries stretching until the end of time. From such a perspective, making contemporary connections is not the result of a naive conflation of exegesis and eisegesis, but rather a self-conscious attempt on the part of a believer to read the Qur'an as speaking to his contemporary context.

It is also important to note that according to Nursi the Qur'anic encouragement of scientific progress is a *hint* rather than a direct and explicit lesson.[113] Nursi suggests two reasons for why it is appropriate that such reference to technology in the Qur'an is merely a hint. The first is that the Qur'an speaks to all ages and all classes; hence, specific references that would be comprehensible only in a particular age would alienate readers in other periods of history. Second, given the *maqāṣid* of the Qur'an to teach about the Creator and eternal life, technological development disconnected from faith, purely for its own sake, would not be worthy of mention in the Qur'an.[114] Nursi is hopeful, however, that there are people who can study nature in its proper worshipful context—in God's name and with the intent to serve God's creatures—and for them such indirect encouragement will suffice: "If there are among you [readers of the Qur'an] respected craftsmen and artists and inspired inventors, who, purely for the benefit of God's servants, serve the general interest and public well-being and betterment of social life, which is a valuable worship, these signs and indications of the Qur'an are surely sufficient for those sensitive people, who of course form a minority, in order to encourage their efforts and appreciate their art."[115]

Thus, so far, we have observed how Nursi interprets the miracle stories in the Qur'an in various interesting ways. In what follows, as a summative illustration of Nursi's approach to miracle stories, I shall discuss his multifaceted interpretation of the Qur'anic miracle of Abraham's survival in the fire.

Nursi on Multiple Meanings of the Story of Abraham's Miracle

Abraham said, "How can you worship what can neither benefit nor harm you, instead of God? Shame on you and on the things you worship instead of God. Have you no sense?" They said, "Burn him and avenge your gods, if you are going to do the right thing." But We said, "Fire, be cool and safe for Abraham."

—Qurʾan 21:66–69

As noted earlier, in the Qurʾan the prophets and messengers are presented as exemplary human beings, including Abraham, who is highlighted as a crucial upholder of monotheism, following the path of previous messengers who proclaimed the oneness of God, such as Noah (e.g., Q. 37:79–83). In the Qurʾan, the audience time and again are called to follow the "creed of Abraham" (*millati ibrahīm*) (Q. 2:130, 2:135, 3:95, 6:161, etc.). As with other figures in the Qurʾan, the story of Abraham is not told all in one breath or with great detail. Instead, the Qurʾan presents snippets and episodes from Abraham's life: his inner search for God, his dialogues with God, and his mission to his pagan people. To offer a brief summary, Abraham searches for God amid his pagan society and questions its idol worship. He turns away from the worship of the idols, dissatisfied with their finitude, saying, "I do not like things that set" (Q. 6:76). Abraham is then guided by God to the path of "truth": the worship of the One. His public mission also starts early: as a youth, he engages his father (Q. 19:42–46) and people, trying to convince them to cease their idolatry.

Two major miracles of Abraham are mentioned in the Qurʾan. First is the birth of Isaac in his old age through his barren wife Sarah, which parallels the story of Mary's virgin conception and Zachariah's having a son in old age—all of which seem to supersede the usual reproduction processes. The other miracle, which is uniquely attributed to Abraham in the Qurʾan, is his survival in the midst of blazing fire. We shall now look at how Nursi interprets this particular story in various ways.

Like all other narratives in the Qurʾan, Abraham's trial by fire is narrated very succinctly. It is referenced in three different suras (Q. 21:68–69, 29:24, 37:97), all of which also refer to Abraham's discussion with his people about idolatry. In each telling of the story, Abraham calls his people to monotheism, saying, "What are these images to which you are so devoted? . . . Listen! Your true Lord is the Lord of the heavens and the earth, He who created them, and I am a witness to this" (Q. 21:52–56; cf. 29:16–17, 37:85–87). The people respond to Abraham with disbelief, unwilling to change their ancestral ways (Q. 21:52). The Qur'an also narrates Abraham's "Socratic" plot aimed at revealing to them what they already know deep down inside. Abraham secretly smashes the idols in the temple, except one, and when the people question him, he suggests that they consider the remaining idol as the culprit. When the people admit that the idols cannot speak or act, Abraham delivers his punch line: "How can you worship what can neither benefit nor harm you, instead of God? . . . Have you no sense?" (Q. 21:66–67; cf. 37:95–96). The Qur'an notes that even before Abraham makes this statement, his audience recognizes that he is right in rejecting idols (Q. 21:64). However, they then turn back on their realization and decide to annihilate him: "They said, 'Burn him and avenge your gods, if you are going to do the right thing'" (Q. 21:68); "The only answer Abraham's people gave was, 'Kill him or burn him!'" (Q. 29:24); "They said, 'Build a pyre and throw him into the blazing fire'" (Q. 37:97–98). It is at this dramatic moment that God saves Abraham from the fire: "But We [God] said, 'Fire, be cool and safe for Abraham.' They planned to harm him, but We made them suffer the greatest loss" (Q. 21:69–70; cf. 29:24, 37:97–98).

As usual, the Qur'anic narrative does not offer much detail about the event: there are no descriptions of how Abraham is thrown into the fire, how he emerges from it, or what the immediate reactions of his people to this miracle were. Given the succinctness of the Qur'anic story, it is perhaps not surprising that some interpreters suggested that no miracle actually happened, including the renowned Muslim commentator Muhammad Asad (1900–1992). In his commentary on Q. 21:68–70, Asad notes, "Nowhere does the Qur'an state that Abraham was actually, bodily thrown into the fire and miraculously kept alive in it: on the contrary, the phrase 'God saved him from the Fire' occurring in 29:24 points, rather, to the fact of his not having been thrown into it."[116] That is, according to Asad's reading, Abraham's audience must have talked about throwing Abraham into a blazing fire but did not get to carry out their plans. God's deliverance of Abraham from the fire consisted in not letting him be thrown into it in the first place. Asad's move here is consistent with his overall approach to the Qur'an in his widely read and insightful commentary *The Message of the Qur'an*. In this commentary, Asad does admit that miracles are possible, and certain miracles, such as the virgin birth, are plainly there in the sacred text. Nevertheless, he does his best to minimize such miraculous moments in the Qur'anic discourse, so as to protect the integrity of reason and common sense. Hence, he argues that what is traditionally understood as Abraham's miraculous survival in fire—or Jesus's healing miracles for that matter—is actually a metaphor. Focusing on the versions of the Abraham story in Q. 29:24 and 37:97, Asad concludes that the Qur'an only makes "apparently an allegorical allusion to the fire of persecution, which Abraham had to suffer, and which, by dint of its intensity, was to become in his later life a source of spiritual strength and inner peace (*salām*)."[117]

Intriguing as it is, Asad's exclusively metaphorical reading of the story is challenged by the fact that its telling in Sura 21 makes reference to the divine command to the fire to be "cool" (*bardan*) for Abraham ("But We [God] said, 'Fire, be cool and safe for Abraham'"; Q. 21:68). If the text meant that Abraham was not literally thrown into fire but was simply threatened by it, the inclusion of God's command that the fire be cool would be awkward. Interestingly, all of Nursi's remarks about Abraham's miracle of surviving the fire refer to this passage in Sura 21, which provides the clearest telling of the miracle. Nursi reads this miracle story in a number of ways, all of which, he feels, are compatible with one another and cohere with the overall purposes of the Qur'an.

As will be recalled, for Nursi, the first implication of this miracle story—like the others—is a provocative invitation to rethink our assumptions about natural causality. The story of fire cooling off for Abraham suggests that "like other natural causes, fire does not act according to its own wishes and nature, blindly, but performs a duty under a [divine] *command*. Thus it did not burn Abraham, peace be upon him, because it was *commanded* not to burn him."[118] In other words, the narration of such an interruption in the usual course of nature interrupts our superficial understanding of natural order. The story invites the reader to see how the usual event of fire burning things and transforming them into ashes is worthy of wonder: it is a *sign* disclosing the agency of the powerful, wise, and merciful One.

Indeed, for Nursi, the miracle story highlights how the natural world is full of "miracles" of divine power—that is, situations that exceed the capacities of the apparent causes and that direct our attention to an all-knowing, wise, and powerful God. Hence, he argues, the story of Abraham's miraculous survival in fire helps us notice how in the summer "delicate green leaves retain their moisture for months in the face of extreme heat." We actually see a reenactment of Abraham's miracle occurring before our very eyes in nature: "The delicate leaves thin as cigarette paper recite the verse, 'Fire, be cool and safe for Abraham' (Q. 21:69) against the heat of the fire, each like the body of Abraham."[119] An ordinary event such as the survival of green leaves under the blazing sun is an *āya*, or sign, revealing God's agency, not because it is rare or because we don't have any scientific study of this process. Rather, such natural events that circumvent the familiar consequences of heat exceed the wisdom and mercy of the "apparent causes" and thus call for the agency of the Creator. Nursi's reading of Abraham's miracle story insightfully interprets the contingency and regularity of the natural world as worthy of wonder and as disclosing the divine.

Nursi also offers a spiritual reading of this miracle story: "See how elevated, subtle, and fine a garment this verse weaves on the loom of *ḥanīfan muslimān* which will not be ripped apart in all eternity."[120] The Arabic term referred to in the original Turkish text of this passage is a Qur'anic idiom used to describe Abraham in Q. 3:97—as "upright and submitting [to God]." That is, the story of Abraham's survival in fire symbolizes how "cloth[ing] your spirit in belief in God" protects you from hellfire. Such an allegorical reading reflects an appreciation of Abraham's profile in the Qur'an as a human being who fully responded to his sustainer and surrendered to him (e.g., Q. 3:92, 26:77–94). In the Qur'an, Abraham not only preaches monotheism but also lives out what he preaches, approaching his sustainer with a peaceful heart (*jā'a rabbahu biqalbin salīm*; Q. 37:84). Hence, for Nursi, the miracle story is inextricably linked with what Abraham stands for in the Qur'an. The reader is to take up the garment of Abraham—that is, to be clothed with recognition and peaceful surrender to one God, thereby escaping hell and the finitude and suffering that accompany deprivation from the Eternal One.[121]

Finally, Nursi also sees "pro-scientific" implications in the story:

[Besides], just as there is an immaterial substance, [that is] belief, which counters the effects of Hell-fire and affords protection against it . . . so there is a physical substance which protects against the effects of worldly fire. *For as is required by the Name of All-Wise, this world is the abode of wisdom, and Almighty God carries out His works under the veil of [apparent] causes.* Therefore, the fire burnt neither Abraham's body, nor his garments; He imbued them with a state which resisted fire. Thus, by this allusion, the verse is *in effect* saying: "O nation of Abraham! Resemble Abraham, so that your garments may be your [shield] against fire, your greatest enemy both here [in this world] and there [in the hereafter]. Clothe your spirit in belief in God, and it will be your shield against Hell-fire. Moreover, there are certain substances which Almighty God has hidden in the earth for you which will protect you from the evils of fire. Search for them, extract them, and clothe yourselves in them!" Thus, one of man's important discoveries and a step in his progress was his finding a substance which fire does not burn; and he clothed himself in garments resistant to fire.[122]

In other words, the miracle story also hints at a potential substance in nature that can be discovered and utilized for human benefit.[123] It is note-worthy how in this quote Nursi smoothly weaves spiritual and pro-scientific readings of the story together. Moreover, Nursi's approach here takes Ibn Rushd's apparently naturalistic interpretation a step further.[124] That is, if one reads these stories as simply unusual and complicated intersections of natural causes, whose repetition may or may not be possible—as Ibn Rushd seemed to do—there would be little implication for the reader's practice. Nursi, on the other hand, sees in the miracle story a divine promise, so to speak, that a similar feat will be granted if humanity asks for it. "The past is a seedbed for the future," he says, and if a miracle has happened, it could be repeated, albeit via different means. If a believer, following the example of the prophets, surrenders to the transcendent maker despite the inclina-tions of his ego and works within the framework of God's "greater *sharia*," then he will be gifted with the discovery of similar marvels.

In sum, Nursi reads the same miracle story in a number of ways, all of which have implications for readers in the here and now. While the first reading of the story emphasizes the contingency of nature and its "miracu-lous" dimension, in the sense of its utter dependence on an unseen mar-velous being, the "pro-science" interpretation stresses the need to take the current arrangement of apparent causes seriously. Thus, the same miracle story invites us to have gratitude for God's mercy, which sustains the world in each moment, and reverence for divine wisdom, through which the world is sustained according to consistent patterns. Readers of the Qurʾan are not only invited to an existential awareness of their vulnerability in a vulnerable world and to gratitude, but are also encouraged to appreciate divine wisdom and to imagine new possibilities in nature. Finally, the story communicates a spiritual lesson, calling the reader to take up Abraham's surrender to God as a shield against the experience of hell in this world and in the next.

In conclusion, let us note how such a multilayered approach reconciles the apparent puzzle in the Qurʾanic discourse on miracles. Nursi shows that when read with the *maqāṣid* or overall purposes of the Qurʾan in mind, the Qurʾanic miracle stories cease to be a "problem" in the middle of a discourse that focuses on the natural. Instead, they enhance the overall Qur'anic emphasis on nature by interrupting our familiarity with it. Moreover, Nursi's case illustrates how a Qur'anic miracle story can have actual implications—how it can be interpreted in a way that both coheres with and enlightens our experience of the world.

CONCLUSION
QUR'ANIC HERMENEUTICS IN THE MODERN AGE

Familiarity is risky. It may bring the illusion that we have comprehended the world around us. By breaking into such familiarity, miracle stories can invite the reader into a world of wonder, gratitude, and discovery. Yet the miracle stories themselves, and the Qur'anic text that contains them, can also become too familiar. This book was meant to make such narratives worthy of note once again by highlighting their potentially far-reaching repercussions. Indeed, the case of miracle stories in the Qur'an discloses the complexity of scriptural interpretation in the modern age. By analyzing samples from Qur'anic reception history and connecting them with modern debates on miracles and epistemology, this book illustrated how a site of apparent conflict between faith and reason, or revelation and science, can become a venue for a fruitful exchange between them.

At the core of this book's analysis, there has been a deceptively simple question addressed to the Qur'anic text: "What do you want us to do?" To be sure, inquiring about the implications of a text is not an innovation of modern hermeneutics; any serious reader of the scriptures in any age must have raised such a question of relevance in various ways. In the case of the Qur'an, as Walid Saleh pointed out, it was a frequent perception in the exegetical tradition that "whoever may be the addressee in any particular verse, the Qur'an was seen ultimately to carry a message, a lesson or warning. The reader always expected a moral to be learned, and this was an expectation that predetermined the mode of reading."[1] Even verses that seemed to address Prophet Muhammad in the singular second-person pronoun could be read as having relevance for all readers who were open to receiving guidance.[2] Other passages, especially those that were understood to contain commandments—such as guidelines for prayer, fasting, marriage, inheritance, diet, and so on—were read very closely to bring out their implications for sacred law, the *sharia*. Indeed, in contemporary studies of Qur'anic interpretation, the issues related to reinterpreting the *sharia* are very popular. This book raised such questions of implication with regard to a Qur'anic motif that typically falls outside the scope of Islamic law, *sharia*, and also seems utterly inapplicable to everyday life. By paying attention not only to *what* the interpreters say about these miracle passages but also to what *implications* were *at stake* for them, we have uncovered an intriguing range of implications of miracle stories.

Indeed, our engagement with the reception history yielded fascinating results. We have witnessed how scriptural texts that seem irrelevant or absurd to many readers at first glance may turn out to be meaningful. To be sure, it was clear from the outset that the case of miracles in the Qur'an presented a special circumstance. Not only did the Qur'anic miracle stories raise important questions about the relevance of sacred texts, but they also seemed to be at odds with the overall Qur'anic discourse, which criticized the demand for miracles and emphasized reflection on nature. As we turned to two classical Muslim interpreters, Ghazali and Ibn Rushd, we discovered that this apparent contradiction was pregnant with profound insights.

In Ibn Rushd's approach, such a perception of the apparent tension in the Qur'an was palpable. As someone from the "demonstrative class," Ibn Rushd saw the Qur'anic references to nature as relevant, as they supported inquiry into nature and allowed him to recognize that there is divine wisdom and purpose manifested in the natural order. In contrast, he did not find Qur'anic miracle stories very exciting and suggested that they be passed over in silence, with no apparent implications for a serious thinker. According to him, accepting the possibility of interruption in natural causality was too costly. For Ibn Rushd, a literal reading of miracle stories implied that our reasoning and science were useless, that there was no link between our minds and the world "out there," and no point in being certain about anything. While Ibn Rushd did not directly answer our question of what to do with these narratives, or how to reconcile the nature passages with miracle passages in the Qur'an, his attitude was helpful in clarifying what these texts may *not* imply for someone who wishes to make sense of the text.

Ghazali, to whose literal reading Ibn Rushd was responding with dismay, was actually in agreement with Ibn Rushd about what these texts did not imply. Ghazali was clear that these passages could not be taken in any way to imply destruction of common sense and the practice of science. What did these stories mean, then? Ghazali provided a very interesting reply by mirroring the apparent tension between the natural and miraculous in the Qur'an. On the one hand, he made a compelling case for reading the miracle stories literally. On the other hand, he questioned the evidentiary value of miracles in establishing faith. This apparently contradictory stance turned out to be a nuanced reading of the Qur'an: miracle stories are *not* meant to serve as primary proofs for faith, just as they are not meant to destroy common sense and our trust in the stability of natural order. Rather, they provoke us to rethink our assumptions about natural causality. They encourage us to see that the natural order is not a logical given, even if we witness the same sequence of events repeatedly. These narratives call the reader to move beyond the "apparent causes," to be wary of confusing the regular proximity of two things with the action of one upon the other, and to find the One acting behind the veils of natural causality. By taking miracle stories seriously, Ghazali suggested a new way of looking at the world around us—that is, taking the natural order not as a given but as a divine gift. In effect, I interpreted his approach as implying, "Appreciate the stability and coherence in your experience of the world as a precious gift to you, and be grateful to the artist who constantly sustains the entire world, including yourself."

We noted that Ghazali's approach to miracle stories not only yielded this existential posture but also created a breakthrough in medieval epistemology, which forms the backbone of our contemporary epistemology. Ghazali's work broke away from naive realism and rationalism and signaled the awareness of the limits—and the horizons—of human knowledge. In order to appreciate both Ghazali's breakthrough and Ibn Rushd's concerns, the book then turned to two crucial Western thinkers who contributed immensely to the making of our modern epistemology.

Few books today combine a close analysis of classical Islamic texts with that of early and late modern Western material. With such an exciting innovation, this book has brought into sharp relief the issues at stake in interpreting miracle stories in the modern age. David Hume and Charles Peirce acted as our translators, so to speak, rendering for us in modern terms the challenges and promises lurking beneath a classical Muslim debate. Moreover, by connecting Islamic texts with Western ones, the book has made Islamic thought more accessible to those of us who are more familiar with Western thought, and vice versa.

Hume vividly illustrated both the promises and dangers of critically engaging with natural causality. On the one hand, his criticism of natural causality and his exposition of the problem of induction, which was very reminiscent of Ghazali's breakthrough, ushered in a new era for modern Western thought. Hume thus represents the transition into "fallible epistemology," an approach to human knowledge that is less pretentious and more in touch with human experience. On the other hand, similar to Ibn Rushd, Hume's puzzling discourse on miracles signaled the need to make room for stability and scientific inquiry.

Indeed, while it harbored a number of inconsistencies and contradictions, Hume's stance vis-à-vis miracles was instructive in highlighting a crucial need. Hume attempted to banish miracles completely from any meaningful discussion, even though such a move flatly contradicted his critical analysis of natural causality. For Hume, as it was for Ibn Rushd, admitting that a particular miracle could have happened seemed too costly: if any miracle stories were allowed, they would create havoc in the emerging Newtonian science and open up the haunting box of skepticism that Hume tried so hard to keep shut. Thus, Hume's overreaction to miracles betrayed the helplessness he felt before skepticism, more than it provided a credible basis for rejecting miracles. Just as he felt compelled to set aside free will so as to allow for the development of a "science of human being," he felt compelled to uphold the absoluteness of natural laws so as to support science. Hence, in Ibn Rushd's ambivalence vis-à-vis the Qur'anic miracle stories and in Hume's hyperbolic rejection of all miracle reports, crucial values were at stake: they feared the destruction of science, rationality, and common sense. I have chosen to take their conundrums as birth pangs, as a crying out for the birth of a new epistemology and existential stance.

While this book has offered a fair-minded and emphatic reading of each figure, I trust that it is clear to my readers that I find the overall approaches of Ghazali, Peirce, and Nursi to be more insightful and coherent than Ibn Rushd's and Hume's. The latter two offer valuable clues in highlighting what readings of miracles *cannot* be accepted if we are to remain authentic to our reason and experience. It is the first three, on the other hand, who are most helpful in going beyond negation to affirmation; they offer substantial responses to our question of whether these narratives may be relevant for us in the here and now. In what follows, I shall reiterate their insights on what miracle stories may imply, with specific emphasis on Peirce and Nursi, who are closer to the contemporary era.

As will be recalled, Ghazali, Peirce, and Nursi explicitly rejected the useless and absurd implications drawn from miracle stories. Nursi, for instance, repeatedly noted that the believer must take the current order in nature seriously, even as she recognizes the "hand" of the divine artist acting behind the scenes. Similarly, while he denounced necessitarianism, Peirce upheld the scientific method. Ghazali, Peirce, and Nursi also agreed that miracle narratives did not function as knock-down proofs for belief. They were all aware of the limited use of miracles in establishing belief, as Hume and Ibn Rushd were.

Instead, for Ghazali, Peirce, and Nursi, these narratives were meaningful because they call for a breakthrough in the way we interpret the natural order around us. To repeat, by noting that the relative stability of the natural order must not be confused with its logical necessity, Ghazali's interpretation heralded a crucial shift from the medieval statistical view of modalities to the view of synchronic alternatives. That is, taking his cue from the miracle stories, Ghazali highlighted that that which has never obtained in our experience does not thereby cease to be a genuine possibility. In a similar vein, Peirce regarded miracle stories as highlighting the very logic of abduction—being open to unprecedented possibilities. It is this openness to new possibilities that lies at the heart of scientific inquiry.

Peirce also retrieved for us insights from Ibn Rushd's emphasis on the link between reason and natural order. He made a case against nominalism, rejecting the claim that our sense of an order in the world is mere imagination. There *are* real patterns or "natural laws" manifested in the world, and our habits of thinking *are* endowed with a *real* connection to these patterns. Otherwise, we would never have been able to discover any regularity in nature nor benefit from our scientific inquiry at all. At the same time, affirming Hume's exposition of the problem of induction, Peirce cautioned against privileging a priori thinking over our instincts and experience, for there is no proof whatsoever that the natural laws we discover are absolute and without exception. Indeed, contrary to the rationalist philosophers' contention, Hume's mistaken logic of possibilities, and the popular views of science, natural laws are not absolute; the growth, diversity, and consciousness present in nature all undermine necessitarian assumptions. Peirce was also refreshingly clear that by discovering general patterns in nature, we do not thereby obviate the need for what he called "a properly executed metaphysics." Indeed, no natural law counts as an explanation of the world if we skip the mention of a "cosmic sheriff" who continuously puts these "laws" in effect.

Likewise, in Nursi's interpretation, miracles of prophets in the Qur'an implied that a believer should look for fresh possibilities in nature, with a worshipful attitude that recognizes both the freedom and the wisdom of the One sustaining the natural phenomena. Like Peirce, Nursi suggested that miracle stories signal that natural laws are not absolute at all. Moreover, a careful observation of the world suggests that the regularity of the world actually coexists with its diversity and spontaneity, which indicates both the wisdom and freedom of the Creator. Such recognition of the hidden potentials of nature as well as the flexibility of natural laws propels not only scientific engagement but also offers a message of hope for personal life. As Nursi and Peirce noted in their own ways, miracle stories suggest that within the impressive regularity of nature there is room for human free will and hope.

In sum, from the perspectives of Ghazali, Peirce, and Nursi, what seems to be an irrational moment in the Qur'an—or the Bible—turns out to be a challenge to rethink the horizons of natural possibility and the role of human instincts. What initially appeared to be a clear tension between science and scripture, as was nicely noted in the case of Ibn Rushd and Hume, was transformed into a profound connection between the two.

Furthermore, Ghazali's and Nursi's approaches displayed how the Qur'anic miracle stories not only can open up new vistas in the way we conceive of the world around us, but also invite us to adopt a particular existential attitude toward it. By calling into attention the contingency of the order around us and by shaking our smug grounds of certainty, these miracle narratives make us face our vulnerability in an utterly contingent world. Even if initially it may be scary and disturbing, the discovery of one's vulnerability is essential for an authentic human existence. Tipping over our paper castles of certainty, so to speak, Ghazali and Nursi read the miracle texts as inviting us to *embrace* our vulnerability by being grateful to the One who maintains our existence in every moment. These stories, then, are primarily about receiving nature, as well as our familiarity with it, as a *gift*. The notion of this gift opens up the possibility of an enduring relationship with the generous giver.

To be sure, divine gifts can take a challenging form, as in the case of sickness, calamity, and separation. Still, in Ghazali's and Nursi's framework, each event can connect a person to the source of majesty and mercy manifested in the world—to the source of *asmā al-ḥusna*, the beautiful attributes of God. Through both its regularity and diversity and both its comforts and challenges, the world calls the person to recognize the stable source of all its passing manifestations of beauty and power. With such recognition, the person is delivered from the clutches of finitude as well as a victim mentality. Especially in Nursi's (and, in a more succinct form, Ghazali's) readings, the miracle stories introduce us to a world of "everyday miracles" and "signs" worthy of wonder and gratitude, and to a posture of cultivating a relationship with the One to whom these signs point.

It is worth emphasizing that in the case of both Ghazali and Nursi, the path to existential awareness and gratitude passed through a rigorous engagement with our commonsensical assumptions about natural causality. Such critical analysis of natural causality, in which Ghazali and Nursi engaged, is a prerequisite for receiving the world around us as a promising sign of the presence of a transcendental source of power and mercy. Otherwise, the idea of "everyday miracles" is evocative but ultimately fragile. Indeed, in various popular circles, it is not uncommon to refer to select ordinary events, such as the birth of a baby, as a "miracle of life." Poetic as such uses are, they may melt away quickly with the influx of "hard facts"— and perhaps it is in this sense that the Qur'an resists being called poetry. After all, as David Weddle put it, the question is this: Given scientific data, what is it about the normal birth of a baby that is miraculous? Are not ordinary babies produced by a "natural process" that does "not require transcendent power"?[3] Both Ghazali and Nursi take such a question seriously. This is not a simple question at all, and it cannot be glossed over, especially in an age where science has advanced tremendously. It is no intellectual luxury that both Ghazali and Nursi critically and rigorously analyze the commonsensical notions of natural causality that underpin our assumptions about the explanatory power of scientific data.

Certainly, both Ghazali and Nursi acknowledge the legitimacy of scientific discourse. At the same time, they resist the temptation to blur the boundaries between science and its philosophical interpretation, between scientific description and scientism or "materialist metaphysics." According to Nursi and Ghazali, it would be one thing to *describe* the process of the evolution of a zygote into a full-fledged fetus in the womb, and completely another thing to assume that such a process is thereby *explained*. In their own ways, they are keen to point out that a scientific description does not really address the question of agency, for it does not inquire into the source(s) of the wisdom, mercy, and power displayed throughout the described processes. Hence, while scientific descriptions may perfectly serve the scientific ends of predicting and controlling natural phenomena, they do not answer the questions about agency.

It is also noteworthy that Nursi, as a child of his own age, attends to the question of science with more intensity than Ghazali. There is clearly a need for such engagement in the modern age, not just in the case of miracles but in appreciating the Qur'an in general. Indeed, even though natural phenomena are such a central theme in the Qur'an, it is often unclear what it is that is worthy of wonder in natural processes, and how natural phenomena constitute "signs of God," as the Qur'an claims. Nursi offers a very interesting response to this important question. He closely attends to our usual descriptions of the natural order and displays a refreshing awareness of the distinction between modern science and its materialist interpretations.[5] Nursi's approach rests on what he considers to be the "mismatch" between natural causes and their effects—for instance, between the emergence of a regular, wisely organized, lively organism and the "apparent causes" that go into its making. To return to the example noted above, the formation of a baby in the womb is a miracle or a sign of God, but not because we lack a scientific description of the embryologic development. Rather, it is because what goes into its making (e.g., the egg and the sperm, the genes, nutrition from the mother's bloodstream, hormones, and so on) does not have the requisite wisdom, planning, power, knowledge, mercy, and care to account for the well-planned and wisely executed process that results in an intricate form of life that is interconnected with the rest of the universe and endowed with consciousness and emotion. Hence, Nursi's God is not a "God of gaps" who competes with scientific description. There is no scientific gap into which the notion of God is being inserted: we know many of the scientific details of the process in the sense that we know what goes into the emergence of a normal baby, a being that is alive, with trillions of cells consisting of hundreds of specialized types and the balanced connections across them. While we may have a good scientific description of *what* happens, we do not thereby possess an explanation of *how come* it happens—how all of these natural causes act as if they have intentionality, as if they have the comprehensive knowledge, wisdom, mercy, and power to weave a baby out of the web of infinite connections in the universe. Indeed, we fail to find any logical connections implied between natural causes and their consequences, and thus a *transcendental* gap remains that leads Nursi, like Ghazali, to interpret these regularities as pointing to a conscious, willing, powerful, and merciful source. This very reinterpretation of natural causality enables both Nursi and Ghazali to interpret the evolution of a baby in a mother's womb as a sign of God, as the Qur'an presents it. They also encourage scientific study, seeing no conflict between identifying apparent natural causes and recognizing the transcendental maker who employs them. In fact, the former process becomes a stepping-stone for the latter. Moreover, a believer's attention to the natural laws and the apparent causes displays respect for the divine arrangement of the world. As Nursi innovatively noted, when carried out with appropriate awareness, following natural order is an act of worship to the One who promulgates the greater *sharia*, or cosmic laws.

It is not uncommon to hear the remark that Muslims have failed to rise to the challenge of the modern era, in contrast to the accomplishments of premodern generations. Frank Griffel notes, for instance, that unlike Ghazali's reckoning with the philosophers' challenge to religion in the medieval era, Muslims could not respond to the challenge of modern science.[4] Griffel is right in that much of Muslim energy in the modern age has been devoted to the issues of identity and reinterpretation of Islamic law, and attempts at reconciling modern science and religion too often overlooked some of the underlying crucial philosophical questions. Hence, Nursi's work is a refreshing exception to that trend in the modern age. It is my hope that this book will initiate further fruitful discussion of his woefully understudied works in this regard.

It is also noteworthy that Nursi's and Ghazali's analysis of natural causality hits two birds with the same stone. Through their analysis, they answer this book's central question of what to make of miracle stories, as well as the question of how to reconcile the apparent tension in the Qur'an between the miraculous and the natural. Their critical analysis of natural causality makes room for both making sense of the Qur'anic reference to natural signs of God *and* the possibility of miracles. Since it turns out that natural causes do not constitute logical explanation, the birth of a normal baby is still a "sign" worthy of attention. And, since natural causes are not linked by any logical necessity, it is possible to read miracle stories without any logical contradiction: in special situations natural causality can be transcended, as in the case of virgin birth. Hence, in Nursi's and Ghazali's readings, the miracle stories and the discourse of "natural signs" in the Qur'an turn out to be intimately linked, calling for a particular spiritual awareness of the natural processes around us. From their perspective, two apparently contradictory features in the Qurʾan are actually revealed to be deeply interlinked and consistent.

Having highlighted the key points of this book about Qurʾanic miracle stories, let me now take a moment to offer broader conclusions about Qurʾanic hermeneutics. Our study in this book suggests that exploring the reception history of the Qurʾan with an attention to the *implications* of the texts can be extremely useful. Indeed, taking a cue from Peirce's pragmatic maxim, which defines meaning exclusively in terms of actual or potential consequences, I shall call this approach to Qurʾanic exegesis an example of "pragmatic hermeneutics." Pragmatic hermeneutics engages with the Qurʾanic texts by asking them, "What do you want me to do? Are you making any generalizable and applicable suggestions or are you simply burdening me with empty concepts and useless implications?" Given that the Qurʾan repeatedly presents itself as providing guidance for humankind, pragmatic hermeneutics is also valid from a phenomenological perspective, being in line with the Qurʾanic élan. Indeed, pragmatic hermeneutics is a moment of hermeneutics of trust: raising the question "What does the text exhort its reader to do?" assumes a level of trust. It presupposes a posture of openness—being open to the possibility that the text may indeed have something meaningful to suggest for its reader, as it claims. As such, it is a helpful approach not only for the Qurʾan but also for the Bible and other sacred scriptures.

The story of the attempted sacrifice of Abraham's son, as a shared story in the Qurʾan and the Bible, is another good example of the promise of pragmatic hermeneutics. Here, the text again first presents us with an apparent conundrum; it seems to glorify senseless violence, as if the point is to be prepared to kill your loved one when God commands it. And, yet, when we give the text the benefit of the doubt and ask the pragmatic question "What is the text calling the reader to do?" such apparent absurdity is replaced by a potentially relevant meaning. Looking at reception history with this question in mind again proves to be useful. Muslim interpreters across the ages read the story as suggesting something completely different from doing violent harm to your innocent beloveds, similar to Christian and Jewish interpreters, who also rejected human sacrifice as incompatible with the biblical telling of the story. There has been an overall consensus in these Abrahamic traditions that the story did *not* imply at all what it seemed to at first.[6] Attending to reception history with an eye to implications derived from the text can indeed be eye-opening.

Thus, this book suggests that studying the scriptures in the modern age calls for paying more attention to their reception history. In this regard, it joins the more recent discourses emerging in Qur'anic studies and, more broadly, in scriptural hermeneutics. Among such discourses is the conversation initiated by the Signifying (on) Scriptures series, a comparative study of scriptures that intends to raise our heads from their fixation on the words on the page, so that we more clearly see the horizons of scriptures. We must pay closer attention to the ways in which scriptures enrich and interact with human thought and praxis in exciting new fields of inquiry, both in Qur'anic studies and in broader scriptural hermeneutics.

I would also like to note that among the best "pragmatic" interpreters of the Qur'an have been those who focused on edification and on self-formation at both the individual and communal levels. Thus, when looking for meaningful readings of a scriptural text, paying attention to such trends in reception history is indispensible. Sufi interpreters, with their clear focus on spiritual growth, have offered remarkable readings in this regard. Theirs is a crucial genre that unfortunately largely fell out of the scope of this book, though Ghazali and Nursi both drew on this tradition and contributed to it. My hope is that the book will provoke further study of Sufi masters and other interpreters, including Rumi and Ibn ʿArabi, to reveal how they interpreted the implications of the Qur'anic stories for self-transformation and everyday life.

Furthermore, our engagement with the interpretation of miracles further illuminates the perennial question of the relation between reason and revelation. At the risk of oversimplifying, I shall note that the relationship between revelation and reason has often been described in terms of polarities. For instance, in Islamic tradition there has been the idea that revelation provides knowledge on matters where reason comes up short and should fall silent, such as the belief in a life after death or in the case of ethical commandments. This view became the predominant Islamic theological position and was meant to emphasize the indispensability of revelation. On the other hand, it has been argued that reason can, on its own, reach the truths of revelation when it is used properly by its experts. The idea was that the Qur'an is so reasonable that one could arrive at the same fundamental Qur'anic conclusions on the basis of reason alone. This position was championed by Muslim philosophers and Muʿtazilite theologians, and it served to highlight the utter reasonability of revelation. In theory, then, it seemed that one had to choose between the indispensability of revelation and its utter reasonability.

Not surprisingly, like most binaries, neither has been quite satisfactory. If we prioritize revelation, reason's function in crucial matters seems defunct: Is it merely there to parrot what is transmitted through revelation? If we affirm the primacy of reason, then the Qur'an seems superfluous—except among the common people, who need parables and symbols to fit their limited reasoning. Our study of the interpretation of miracle stories demonstrated that in the "real world" of interpretation such binaries do not rule, and there can be a way out of such an impasse in theory as well. Especially in the approach of the interpreters who found the Qur'anic miracles meaningful in their plain sense—that is, Ghazali and Nursi (and Peirce in the case of biblical miracles)—we did witness a dynamic and dialectical interaction between reason and revelation that disclosed the need for both.

I find Peirce's "logic of abduction" most helpful in describing this dynamic relation between reason and revelation. As will be recalled, Peirce noted that in making a discovery one needs a creative moment, an insightful suggestion that can be provided by neither induction nor deduction. At the same time, that creative moment—that guiding suggestion—is not the end but the beginning: in response to that suggestion, one needs to form a hypothesis and proceed to test it. Both the creative moment of abduction and the step of forming a hypothesis and experimenting are indispensable for a successful inquiry. Such connection between abduction and testing seems to best represent a positive dynamic link between reason and revelation: revelation offers precious insights, without which no useful "inquiry" into the meaning of life and interpretation of existence can take place. These insights, like all abductions, still need to be "tested out," so to speak, by the reader's reasoning and experience. To my mind, in both Ghazali's and Nursi's (and, in a more indirect way, Peirce's) interpretations, the scriptural stories were in effect treated as abductive insights, which were then "tested" in light of logic and empirical data by engaging with our commonsensical judgments about nature. Even Ibn Rushd's Qur'anic interpretations were partially a reflection of such a relationship. It must have been his exposure to the Qur'anic discourse on nature that allowed him to appreciate and further the Aristotelian legacy so well, and to develop his famous arguments for God, which benefited not only his Muslim but also his Christian readers. It is my contention that this kind of interactive dynamic is present in many acts of scriptural interpretation, especially in the exciting and insightful ones. Accordingly, the way we portray the relationship between reason and revelation is in need of revision. It is time to go beyond the idea that one has to be de-emphasized for the sake of the other, or that they can work independently of each other.

In conclusion, by using the miracle stories as a sample case, this book demonstrated how apparently "dead" or irrelevant scriptural texts could quicken to a life of meaning and relevance, like Moses's staff coming alive. When read closely, the "fire" of apparent contradiction running across the scriptural discourses can blossom into profound connections, like Abraham's fire becoming a source of peace. And, of course, we may add a nuance to this optimistic ending: approaching the Qurʾanic text, or any scriptural text for that matter, with an attention to its implications does not guarantee the presence of a meaningful implication. Rather, it simply poses a just challenge to it, which opens up the possibility of doing more justice to the text. After all, a scripture that does not have any potential whatsoever to make any difference in our lives is a "problematic" text, by the very standards of the scripture itself. It would be a slight to the Qurʾan, and other sacred scriptures, if we were to shy away from posing questions to them that matter to us. These cherished stories do offer insightful messages, and, as Peirce was fond to quote the biblical dictum, "Ye shall know them by their fruits."

INTRODUCTION

1. Standard Egyptian numbering of the Qur'an and M. A. S. Abdel Haleem's English translation (Oxford University Press, 2004) are used throughout this book, unless otherwise noted. Citations to the Qur'an appear parenthetically in the text, abbreviated as "Q."

2. For an introduction to this innovative project, see Wimbush, "Introduction."

3. Rahman, *Major Themes of the Qur'an*, 69–70 (italics in original).

4. Ibid., 77.

5. Ibid., 68.

6. Indeed, in the Qur'an—sometimes in the very same passage—the term *āya* is used in these two different but related senses (e.g., Q. 13:1–3). The Qur'an often associates the rejection of the prophetic message with a rejection of the natural signs (e.g., Q. 12:103, 105).

7. Rahman, *Major Themes of the Qur'an*, 70.

8. Grill, "Miracles," 397–99.

9. For instances of contemporary mention of this traditional view, see Nasr, *Heart of Islam*, 24, and Ali, *Scientific Miracles of the Glorious Qur'an*, 10–12.

10. Sells, *Approaching the Qur'an*, 7.

11. Bulut, *Kuran ışığında mucize*, 231–32. See also Boullata, "Rhetorical Interpretation," 139–42.

12. To be sure, the traditional scholars also noted that Muhammad was gifted some miracles besides the Qur'an, even though the Qur'an was his central miracle. They approvingly passed down the reports that Muhammad performed a number of physical miracles, such as feeding many with little food, bringing down rain with his prayer, and splitting the moon into two halves. At the same time, traditional scholarship insisted that such miracles were not central to Prophet Muhammad's mission, unlike the ancient prophets.

13. For instance, Fakhr al-Dīn al-Rāzī (d. 1209) interprets Moses's miracles as giving clues about the existence of an all-powerful creator. Al-Rāzī, *Tafsīr al-kabīr*, 204.

14. Weddle, *Miracles*, 1.

CHAPTER I

1. As Tim Winter notes, Ghazali came to be called the "proof of Islam," not so much for his "unique originality" but for his "programmatic attempt to retrieve an original unity" manifest in the Qur'anic discourse. Winter, introduction to *The Cambridge Companion*, 6.

2. Marmura, "Translator's Introduction," xvi. My summary of Ghazali's biographical background is drawn from this introduction (xvi–xix), with details added from Frank

Griffel's richly nuanced account of Ghazali's life. Griffel, *Al-Ghazālī's Philosophical Theology*, 19–59.

3. See Ghazali's autobiography, as translated by W. Montgomery Watt. Ghazālī, *Faith and Practice of al-Ghazālī*, 21.

4. Ibid., 26.

5. Ibid., 56.

6. Griffel, *Al-Ghazālī's Philosophical Theology*, 43–44.

7. See Gianotti, *Ghazālī's Unspeakable Doctrine*, 27.

8. Marmura, "Translator's Introduction," xviii.

9. Marmura, "Ghazali and Ashʿarism Revisited," 37, 46–51. For an analysis of Ghazali's comment that the best theological discourse can only lead one to "[knock] at the doors of gnosis," see ibid.

10. According to Timothy Gianotti, Ghazali only indirectly speaks of "the gnosis of the spiritual verities, a theoretical knowledge that comes through the seeker's first-hand 'eye-witnessing' or experience of the higher realities. This is what he terms the 'knowledge of the Unveiling' (*ʿilm al-mukāshafa*), an experiential mode of knowing bestowed upon God's prophets and God's 'friends,' or *awliyāʾ*." Gianotti, *Ghazālī's Unspeakable Doctrine*, 27.

11. Watt, "Al-Ghazālī," 110. Ghazali explicitly rejects a contrast between publicly available theology and the more profound and private Sufi discourse, saying that "he who says that reality disagrees with the Law and the esoteric contradicts the exoteric is closer to unbelief than to belief." He goes on to explain in five categories how "the secrets" that are accessible to the few need not contradict the explicit declarations that the majority understand. See Ghazālī, *Foundations of the Articles of Faith*, 38. Furthermore, as Griffel notes, "To say that al-Ghazālī's theological teachings underwent a change cannot, in fact, be maintained." Griffel, *Al-Ghazālī's Philosophical Theology*, 8.

12. Ghazālī, *Clear Criterion*, 171. Cf. Ghazālī, *On the Boundaries of Theological Tolerance*, 128. Ghazali wrote *The Criterion for Distinction* to counter fanaticism on the part of certain theologians who too quickly declared other believers to be infidels. He offers a conciliatory approach across different schools of thought, always emphasizing the fundamentals of faith that unite all. For a fine introduction to the text, see Jackson, introduction to *On the Boundaries*, 3–64.

13. Ghazālī, *Foundations of the Articles of Faith*, 8; see also 56, 88, 90.

14. Ghazālī, *Iqtiṣād*, 206–10.

15. Bulut, *Kuran ışığında mucize*, 82. As Bulut notes, scholars after Ghazali continued to hold a similar view, including Muḥammad bin ʿAbd al-Karīm al-Shahrastānī (d. 1153), Aḥmad bin ʿAbd al-Ḥalīm Ibn Taymiyya (d. 1328), and Saʿd al-Dīn al-Taftazānī (d. 1390).

16. Ibid., 104. Here, Bulut notes that these theologians all agreed that the miracles cannot be *dalīl samʿī*—that is, they cannot prove the prophecy on the basis of tradition—because that would be circular reasoning.

17. Among them was Muḥammad ibn Yūsuf al-Sanūsī (d. 1490), who argued that miracles are events that can only be explained as God's actions on behalf of a true prophet and therefore provide a strong rational argument for the truthfulness of God's messengers. See al-Sanūsī, *Sharḥ Sanūsiyya al-kubra*, cited in ibid., 108.

18. Bulut notes that ʿAlī ibn Abī ʿAlī al-Āmidī (d. 1233), Saʿd al-Dīn al-Taftazānī (d. 1390), and ʿAḍūd al-Dīn ʿAbd al-Raḥmān al-Ījī (d. 1355) were among those who considered miracles as contextual evidence for the truthfulness of the prophet. Bulut, *Kuran ışığında mucize*, 105.

19. See Ibn Taymiyya, *Al-Nubūwwāt*, 49, cited in ibid., 106.

20. Among the scholars who used this metaphor were al-Juwaynī, al-Shahrastānī, al-Taftazānī, Abuʾl Ḥasan ʿAlī al-Māwardī (d. 1058), and al-Āmidī (Bulut, *Kuran ışığında mucize*, 96–97, 107; also see al-Rāzī, *Uṣūl al-dīn*, 95–96). In his *Al-Nubūwwāt*, Ibn

Taymiyya disagrees with this view, saying that the absence of an explicit preexisting agreement between God and humanity disqualifies miracles from being conventional evidence (Bulut, *Kuran ışığında mucize*, 198–201).

21. Some theologians, such as Qāḍī ʿAbd al-Jabbār and ʿAbd al-Qāhir al-Baghdādī, even assert that in this case the performance speaks louder than the words. Bulut, *Kuran ışığında mucize*, 96–97.

22. Ghazālī, *Foundations of the Articles of Faith*, 91.

23. Batak, "Tehâfütü'l felâsife ile," 381.

24. Yet, even when one admits the legitimacy of the king metaphor, it seems that the existence of a wise creator is not proven but rather assumed by the miraculous event, as we shall note in the next chapter. It seems, then, that a miracle can only support the belief that a human being is a messenger of the unseen creator, and in the aforementioned works Ghazali uses miracles as such. Cf. al-Rāzī, who interprets Moses's miracles as giving clues about the existence of an all-powerful creator. Al-Rāzī, *Tafsīr al-kabīr*, 204.

25. Ghazali notes that the Qurʾan's eloquence is the foremost miracle of Muhammad. Ghazālī, *Iqtiṣād*, 206–8.

26. Ghazālī, *Incoherence*, 3; Ghazālī, *Iqtiṣād*, 210–11.

27. Ghazālī, *Deliverance from Error*, 63. I found that this translation by Abūlaylah is more eloquent than Watt's translation in *The Faith and Practice of al-Ghazālī*, 22.

28. It should be noted that these two philosophers were not only Aristotelian but also Neoplatonists, with their distinct theories of emanation. And, despite the difference in their opinions on soul, epistemology, and eschatology, Ghazali's criticisms apply to both. Marmura, "Translator's Introduction," xix.

29. Ghazālī, *Incoherence*, 163.

30. Ibid. See also the parallel Arabic text on the facing page.

31. See Ghazālī, *Clear Criterion*, 152–57 (cf. Ghazālī, *On the Boundaries of Theological Tolerance*, 96–103); Ghazālī, *Foundations of the Articles of Faith*, 39–53.

32. Ghazālī, *Foundations of the Articles of Faith*, 44–45. What is translated as "legal evidence" refers to "sacred law" and is shorthand for the Qurʾan and prophetic tradition.

33. Ibid.

34. Ibid., 49–50; Jackson, introduction to *On the Boundaries*, 57.

35. For an excellent brief discussion of Ghazali's views on metaphorical interpretation, see Griffel, *Al-Ghazālī's Philosophical Theology*, 111–16. Also see Griffel, "Relationship Between Averroes and al-Ghazālī," 59.

36. Ghazālī, *Foundations of the Articles of Faith*, 47.

37. Ibid., 48.

38. Ibid., 48–49.

39. Translation from Asad, *Message of the Qurʾan*, 425.

40. Ghazālī, *Incoherence*, 166. Cf. Avicenna, according to whom "4 is necessary of existence not by itself but on the supposition of 2+2, and burning is necessary of existence not by itself but on the supposition of contact on the part of a naturally active force with a naturally passive force, I mean one which burns and [one which] is burned." Avicenna, *Al-Najāt*, 224, cited in Kogan, *Averroes and the Metaphysics of Causation*, 29. As Kogan explains, for Avicenna "relations between ideas and matters of fact like cause and effect exhibit one and the same kind of necessity, although it has both logical and ontological manifestations" (29). On Avicenna's understanding of natural causation in logically necessary terms, see also Marmura, "Ghazali and Demonstrative Science," 198.

41. Marmura, "Ghazali and Demonstrative Science," 188.

42. Ghazālī, *Incoherence*, 167. As Harry A. Wolfson notes, this example of fire and burning was also used by earlier theologians, such as Abuʾl-Hudhayl al-ʿAllāf (d. ca. 841) and Muḥammad Abū ʿAlī al-Jubbāʾī (d. 915). Wolfson, *Philosophy of the Kalām*, 544.

43. Ghazālī, *Incoherence*, 167.

44. Ibid., 167–68.

45. Ghazālī, *Iqtiṣād*, 89.

46. Ghazālī, *Faith in Divine Unity*, 16–17. This example is again acceptable for Ghazali only for its function as a metaphor, and even the king's writing in the parable is only possible through the divine power (ibid., 17).

47. Ibid., 17.

48. Rahman, review of *Islamic Occasionalism*, 233.

49. A similar point is made by Harold W. Noonan with regard to Hume's thought. See Noonan, *Hume on Knowledge*, 108.

50. Ghazālī, *Foundations of the Articles of Faith*, 62. Ghazali notes explicitly that "every event that comes into existence after having been non-existent has to have a cause." If one asks how we know this, Ghazali answers that it is an intuitively known axiom: "This [principle] is attained through rational necessity [*hadha mudrikuhu ḍarūra al-ʿaql*]." Indeed, "just as the sudden emergence [*ṭarayān*] of existence requires a cause [*sabab*], so does the emergence of extinction require a cause" (Ghazālī, *Al-Ghazālī on Divine Predicates*, 2, 62). Similarly, he notes, "anyone with the least traces of brain in his head will, upon reflecting upon the import of these verses and examining the wonders of God's handiwork, in Heaven and on earth as well as the beauties of nature in animal and plant, realizes that this wonderful [universe] with its consummate order requires a creator to direct it and a maker to govern it and watch it over" (Ghazālī, *Foundations of the Articles of Faith*, 58–59).

51. According to Ghazali, a real agent "should be a willer, chooser, and a knower" of its object (Ghazālī, *Incoherence*, 55). Griffel notes that by defining "agent" (*fāʿil*) in these terms Ghazali is departing from the Avicennan definition of the same term: "For al-Ghazali it means 'voluntary agent'; for Avicenna, *simply* 'efficient cause'" (Griffel, *Al-Ghazālī's Philosophical Theology*, 153, italics added). By shifting definitions, Ghazali is introducing not just a linguistic shift but also a conceptual shift. He is rejecting, like other Ashʿarites, that something can be a *genuine* efficient cause if it lacks the will and knowledge needed to perform the act.

52. William Courtenay notes that "no medieval author with whom I am familiar doubted that everything (excluding God) must have one or more causes, although this thesis was not always stated in causal language. When we speak of critiques of the 'principle of causality,' therefore, we are referring to questions about the necessity, demonstrability, validity and knowability of particular causal relationships (especially within the natural order)." Courtenay, "Critique on Natural Causality," 79.

53. Ghazali is not simply shifting epistemologies for the sake of his theological aims, contrary to what Kogan seems to suggest: "Interestingly, an occasionalist like Ghazali could accept the second proposition [that no effect exists without a cause] if it were clear that the cause which any given effect *must* have, is God." Kogan, *Averroes and the Metaphysics of Causation*, 74 (italics in original).

54. Ghazālī, *Incoherence*, 166 (italics added).

55. Marmura, "Ghazali and Demonstrative Science," 187.

56. Fakhry, *Islamic Occasionalism*, 62.

57. Ghazālī, *Iqtiṣād*, 222; translated by Fakhry in *Islamic Occasionalism*, 62.

58. Fakhry, *Islamic Occasionalism*, 63. See also Ghazālī, *Iqtiṣād*, 223–24.

59. Fakhry, *Islamic Occasionalism*, 63.

60. Kogan, *Averroes and the Metaphysics of Causation*, 105.

61. Griffel, "Al-Ghazālī." See also Griffel, *Al-Ghazālī's Philosophical Theology*, 167–72.

62. Griffel, "Al-Ghazālī."

63. Kukkonen, "Possible Worlds in the *Tahāfut al-tahāfut*," 347.

64. Ibid., 480.

65. Ghazālī, *Incoherence*, 169–70 (italics added). Ṣāliḥ Qubba was one of the theologians who asserted these kinds of fantasies. See Halevi, "Theologian's Doubts," 28, and Watt, *Free Will and Predestination*, 81.

66. Ghazālī, *Incoherence*, 174.

67. Dutton, "Al-Ghazali on Possibility," 39 (italics added).

68. Here Ghazali's move is similar to Hume's mitigated skepticism, as we shall discuss in chapter 3.

69. Ghazālī, *Incoherence*, 170.

70. Ibid., 171.

71. Ibid., 176 (italics added).

72. Again, Ghazali is clear that in his admission of the *logical possibility* of a dead man seen in action, he is not thereby suspending the causal maxim, which demands that a coherent and wise result will not come into existence with no cause, nor will it be attributed to an ignorant and lifeless being. Hence, the opponent's claim that "the well-designed act ceases to indicate the [existence of] the knowledge of the agent" is not true. Part of Ghazali's answer to the charge of absurdity amounts to saying, "No, I do not go against any logical principle by accepting the conceivability of such a situation."

73. Marmura, "Ghazali and Demonstrative Science," 195. See also Marmura, "Al-Ghazālī," 149.

74. Marmura, "Ghazali and Demonstrative Science," 195. Here, Marmura specifically mentions Avicenna, but this also applies to Ibn Rushd, as we shall observe in the next chapter.

75. Indeed, as alluded to earlier, Ghazali's insistence that causes and effects are, in fact, all created by God at all times is in line with Ashʿarite occasionalism, which, by his time (the eleventh century), was becoming the dominant school in Islamic theology. Ashʿarite occasionalism, named after al-Ashʿarī (d. 936), "regarded all temporal existents as the direct creation of God, decreed by His eternal attribute of will and enacted by His attribute of power. What humans habitually regard as sequences of natural causes and effects are in reality concomitant events whose constant association is . . . [freely] decreed by the divine will. . . . God is the sole cause: all events are His direct creation." Marmura, "Translator's Introduction," xvi. For different tendencies within occasionalism, its development in the history of Islamic theology, and its implications for human free will, which are beyond the scope of our discussion, see Fakhry, *Islamic Occasionalism*, 22–55, and Watt, *Free Will and Predestination*, 135–64.

76. Ghazālī, *Incoherence*, 171.

77. Marmura, "Ghazali and Demonstrative Science," 195.

78. Ghazālī, *Miʿyār al-ʿilm*, 58; quoted and translated by Marmura in "Ghazali and Demonstrative Science," 195–96 (italics added).

79. Commenting on the founder of the school that Ghazali defended, Halevi writes, "Ashʿarī saw God's action as moving the world with measured regularity in a *habitual* way interrupted only occasionally by miracles. To be sure, this position does not make Ashʿarī a follower of Aristotle, but it does show him disengaged from that wildly speculative theology whose proponents vigorously effaced the mildest blush of naturalism." Halevi, "Theologian's Doubts," 22–23 (italics added).

80. Indeed, Ghazali notes that it is permissible to talk of "habitual causes" and "habitual effects" in constructing syllogisms so long as one does not let this shorthand usage become ossified into an assumption of self-sufficient and logically necessary causal connections. Marmura, "Ghazali and Demonstrative Science," 193. See Griffel's *Al-Ghazālī's Philosophical Theology* for five conditions that Ghazali in effect lays down for any viable account of cosmology, one of which is to "account for our coherent experience of the universe and [to allow] predictions of future events" (185). See also Marmura, "Ghazālian Causes and Intermediaries," 99–100.

81. Ghazālī, *Iqtiṣād*, 95–96 (my translation, italics added). See also Ghazālī, *İtikatta ölçülü olmak*, 129.

82. Marmura explains, "The doctrine of generation [*al- tawallud*] was espoused by the Mu'tazilite school of *kalām*, a doctrine al-Ghazali in the *Incoherence* identified with philosophers' causal theory." Marmura, "Al-Ghazālī," 148.

83. Ghazālī, *Iqtiṣād*, 96 (my translation, italics added).

84. Ibid., 97 (my translation).

85. Ghazālī, *Incoherence*, 175.

86. Ghazālī, *Al-Qisṭās al-mustaqīm*, 80.

87. Ghazālī, *Correct Balance*, 316.

88. Ibid.

89. Ibid.

90. McCarthy, introduction to *Freedom and Fulfillment*, l–li.

91. Kukkonen, "Possible Worlds in the *Tahāfut al-falāsifa*," 494. Kukkonen borrows the terms "metaphysics of contingency" and "metaphysics of grace" from Lenn Goodman.

92. Indeed, Ghazali notes that it is God who causes the human mind to expect the hitherto observed natural order to continue. See Ghazālī, *Incoherence*, 171.

CHAPTER 2

1. Much of the following biographical background is summarized from Butterworth, "Biographical Sketch of Averröes," xiii–xix.

2. Ibn Rushd composed commentaries on all of Aristotle's logical works, including *Rhetoric* and the *Poetics*; on most of the major works related to physical science (namely, the *Physics*, *On the Heavens*, *On Generation and Corruption*, *Meteorologica*, and *On the Soul*); on the *Metaphysics*; and on the *Nicomachean Ethics*. Ibid., xv.

3. Ibid., xiv.

4. Kogan, *Averroes and the Metaphysics of Causation*, 12.

5. For an analysis of the ways in which Averroes's works, as well as other Arabic scientific and philosophical works, were translated into Latin during the Renaissance, see Burnett, "Second Revelation."

6. This original title could be most literally translated as *The Book of Decisively Judging the Statement and Determining the Connection Between the Law [Scripture] and Wisdom [Philosophy]*. Butterworth, "Translator's Introduction," xix. While *al-shar'* is often translated as "the Law," it does not merely refer to rules of conduct (*sharia*) believed to be revealed by God, but also bears the connotation of the entire discourse believed to be God's word—that is, the scripture.

7. The verse continues, ". . . so that he might be a firm believer" (Q. 6:75).

8. Ibn Rushd, *Decisive Treatise*, 2. Please note that this English translation is published with the parallel Arabic text of *Faṣl al-maqāl* on one side of the page. Thus, the page numbers for the English translation and Arabic original are the same.

9. To be sure, Ibn Rushd was not the first to suggest such a technical preparation for understanding the Qur'an. Ghazali himself, in his *The Correct Balance*, had tried to demonstrate the usefulness of Aristotelian logic in understanding the Qur'an.

10. Ibn Rushd, *Decisive Treatise*, 5–7.

11. Ibid., 1.

12. Ibn Rushd, *Averroes on the Harmony*, 49; Ibn Rushd, *Decisive Treatise*, 8–9.

13. Ibn Rushd, *Manāhij*, 153–54; translated by Najjar in "Ibn Rushd's Theory of Rationality," 204 (italics added).

14. Ibn Rushd, *Averroes on the Harmony*, 33–34.

15. Griffel, "Relationship Between Averroes and al-Ghazālī," 60 (italics in original).

16. Ibn Rushd, *Decisive Treatise*, 20–21.

17. In the conclusion of his *Exposition*, under the title "Canon of Interpretation" (*qānūn al-taʾwīl*), Ibn Rushd offers a similar but more detailed division of types of Qurʾanic passages, which can be schematized as follows: (1) passages in which plain sense *is* the intended meaning, and (2) passages in which plain sense is meant to *represent* the intended meaning. The latter passages include (a) those that *all classes* recognize as a metaphor for something that is known; (b) those that *all classes* would recognize as metaphors but, because it is difficult to comprehend what they stand for, should not be interpreted by anyone; (c) those that are only recognized by the demonstrative class to be metaphorical and can only be legitimately interpreted by them; and (d) those that could well be metaphorical, but it is not clear whether they are. In this case, it is *safer* not to interpret them metaphorically, especially for the common people. An example of this would be the corporeality of the afterlife; it can well be interpreted metaphorically, but it is not clear whether that is required. Ibn Rushd, *Manāhij*, 248–51; Ibn Rushd, *Faith and Reason in Islam*, 128–31.

18. Ibn Rushd, *Faith and Reason in Islam*, 124.

19. Ibn Rushd, *Incoherence of the Incoherence*, 362.

20. Ibn Rushd, *Decisive Treatise*, 21.

21. One may ask how one decides what is essential in faith and what is not. Ibn Rushd here refers to the traditional concept of consensus or *ijmāʿ* in Islamic law. Traditionally, this concept refers to the idea that the interpretations that are agreed upon by the faith community are binding for that entire community. Yet, even if the *concept* of consensus is clear in the tradition, its *content* and *conditions* are often less clear. Whose consent is required for the consensus to obtain—experts or the general public of believers? In Islamic *law*, the issue was practically resolved: it was the early generations of Muslims and the scholars who counted in the formation of the authoritative consensus. As for *theological* interpretations, Ibn Rushd insists that there is no such consensus obtained as yet. However, since the demonstrative class is the expert on allegorical interpretation, only the philosophers' consensus counts when there is the question of whether a passage's literal sense can be suspended (Ibn Rushd, *Averroes on the Harmony*, 24, 31–32). As Josef van Ess noted, even though in *legal* matters the idea that every interpretation, as long as it is made with appropriate intention and expertise, is correct was formulated eventually (*kull mujtahid muṣīb*, lit. "every [qualified] interpreter is in right"), it was not formulated in theology (see van Ess, *Flowering of Muslim Theology*, 20).

22. As Taneli Kukkonen notes, "Because both al-Ghazālī and Averroes see themselves as in genuine dialogue, they are exceedingly careful in laying out correctly both their own positions and that of their opponents and in trying to explicate the underlying concerns informing each point of view. As a consequence, the resultant texts display an exceptional degree of self-consciousness concerning the philosophical commitments made in adopting any given viewpoint." Kukkonen, "Possible Worlds in the *Tahāfut al-tahāfut*," 331.

23. Ibn Rushd, *Incoherence of the Incoherence*, 318; Ibn Rushd, *Tahāfut al-tahāfut*, 505.

24. Kogan, *Averroes and the Metaphysics of Causation*, 3 (italics added).

25. See Wolfson, *Philosophy of the Kalām*, 551–58.

26. Ibn Rushd, *Incoherence of the Incoherence*, 318–19; Ibn Rushd, *Tahāfut al-tahāfut*, 505.

27. Kogan, *Averroes and the Metaphysics of Causation*, 97 (italics in original).

28. Ibn Rushd, *Incoherence of the Incoherence*, 318.

29. Cf. Kogan, *Averroes and the Metaphysics of Causation*, 125–28.

30. According to Kant, there is a crucial distinction between the general principle of causality—the principle that every event b must have a cause a—and particular causal

patterns. The former is an intuitive principle and is synthetic a priori while the latter is an empirical judgment that cannot ever be deemed logically necessary. See Kant, *Critique of Pure Reason*, 127 (A95/B127).

31. Ibn Rushd, *Incoherence of the Incoherence*, 318.

32. Ibid.; "*ṣināʿat al-manṭiq taḍaʿu waḍʿan anna hahuna asbāb wa musabbabāt*" (Ibn Rushd, *Tahāfut al-tahāfut*, 507).

33. Ibn Rushd, *Incoherence of the Incoherence*, 320 (italics added).

34. Ibid., 319–20 (italics added).

35. Ibid., 320 (italics added).

36. Ibn Rushd also disagrees with Ghazali over divine will. Thus, while Ghazali talks of an inherently contingent event being actualized by God, Ibn Rushd thinks that this is a misnomer. Rather, Ibn Rushd argues, God is the one who knows what is best and will only act to actualize the best, and thus it is unreasonable to say that God could possibly do otherwise. See Kogan, *Averroes and the Metaphysics of Causation*, 222–26.

37. In fact, the concept of ʿāda or habit of God had previously been similarly criticized by other theologians, such as the Ẓahirī scholar Ibn Hazm (d. 1064) and the Muʿtazilite scholar Abu Rashid (d. 1068). Their criticism was that "habit" is too loose a term to adequately represent the order in the world. Wolfson, *Philosophy of the Kalām*, 547.

38. Ibid., 547–48.

39. Ibn Rushd, *Incoherence of the Incoherence*, 320; Wolfson, *Philosophy of the Kalām*, 558.

40. Ibn Rushd, *Incoherence of the Incoherence*, 320.

41. Halevi, "Theologian's Doubts," 24.

42. Kukkonen, "Possible Worlds in the *Tahāfut al-falāsifa*," 492.

43. See, for instance, Ibn Rushd, *Incoherence of the Incoherence*, 318–20, 325, 331.

44. Ibn Rushd, *Faith and Reason in Islam*, 114; Ibn Rushd, *Manāhij*, 222. This is the same argument that David Hume used against the design argument half a millennium later.

45. Ibn Rushd, *Faith and Reason in Islam*, 114; Ibn Rushd, *Manāhij*, 222.

46. Ibn Rushd, *Faith and Reason in Islam*, 86; Ibn Rushd, *Manāhij*, 201 (italics added).

47. Ibn Rushd, *Faith and Reason in Islam*, 85; Ibn Rushd, *Manāhij*, 200.

48. Ibn Rushd, *Faith and Reason in Islam*, 84; Ibn Rushd, *Manāhij*, 199 (italics added).

49. Ibn Rushd, *Faith and Reason in Islam*, 85; Ibn Rushd, *Manāhij*, 200.

50. Ibn Rushd, *Faith and Reason in Islam*, 114 (italics added). "Al-asbāb muaththira biidhnillah fi musabbabātiha"; Ibn Rushd, *Manāhij*, 232. Similarly, Ibn Rushd says that "He [God] is the Inventor of Causes and their causal efficacy is by His leave and His preserving them in existence." Ibn Rushd, *Faith and Reason in Islam*, 114.

51. Mermer and Ameur, "Beyond the Modern," 144.

52. Ibn Rushd, *Incoherence of the Incoherence*, 332; Ibn Rushd, *Tahāfut al-tahāfut*, 520.

53. Ibn Rushd, *Incoherence of the Incoherence*, 315.

54. Ibn Rushd notes that "these [principles of religion] are the principles of the acts through which man becomes virtuous, and that one can only attain knowledge after the attainment of virtue. One must not investigate the principles which cause virtue before the attainment of virtue, and since the theoretical sciences can only be perfected through assumptions and axioms which the learner accepts in the first place, this must be still more the case with the practical sciences." Ibid.

55. Ibn Rushd, *Faith and Reason in Islam*, 92; Ibn Rushd, *Manāhij*, 208.

56. Ibn Rushd, *Faith and Reason in Islam*, 93; Ibn Rushd, *Manāhij*, 209.

57. Ibn Rushd, *Incoherence of the Incoherence*, 316.

58. Ibn Rushd, *Faith and Reason in Islam*, 95–96; Ibn Rushd, *Manāhij*, 212.

59. Ibn Rushd, *Manāhij*, 215; translated by Fakhry in *Averroes*, 92.

60. Ibn Rushd continues, "And may he understand that the argument on which the learned base their belief in the prophets is another, to which Ghazali himself has drawn attention in another place, namely the act which proceeds from that quality through which the prophet is called prophet, that is the act of making known the mysterious and establishing religious laws which are in accordance with the truth and which bring about acts that will determine the happiness of the totality of humankind." Ibn Rushd, *Incoherence of the Incoherence*, 315–16.

61. Ibid., 322.

62. As will be recalled, in *Incoherence of the Philosophers*, Ghazali attributes this kind of interpretation to some philosophers (Ghazālī, *Incoherence*, 163). The medieval Qurʾan commentator al-Rāzī also mentions this allegorical interpretation in his exegesis of the Moses story and does not think that it is called for (see al-Rāzī, *Tafsīr al-kabīr*, 204).

63. Ibn Rushd, *Incoherence of the Incoherence*, 322.

64. For a summary of Ibn Sīna's explanations of miracles through reference to the natural but special powers of the prophet, see Rahman, *Prophecy in Islam*, 45–52.

65. Kogan, *Averroes and the Metaphysics of Causation*, 76–77.

66. Ibn Rushd, *Incoherence of the Incoherence*, 315.

67. Kogan, *Averroes and the Metaphysics of Causation*, 83–84.

68. Interestingly, this position has been taken up in the modern era as well. As I shall note in chapter 5, the Muslim theologian Shibli Nuʿmani interpreted Qurʾanic miracle stories as referring to unusual but natural events unknown to their audience at the time.

69. Fakhry, *Islamic Occasionalism*, 108.

70. Kogan, *Averroes and the Metaphysics of Causation*, 85–86.

71. Aristotle, *Physics*, bk. 2, 196b33–197a5.

72. "Still," Kogan writes, "there seems to be no reason to claim that his novel theory of miracles was without special theological relevance to those in his *milieu* who were equipped to understand it. A philosophical theology is a theology nonetheless." Kogan, *Averroes and the Metaphysics of Causation*, 86.

73. Ibn Rushd does not indicate whether these spontaneous events were pre-planned, unlike, for instance, Maimonides in *Guide to the Perplexed*, 2:25. Cf. Griffel, who argues that Ghazali could be interpreted as having entertained the idea that "miracles are programmed into God's plan for His creation, so to speak, from the very beginning and do not represent a direct intervention or a suspension of God's lawful actions." Griffel, "Al-Ghazālī."

74. Kogan, *Averroes and the Metaphysics of Causation*, 265.

75. As Goodman noted, Ibn Rushd's was a metaphysics of wisdom: "As for the intellectualist *metaphysic of wisdom*, which leads Aristotle to say, in his immanentist language, that nature does nothing in vain, it leads to the necessity of all true beings—the eternity of matter, form, species, minds, and the celestial bodies that form what are later called the 'principal parts' of the cosmos. Being is necessary by its nature, and the task of science is to discover in specific and in general terms the grounds of that necessity. In so doing the philosopher discovers and makes his own the wisdom of nature, which is divine." Goodman, *Avicenna*, 59.

CHAPTER 3

1. Norton, "Introduction to Hume's Thought," 1.

2. It is possible that Hume knew of Ibn Rushd's *Incoherence of the Incoherence*, which cites Ghazali's arguments completely before criticizing them. Hence, the similarity of Hume's critique of natural causation to Ghazali's, and of his critique of the design

argument to Ibn Rushd's critique of Ghazali, may well spring from historical influence, though exploring such historical lines of influence fall outside the scope of this book.

3. This biographical background of Hume is mainly summarized from Noonan, *Hume on Knowledge*, 1–5.

4. See, for instance, Capaldi, *David Hume*, and Noonan, *Hume on Knowledge*, 17–18.

5. Norton, "Introduction to Hume's Thought," 3.

6. Hume, *Enquiry*, sec. 4, pt. 1, p. 25, gp. 22. Unless otherwise noted, all references to David Hume's works are from the online Past Masters text, published by InteLex at http://www.nlx.com. Following the scholarly convention adopted in this online source, the citations specify book, section, part, and/or paragraph numbers, as well as the page numbers ("p." and "gp.") in the original written texts on which the online version is based.

7. Ibid., sec. 4, pt. 1, p. 26, gp. 24.

8. Ibid., sec. 4, pt. 1, p. 29, gp. 26 (italics added).

9. Ibid., sec. 4, pt. 1, p. 27, gp. 24.

10. Hume, *Treatise*, bk. 1, pt. 3, sec. 3, para. 3/9, p. 79 (italics added).

11. Norton, "Introduction to Hume's Thought," 9.

12. Hume, *Enquiry*, sec. 4, pt. 2, p. 32, gp. 29.

13. As Harold Noonan explains, "Hume approaches this question, as he must, given his Copy Principle, by looking for an impression or impressions from which the idea [of causation] can be derived. In the first place he notes that no *quality* of the things we call causes or effects can be the origin of our idea of causation, for we cannot discover any single quality common to them all." Noonan, *Hume on Knowledge*, 99.

14. Hume, *Treatise*, bk. 1, pt. 3, sec. 2, para. 11/16, p. 77.

15. Fogelin, *Hume's Skepticism*, 42.

16. Hume, *Treatise*, bk. 1, pt. 1, sec. 1, para. 8/12, p. 4; Hume, *Enquiry*, sec. 4, pt. 2, p. 32, gp. 29. Also see Schmidt, *David Hume*, 73.

17. Hume explains, "Our memory presents us only with a multitude of instances wherein we always find like bodies, motions, or qualities, in like relations. From the mere repetition of any past impression, even to infinity, there never will arise any new original idea, such as that of a necessary connexion; and the number of impressions has in this case no more effect than if we confined ourselves to one only." Hume, *Treatise*, bk. 1, pt. 3, sec. 6, para. 3/16, p. 87.

18. Ibid.

19. Hume, *Enquiry*, sec. 4, pt. 2, p. 36, gp. 32 (italics added).

20. Ibid., sec. 4, pt. 2, p. 32, gp. 29 (italics added).

21. Ibid., sec. 5, pt. 1, p. 44, gp. 39. See also Hume, *Treatise*, bk. 1, pt. 3, sec. 13, para. 19/20, p. 153. For more references to habit or custom in Hume's works, see Schmidt, *David Hume*, 73–74, 79–81.

22. Hume observes that "the mind has a great propensity to spread itself on external objects. . . . The same propensity is the reason why we suppose necessity and power to lie in the objects we consider, not in our mind, that considers them." Hume, *Treatise*, bk. 1, pt. 3, sec. 14, para. 25/36, p. 167.

23. Guyer, "Introduction," 3.

24. Fogelin, *Walking the Tightrope of Reason*, 13.

25. For a lucid discussion of Hume's skeptical arguments, including the ones concerning the existence of an external world and enduring self, see Hookway, *Scepticism*, 90–107.

26. Hume, *Treatise*, bk. 1, pt. 4, sec. 7, para. 2/15, p. 264 (italics added). Noonan notes that these observations reflect a practical circumstance in Hume's life: "It is hard not to read this section of the *Treatise* without seeing it as expressing, not merely a theoretical

solution to a theoretical problem, but the *practical* lesson that Hume had learnt from his own recent breakdown about the way he must conduct his own life in order to control the 'melancholy and indolence' to which he found himself to be susceptible." Noonan, *Hume on Knowledge*, 14; on his breakdown during his composition of the *Treatise*, see 2.

27. Thus, Hume says, "Most fortunately it happens, that since reason is incapable of dispelling these clouds, Nature herself suffices to that purpose, and cures me of this philosophical melancholy and delirium, either by relaxing this bent of mind, or by some avocation, and lively impression of my senses, which obliterate all these chimeras. I dine, I play a game of backgammon, I converse, and am merry with my friends; and when, after three or four hours' amusement, I would return to these speculations, they appear so cold, and strained, and ridiculous, that I cannot find in my heart to enter into them any further." Hume, *Treatise*, bk. 1, pt. 4, sec. 7, para. 9/15, p. 269.

28. Ibid., bk. 1, pt. 4, sec. 7, para. 11/15, p. 270.

29. Hume, *Enquiry*, sec. 5, pt. 2, p. 55, gp. 47 (italics added).

30. Ferreira, *Scepticism and Reasonable Doubt*, 45 (italics added).

31. Hume, *Treatise*, bk. 1, pt. 4, sec. 7, para. 10/15, p. 269 (italics in original).

32. Ferreira, *Scepticism and Reasonable Doubt*, 55.

33. Stroud, *Hume*, 94–95, 243–45. Indeed, Stroud hopes that someday there can be a more reasonable account of how to transition from the loss of using reason to critical belief. Similarly, Paul Russell thinks that Hume's solution to radical skepticism "is highly paradoxical because this position is the outcome of 'conflicting' and 'irreconcilable' forces: viz. reason and the imagination." Russell, review of *Hume's Skepticism*, 395.

34. Hookway, *Scepticism*, 105. Similarly, I. M. Fowlie notes that one may appreciate Hume's move from radical skepticism to mitigated skepticism as an account "of what Hume *himself* has been caused, by a variety of non-rational factors, to believe. We, his readers, may find this record interesting, but it gives us no reason why *we* should believe these things ourselves." Fowlie, review of *Hume's Skepticism*, 127.

35. Fowlie, review of *Hume's Skepticism*, 127–28. Also see Schmidt, *David Hume*, 5, for a similar remark.

36. Hume, *Enquiry*, sec. 5, pt. 2, p. 55, gp. 47.

37. Hume, *Dialogues Concerning Natural Religion*, part 11, cited in Fowlie, review of *Hume's Skepticism*, 127.

38. See P. Russell, "Hume on Religion"; Schmidt, *David Hume*, 71.

39. Hume, *Treatise*, bk. 1, pt. 3, sec. 3, para. 4/9, pp. 80–82.

40. Noonan, *Hume on Knowledge*, 105 (italics in original). Such skepticism of the causal principle puts additional strain on Hume's argument. That is, his very attempt to find *causes* for causal thinking seems to contradict his insistence that the causal maxim is not intuitive. It sounds ironic that Hume concluded that it is habit that *produces* causal thinking, that the mind is *determined* by habit to infer causal relations, and that nature has *implanted* in the human mind the propensity to designate objects that occur in repeated sequences as causes. See Giacaman, "Ducasse's Critique of Hume"; cf. Fogelin, *Hume's Skepticism*, 47. Needless to say, Hume's analysis has been criticized for being inconsistent. See Russell, *History of Western Philosophy*, 606; Rosenberg, "Hume and the Philosophy of Science," 73.

41. Russell, "Hume on Religion."

42. As Noonan aptly explains, such a critique is not justified by Hume's own principles: "Given the Separability and Conceivability Principles any object X, whose coming into existence is the effect of a particular cause C, might have come into existence in the absence of C. But it does not follow that X might have come into existence without *any* cause." Noonan, *Hume on Knowledge*, 106.

43. Hume, *Enquiry*, sec. 7, pt. 1, p. 72, gp. 60.

44. Hume, *Treatise*, "Introduction," para. 3/10, p. xiv.

45. P. Russell, "Hume on Religion." At other times, Hume imagines that we could be "assured" that "the wisdom and contrivance" in the universe are the result of a "blind force" randomly inducing "unguided matter"! Hume, *Dialogues Concerning Natural Religion*, pt. 8, para. 7/12, p. 184. See also Gaskin, "Hume on Religion," 326–28.

46. Norton, "Introduction to Hume's Thought," 7.

47. Indeed, "the target of Hume's apparent attack on induction was not empirical knowledge, but rather the pretense of the rationalists that the results of induction could be certified as necessarily true" (Rosenberg, "Hume and the Philosophy of Science," 77). Hume's insistence that we cannot rationally justify any causal link between objects does not deprive us of attaining "morally certain" knowledge of our daily use of causal reasoning (Wilson, *Hume's Defense of Causal Inference*, 106).

48. Indeed, Hume may be credited as introducing the "phenomenological turn" in Western thought. See Norton, "Introduction to Hume's Thought," 8.

49. See Earman, *Hume's Abject Failure*; Johnson, *Hume, Holism, and Miracles*.

50. Hume, *Enquiry*, sec. 10, pt. 1, p. 110, gp. 89.

51. Ibid., sec. 10, pt. 1, p. 113, gp. 92.

52. Ibid., sec. 10, pt. 1, p. 114, gp. 93.

53. Ibid., sec. 10, pt. 1, p. 113, gp. 92.

54. Ibid., sec. 10, pt. 1, p. 114, gp. 93 (italics in original). For similar remarks about gauging miracle reports by a Muslim theologian, Shibli Nuʿmani (1857–1914), see his "Nature of Prophethood and Miracle," 97–98.

55. Hume, *Enquiry*, n. 22, p. 115, gp. 93 (italics in original).

56. Ibid., sec. 10, pt. 1, p. 115, gp. 94.

57. Ibid., sec. 10, pt. 2, p. 116–19, gp. 94–97.

58. Ibid., sec. 10, pt. 2, p. 128, gp. 106 (italics added).

59. Ibid., sec. 10, pt. 2, p. 129, gp. 107.

60. Hume, *Treatise*, bk. 1, pt. 3, sec. 6, para. 7/16, p. 89. See Noonan, *Hume on Knowledge*, 118.

61. Fogelin, *Defense of Hume*, 25–26, 31, and 52.

62. Hume, *Enquiry*, sec. 10, pt. 2, p. 127, gp. 105 (italics added).

63. Hume notes, "But suppose, that all the historians who treat of England, should agree, that, on the first of January 1600, Queen Elizabeth died; that both before and after her death she was seen by her physicians and the whole court, as is usual with persons of her rank; that her successor was acknowledged and proclaimed by the parliament; and that, after being interred a month, she again appeared, resumed the throne, and governed England for three years: I must confess that I should be surprised at the concurrence of so many odd circumstances, but should not have the least inclination to believe so miraculous an event." Ibid., sec. 10, pt. 2, p. 128, gp. 106.

64. I am indebted to Jamie M. Ferreira for this insight, which she shared during a conversation. See also Fogelin, *Defense of Hume*, 90n5; cf. Schmidt, *David Hume*, 345.

65. See, for instance, Yandell, *Hume's "Inexplicable Mystery,"* 315–38, and Earman, *Hume's Abject Failure*, 22.

66. Hume, *Enquiry*, sec. 7, pt. 1, p. 65, gp. 54.

67. Paul Russell notes that "skepticism and the naturalism of the *Treatise* should be viewed not so much as ends in themselves as powerful weapons which Hume wields in order to refute Christian dogmatism and to construct a secular moral and political outlook. In short, contrary to most Hume scholars I take the view that Hume's fundamental philosophical intentions are best characterized as 'atheistic' or anti-Christian in nature rather than as simply secular or naturalistic." Russell, review of *Hume's Skepticism*, 396.

68. Cf. Stanley Tweyman, who argues that belief in an intelligent designer of the world is a natural belief according to Humean criteria. See Tweyman, *Essays on the Philosophy of David Hume*, 73–97.

69. For instance, James Sennett and Douglas Groothuis write, "Only in its application to religious concepts, it seems, is a Humean distrust of the basic categories of human experience warranted today. But of course *such a double standard*, properly exposed to the light of metaphilosophical awareness, cannot hope to survive." See Sennett and Groothuis, *In Defense of Natural Theology*, 16–17 (italics added).

70. David L. Weddle summarizes well Hume's concern in his treatise on miracles: "After all, if God could transgress the boundary between heaven and earth and interfere with the rationality [sic] of natural order, then where would science and philosophy be? What would become of their joint enterprise to master the secrets of physical forces and human actions?" Weddle, *Miracles*, 16.

71. Fogelin, *Defense of Hume*, 58–62.

72. James, *Writings of William James*, 327.

CHAPTER 4

1. Hookway, *Truth, Rationality, and Pragmatism*, 1.

2. Peter Ochs notes that in his early critique of Cartesianism Peirce committed some of the same mistakes he criticized in Descartes's thought. See Ochs, *Peirce, Pragmatism*, 53–58.

3. These papers, which were published in the *Journal of Speculative Philosophy*, are "Questions Concerning Certain Faculties Claimed for Man" (1868), "Some Consequences of Four Incapacities" (1868), and "Grounds of Validity of the Laws of Logic: Further Consequences of Four Incapacities" (1869).

4. Unless otherwise noted, all quotations from Peirce's works are from the online Past Masters text, *The Collected Papers of Charles Sanders Peirce* (henceforth cited as *CP*), published by InteLex at http://www.nlx.com. Following the scholarly convention, after each quote I note the volume number, the paragraph number, and the known or estimated date of composition. Italics are from the original unless otherwise noted.

5. Legg, "Real Law," 131.

6. Misak, "Peirce on Vital Matters," 153.

7. In fact, Hume makes a similar comment about his own accomplishment. See Hume, *Treatise*, bk. 1, pt. 4, sec. 1, para. 8/12, p. 183.

8. Ochs, *Peirce, Pragmatism*, 76.

9. Ochs notes that Peirce, early on, argues inconsistently with this thesis himself and criticizes Cartesianism via a single-thread kind of argument. Ibid., 56.

10. I am indebted to Peter Ochs for alerting me to this point.

11. Ochs, *Peirce, Pragmatism*, 261.

12. Cf. James's definition, in which the terms "conceivable" and "possible" are dropped, as noted in Pihlström, "Peirce's Place in the Pragmatist Tradition," 34. Pihlström also notes that "the Peircean formulation allows that conceptions, though always conceptions of 'conceivable practical effects,' 'reach far beyond the practical'; it is only required that we maintain a connection with some possible practical effect" (37).

13. Indeed, Peirce's insistence that "the road of inquiry should not be blocked" would not allow for such a rigid closure. Peirce uses the phrase "do not block the road of inquiry" repeatedly. See, for instance, *CP* 6.64, 1892; 6.273, 1893; 1.153, 1897; 8.243, ca. 1905.

14. Pragmatism "will serve to show that almost every proposition of ontological meta-physics is either meaningless gibberish—one word being defined by other words, and they by still others, without any real conception ever being reached—or else is downright absurd; so that all such rubbish being swept away, what will remain of philosophy will be a series of problems capable of investigation by the observational methods of the true sciences." *CP* 5.423, 1905.

15. Similarly, David Gruender's comparison of Peirce's pragmatism with Carnap's logical positivism highlights three differences between them. Gruender notes that while both Peirce and Carnap look to scientific inquiry as a model for philosophy, define con-cepts in reference to their tangible difference, and think that much of metaphysics is nonsense and that logical analysis will help clarify philosophical issues, they also differ in significant respects. Peirce's pragmatic method is different from Carnap's verifica-tionism in that, unlike Carnap, Peirce did leave room for a properly conducted metaphys-ics, was committed to realism with respect to universals, and rejected the idea that the "language of theory" and the "language of observation" can be sharply separated. See Gruender, "Pragmatism, Science, and Metaphysics," 272.

16. Corrington, *Introduction to C. S. Peirce*, 39.

17. Peirce also notes that "the end of thought is action only in so far as the end of action is another thought." *CP* 8.272, ca. 1902.

18. In fact, as Hookway notes, Peirce's pragmatism is "a form of empiricism that employs a much richer understanding of *experience* than is familiar from the work of Hume and from twentieth-century logical empiricists." Hookway, *Truth, Rationality, and Pragmatism*, 4.

19. Cf. James, *Psychology*, 134–50.

20. See, for instance, *CP* 5.492, ca. 1906.

21. Intriguingly, Peirce notes that "in order to gain a habit in the outer world, such as to be able to perform a physical act, the repetition does not have to be in the 'outer world'; it may well be that by imagining the reiterations in one's 'inner world' one can perfect an action." *CP* 5.487, ca. 1906.

22. Hookway, *Truth, Rationality, and Pragmatism*, 9–10 (italics added). For the impor-tance of Peirce's contribution to semiotics and interpretation theory, see Sheriff, *Fate of Meaning*.

23. Hookway, *Truth, Rationality, and Pragmatism*, 9–10.

24. See also *CP* 2.148, 1902.

25. This example is from Legg, "Naturalism and Wonder," 206. Here, Legg also notes that what Peirce calls abduction is close to what today is called an "argument to the best explanation."

26. Peirce explains, "Abductive inference shades into perceptual judgment without any sharp line of demarcation between them; or, in other words, our first premisses, the perceptual judgments, are to be regarded as an extreme case of abductive inferences, from which they differ in being absolutely beyond criticism." *CP* 5.181, 1903.

27. Rosenthal, "Peirce's Pragmatic Account of Perception," 193.

28. Hookway, *Peirce*, 229.

29. Ochs, *Peirce, Pragmatism*, 168.

30. Hookway, "Abstract of Chapter 11."

31. Hookway, *Truth, Rationality, and Pragmatism*, 205.

32. Ibid., 205–6.

33. Corrington, *Introduction to C. S. Peirce*, 55.

34. Hookway, *Truth, Rationality, and Pragmatism*, 221.

35. In a lecture on pragmatism, Peirce conducted a simple experiment by asking the audience to guess what would happen if he dropped the stone in his hand. The audience

responded unanimously that it would fall (5.94, 1904). Susan Haack rightly notes that the point of Peirce's experiment was not to prove the possibility of induction by showing that the stone indeed fell, but rather to make the people self-conscious of the fact that if there is any prediction at all, it is only possible if there are real laws operating in nature. See Haack, "Not Cynicism but Synechism," 7.

36. As Griffel noted, "We must point out that al-Ghazālī was not a nominalist in the sense of his contemporary Roscelin (d. *c.* 1120) or William of Ockham (d. 1347) in the Latin West. These nominalists outspokenly denied any ontological coherence between things and their formal (and universal) representations in our minds." Griffel, *Al-Ghazālī's Philosophical Theology*, 176–77.

37. Peirce also rejects any kind of a priori argument in defense of the fixed nature of universal laws. See *CP* 6.49, 1892; 1.144, ca. 1897.

38. If we are correct in our conclusion that for Ibn Rushd natural laws admit no exception and miracles are extraordinary spontaneous events brought about by a peculiar intersection of natural causes, then Ibn Rushd's view coincides with version *B* of necessitarianism in Peirce's scheme. This version of necessitarianism allows some unrepeatable and wondrous intersections of events, while maintaining that natural laws are necessary.

39. Peirce notes that "necessitarianism cannot logically stop short of making the whole action of the mind a part of the physical universe. Our notion that we decide what we are going to do, if, as the necessitarian says, it has been calculable since the earliest times, is reduced to illusion. Indeed, consciousness in general thus becomes a mere illusory aspect of a material system. . . . On the other hand, by supposing the rigid exactitude of causation to yield, I care not how little—be it but by a strictly infinitesimal amount—we gain room to insert mind into our scheme, and to put it into the place where it is needed, into the position which, as the sole self-intelligible thing, it is entitled to occupy, that of the fountain of existence; and in so doing we resolve the problem of the connection of soul and body." *CP* 6.61, 1892.

40. Turley, "Peirce on Chance," 245.

41. Burch, "Charles Sanders Peirce."

42. Corrington, *Introduction to C. S. Peirce*, 174.

43. Actually, as Turley notes, Peirce entertained determinism for quite a while, until his late fifties, and then realized that it does not do justice to our experience. Moreover, before transitioning into admitting "pure chance," Peirce first entertained the idea of "a tiny element of chance" in the world. Turley, "Peirce on Chance," 244.

44. Ibid., 243; Turley, "Peirce's Cosmic 'Sheriff,'" 718. In theological vocabulary, the "pure chance" element in nature that Peirce attempts to describe corresponds to the freedom of divine will, as Ghazali has indicated and (as we shall see in the next chapter) as Nursi also notes in his interpretation of miracles.

45. Corrington, *Introduction to C. S. Peirce*, 56.

46. According to Peirce, suggesting that the laws in nature evolved "supposes them not to be absolute, not to be obeyed precisely. It makes an element of indeterminacy, spontaneity, or absolute chance in nature." *CP* 6.13, 1891.

47. Corrington, *Introduction to C. S. Peirce*, 194–96; Ochs, *Peirce, Pragmatism*, 139. Also see *CP* 6.63, 1891.

48. See Turley, "Peirce's Cosmic 'Sheriff,'" 717–18.

49. For a discussion of the "pragmatic" implication of the concept of God in Peirce, see ibid.

50. Robert Burch summarizes what Peirce's agapistic evolution is meant to account for: "What the directly measured facts of scientific practice seem to tell us, then, is that, although the universe displays varying degrees of *habit* (that is to say, of partial, varying,

approximate, and statistical regularity), the universe does not display deterministic *law*. It does not directly show anything like total, exact, non-statistical regularity. Moreover, the habits that nature does display always appear in varying degrees of entrenchment or 'congealing.' At one end of the spectrum, we have the nearly law-like behavior of larger physical objects like boulders and planets; but at the other end of the spectrum, we see in the human processes of imagination and thought an almost pure freedom and spontaneity; and in the quantum world of the very small we see the results of almost pure chance." Burch, "Charles Sanders Peirce" (italics in original).

51. Ayers, "Peirce on Miracles," 242.

52. Legg, "Naturalism and Wonder," 302–6.

53. Ibid., 304.

54. Peirce, "Logic of Drawing History," 911.

55. Legg, "Naturalism and Wonder," 304. Cf. Fogelin's analogy of miracle testimonies in the case of a person who recounts too many wondrous memories. Fogelin, *Defense of Hume*, 10–13.

56. Legg, "Naturalism and Wonder," 304. Cf. Hume's remark *"It is strange*, a judicious reader is apt to say, upon the perusal of these wonderful historians, *that such prodigious events never happen in our days*. But it is nothing strange, I hope, that men should lie in all ages." Hume, *Enquiry*, sec. 10, pt. 2, p. 119, gp. 97 (italics in original).

57. Legg, "Naturalism and Wonder," 304–5.

58. Peirce, "Logic of Drawing History," 910, cited in Legg, "Naturalism and Wonder," 302 (italics added). And Peirce continues to give examples: "We were told that if there ever were any kings in Rome, all that has come down about them is mythical; that there never was any such poet as Homer, far less any such city as Troy, or any such state of Greek society as is described in the *Iliad* and *Odyssey*; that only a minority of the dialogues of Plato are genuine; that the writings attributed to Aristotle were gradually composed in the Peripatetic school; that Manetho's account of Egyptian history is ridiculous, etc., etc." Ibid. See also *CP* 7.164–255, ca. 1901.

59. Rather, as Legg suggests, the proper attitude would be to see "such a phenomenon [as] potentially valuable as it presents an opportunity for inquiry, a chance to find out something new." Legg, "Naturalism and Wonder," 309.

60. Peirce makes a similar remark elsewhere: "I do not think, by the way, that it is generally known that some of the early Fathers of the Church refused to believe in physical miracles; and apparently attributed them to a superhuman hypnotic power, reminding one of what the Hindoo jugglers have made British officers think they saw. St. Augustine, on the contrary, while holding it impious to think them to be violations of Nature's Laws, regards them apparently as occurrences that are to us what the reading of a letter by a man might seem to a dog to be, namely, a manifestation of some higher mastery of things than would be compatible with his nature." *CP* 6.92, 1903.

61. The Charles S. Peirce Papers, Houghton Library, Harvard University, MS #674, p. 14 (variant), fn. 3, cited in Turley, "Peirce's Cosmic 'Sheriff,'" 718 (italics added).

CHAPTER 5

1. For a helpful overview of the Muslim attitudes toward science during this period, see Iqbal, *Science and Islam*, 131–53.

2. Özervarlı, "Reconstruction of Islamic Social Thought," 536. Özervarlı also notes that Charles MacFarlane, a British visitor to the Galatasaray Medical School (Mekteb-i Tıbbiye) in Istanbul, was "shocked by the number of materialistic books he found at the school. When MacFarlane asked one of the students whether their medical practices

were not somewhat contrary to his religion, he laughed and said, 'Eh! Monsieur, ce n'est pas au Galata Serai qu'il faut venir chercher la religion!'" MacFarlane, *Turkey and Its Destiny*, 2:268–69, cited in ibid.

3. Özervarlı, "Said Nursi's Project," 317.

4. Ibid., 318. For further description of the polarization among Ottoman intelligentsia, see Mermer and Ameur, "Beyond the Modern," 119–22.

5. Özervarlı lists the following Ottoman intellectuals, along with Nursi, as having invested in revival, especially in Islamic theology: Abdullah Harputi (1842–1916), Şeyhulislam Musa Kazım (1858–1920), Filibeli Ahmed Hilmi (1865–1914), İzmirli İsmail Hakkı (1868–1946), Elmalili Hamdi Yazır (1878–1942), and Ahmed Hamdi Akseki (1887–1951). He notes that Nursi differed from his Ottoman contemporaries especially during his New Said period, in that he refused to take up any government posts, emphasized a Qur'anic theology, and addressed the common people rather than a scholarly audience. Özervarlı, "Said Nursi's Project," 318–19. For an extremely useful survey of these Ottoman thinkers as well as some of the early modern Indian and Egyptian Muslim theologians, see Özervarlı's study *Kelāmda yenilik*.

6. Nursi's transformation could be compared to Ghazali's spiritual crisis: "In both, one takes notice of that spiritual struggle, that 'dark night of the soul,' which ends in their case with the victory of the 'heart' over the 'soul' (*nafs*), culminating in the birth of a new intellect, as it were, and a new Qur'anic Man." Mermer and Ameur, "Beyond the Modern," 129n25. For a summary of Nursi's biography, see Turner and Horkuc, *Said Nursi*, 5–19; see also Vahide, *Author of the Risale-i Nur*.

7. For details on this institution, which was founded by V. Mehmet Reshad and Şeyhülislam Musa Kazım Efendi in 1918, see Albayrak, *Son devrin İslam akademisi*.

8. Vahide, *Islam in Modern Turkey*, 106.

9. Keddie, *Islamic Response to Imperialism*, 102, cited in Iqbal, *Science and Islam*, 149.

10. Turner and Horkuc, *Said Nursi*, 17.

11. For a very interesting analysis of Said Nursi's personal transformations vis-à-vis the major political transformations at the time, see Davudoglu, "Bediuzzaman and the Politics."

12. The Old Said had already noted the circularity implied in some of the religious discourse that attempted to argue for faith by citing religious sources. For instance, he wrote, "Mere description of one's thesis is not sufficient; we want evidence [Ar. *burhān*, Tk. *bürhan*]." Nursi, *Muhakemat*, in *Risale-i nur külliyatı*, 2:1994 (my translation). Henceforth, the *Risale-i nur külliyatı*, a comprehensive compilation of Nursi's works in two volumes, will be cited as *RNK*. Whenever I refer to this source, I specify the particular book under discussion. Please note that this text is also available online at www.risaleinur.com.tr.

13. Özervarlı, "Said Nursi's Project," 328.

14. Ibid., 321; Nursi, *Lem'alar*, *RNK*, 1:710–13.

15. For a brief discussion of Nursi's approach to political issues, see Yazicioglu, "Saʿid Nursi."

16. Nursi, *Hutbe-i Şamiye*, *RNK*, 2:1963.

17. Nursi, *Mesnevi-i Nuriye*, *RNK*, 2:1329; Nursi, *Lem'alar*, *RNK*, 1:643; Nursi, *Flashes*, 160.

18. Mermer and Ameur, "Beyond the Modern," 129.

19. Nursi, *Mesnevi-i Nuriye*, *RNK*, 2:1391–95; Nursi, *Lem'alar*, *RNK*, 1:643–56; Nursi, *Flashes*, 159–66.

20. *Ihya* (revival) and *tajdīd* (renewal) are classical Islamic terms referring to distinctive moments of revitalization in Muslim history that are associated with the divine promise noted in a famous saying attributed to Prophet Muhammad. According to this

saying or *hadith*, in each age God will send a person from the Muslim community to revive the faith. See Leaman, "Nursi's Place in the *Ihya*'," as well as the proceedings in *The Reconstruction of Islamic Thought in the Twentieth Century and Bediuzzaman Said Nursi*, including Turner, "Renewal in Islam and Bediuzzaman," and Masala, "Line from Mevlana to Bediuzzaman." Cf. Algar, "Centennial Renewer." While he cautions against quick conclusions, Algar suggests that perhaps Nursi was indeed the last *mujaddid* to have emerged in modern Islam (310–11).

21. For Said Nursi's view on Christian-Muslim relations, see Michel, "Muslim-Christian Dialogue"; Markham and Birinci-Pirim, *An Introduction to Said Nursi*, 51–60; Markham, *Engaging with Bediuzzaman Said Nursi*, 43–66.

22. For instance, see Nursi, *Sözler*, *RNK*, 1:49–55, 97–109, 160–203, and Nursi, *Muhakemat*, *RNK*, 2:1985–2010.

23. Nursi, *Sözler*, *RNK*, 1:195–96; Nursi, *Mesnevi-i Nuriye*, *RNK*, 2:1363; Nursi, *Words*, 443–44.

24. In the preface to his excellent work *Approaching the Qur'an*, Sells offers a good example of how differences in context, intent, and speaker result in different meanings of the same utterance. The meaning of a simple statement, such as "Islam is a religion of peace," can range widely; it might be an apologetic statement or an apocalyptic one, a proud statement about history or an interreligious gesture of trust (ibid., xiii).

25. He derives this implication from Q. 18:109: "Say [Prophet], 'If the whole ocean were ink for writing the words of my Lord, it would run dry before those words were exhausted'—even if We were to add another ocean to it." Cf. Q. 2:30, 16:68.

26. Nursi, *Words*, 146 (modified translation); Nursi, *Sözler*, *RNK*, 1:50. Unless otherwise noted, all English translations of quotes from the major books of Nursi's magnum opus, which are contained in the first volume of the *Risale-i nur*—namely, *Sözler*, *Lem'alar*, *Mektubat*, and *Şualar*—are from Şükran Vahide's respective translations entitled *The Words*, *The Flashes*, *The Letters*, and *The Rays*. In consultation with the original Turkish, I have made occasional modifications to her translations, enclosing these in square brackets.

27. Nursi, *Rays*, 148. Nursi notes that unlike an inspired saint who converses with his sustainer through the "telephone of his heart," the messenger of God receives revelation from the Lord of *all the universe*. Nursi, *Sözler*, *RNK*, 1:51; Nursi, *Words*, 148.

28. Nursi, *Sözler*, *RNK*, 1:51 (my translation, italics added); Nursi, *Words*, 377.

29. Nursi invokes the traditional concept of *tanazzulat al-ilahiyya ila 'uqul al-bashar* (literally, God condescending to the level of human intellect), which means that God speaks in a language that a human being can understand. See Nursi, *Words*, 200, 401. Ghazali had explained *tanazzulat al-ilahiyya* as "the bounty of God and His kindness towards His creatures in descending from the throne of His majesty to the level of their understanding." Ghazālī, *Recitation and Interpretation*, 56.

30. Nursi, *Words*, 402. Nursi notes, "As is indicated by the Hadith [prophetic saying] '*Each verse has an outer meaning, an inner meaning, a limit, and an aim, and each has roots, and boughs, and branches*,' the words of the Qur'an have been positioned in such a way that all its phrases, words even, and even letters, and sometimes even an omission, has many aspects [of meaning]." Ibid., 401 (italics in original); also 263, 410. See Nursi, *Sözler*, *RNK*, 1:175–76.

31. The idea is that Qur'anic verses can have more than one meaning. This is a traditional maxim that plays a crucial role in the works of all major traditional exegetes. Their conviction that the word of God cannot be exhausted justifies a rule of polysemy in the exegetical tradition: any interpretation that does not undo the plain sense of a given verse *is* an aspect of its intended meaning. See Saleh, *Classical Tafsīr Tradition*, 2. Ghazali similarly argues that the individual reader of the Qur'an should not be misled to think

that the Qur'an signifies only those meanings that have been handed down from early authorities. See Ghazālī, *Recitation*, 86.

32. I am grateful to Dr. Ali Mermer for also clarifying this point in Nursi's text.

33. Nursi, *Words*, 376 (modified translation); Nursi, *Sözler*, RNK, 1:161.

34. Nursi, *Words*, 444. See also Mermer and Ameur, "Beyond the Modern," 126–27.

35. Nursi, *Sözler*, RNK, 1:241; Nursi, *Words*, 397, 558.

36. As al-Daghamin summarizes, for Ghazali, the overall purposes of the Qur'an can be narrowed to six, three of which are basic and three of which are complementary. The basic purposes are "definition of the One called on; definition of the Straight Path that has to be followed to journey towards Him; and definition of the state whereby He may be reached. The other three are complementary: description of the state of those who respond to the call and of the subtleties of the Divine art manifested on such people; description of the condition of the deniers and their abasement and ignorant obduracy in the face of the truth; teaching how the way-stations on the journey to God Almighty are established and how the provisions necessary for the journey, and the necessary capacity and awareness, may be obtained." According to Fakhr al-Dīn al-Rāzī (d. 1209), the Qur'an revolves around four matters: godhead, prophethood, the hereafter, and divine decree and determination (*al-qaḍā* and *al-qadar*). Abu Ishaq Ibrahim ibn Musa al-Shatibī (d. 1388) notes that divine unity, prophethood, the resurrection of the dead, and instruction in the law are the major aims in the Qur'an. Al-Daghamin, "Aims of the Qur'an," 356–58.

37. For instance, "the Qur'an does not mention the sun for its own sake. Rather, it refers to it for the sake of the One who illuminates it." Nursi, *Sözler*, RNK, 1:167 (my translation); cf. Nursi, *Words*, 279. See also Nursi, *Muhakemat*, RNK, 2:1986.

38. See Nursi, *Words*, 143–44, 273–74.

39. Nursi, *Sözler*, RNK, 1:95; Nursi, *İşaratü'l i'caz*, RNK, 2:1159; Nursi, *Emirdağ lâhikası*, RNK, 2:1848; Nursi, *Letters*, 244; Nursi, *Words*, 151.

40. Nursi, *Words*, 254; Nursi, *Sözler*, RNK, 1:97.

41. Nursi, *Muhakemat*, RNK, 2:1986.

42. Nursi writes, "Most of Man's 'earthly' cogitations, his inconvertible and even self-evident truths are built on 'customariness' (*ulfah*), the source of *compounded* ignorance. A corruption of serious consequences therefore resides in the very foundation of his knowledge. It is owing to this almost perpetual state of affairs, that the Qur'ān constantly directs the gaze of mankind towards the recurrent vicissitudes ('*adiyāt*), beckoning them fervently to look closer at the veils of the ordinary. . . . Indeed, it is through these that the lights of the Qur'ānic stars pierce the dark vaults and tenebrous shrouds of the mind succumbed to 'customariness' (*ulfah*)." Nursi, *Al-Mathnawī al-'Arabi al-nūri*, 324, cited in Mermer and Ameur, "Beyond the Modern," 146 (italics in original).

43. Nursi, *Words*, 150 (modified translation).

44. See, for instance, Nursi, *Sözler*, RNK, 1:26, 92. Nursi argues that the Qur'anic perspective rejects the tendency to see a three-legged baby as more astonishing than a "normal baby," or to see the survival of an insect in water as more amazing than the nourishment of young with breast milk. See also Nursi, *Words*, 151.

45. Nursi, *Sözler*, RNK, 1:26, 38–9, 83, 88, 91, 99, 261–62, 264, 275, 307, 311; Nursi, *Mektubat*, RNK, 1:417, 487; Nursi, *Lem'alar*, RNK, 1:921, 940; Nursi, *Şualar*, RNK, 1:1355, 1368, etc.

46. Nursi, *Sözler*, RNK, 1:121; Nursi, *Words*, 214.

47. Nursi, *Lem'alar*, RNK, 1:677, 698; Nursi, *Words*, 60. Nursi regards such intuition as the starting point for any concept of causality.

48. Nursi, *Flashes*, 182.

49. Nursi explains, "What misleads those who *worship* apparent causes [*asbāb ẓāhiriyya*] is the two things coming together or being together, which is called [conjunction

(*iqtirān*)]. They suppose the two things cause one another." Nursi, *Flashes*, 182 (modified translation, italics added); Nursi, *Lem'alar*, RNK, 1:653. Note that Nursi's example of the garden has a similar function to Ghazali's example of a blind person beginning to perceive colors, as we saw in chapter 2. See Ghazālī, *Tahāfut al-falāsifa*, 168.

50. Nursi, *Flashes*, 236 (modified translation).

51. Nursi, *Flashes*, 308, 340; Nursi, *Lem'alar*, RNK, 1:712, 727.

52. Nursi, *Words*, 435 (modified translation).

53. Ibid., 711–12 (italics added).

54. This verse is quoted repeatedly in Nursi's corpus, more than 130 times. See Nursi, *Sözler*, RNK, 1:26, 51, 53, 61, 63, 165, etc.

55. Nursi, *Words*, 435. For an example of Nursi's "reading" of divine names, or *asmā al-ḥusna*, on the "pages of the universe," see Nursi, *Sözler*, RNK, 1:286; Nursi, *Words*, 655. Here, Nursi traces names of God such as The All-Wise, The Orderer, The Giver of Forms, The Beautiful, The Munificent, The Bestower, The Merciful, and The Loving through a reflection on natural things, such as a flower, a human being, and so on.

56. Mermer and Ameur argue that "all that Ash'ari discourse did was merely to project the Qur'anic conclusions onto the world without justifying them. They did not engage in a parallel reading of the cosmic signs even though the Qur'an constantly refers the interlocutor to the world and teaches how it should be looked at in order to gain knowledge of the cosmos, oneself and God." Hence, "unwittingly," the Ash'arite discourse neglected "the knowledge of God that can be gained through the knowledge of 'causal relations.'" Mermer and Ameur, "Beyond the Modern," 143.

57. For instance, Kogan, *Averroes and the Metaphysics of Causation*, 96, 265. For a similar criticism directed at Ghazali, see Giacaman and Bahlul, "Ghazali on Miracles," 43–44.

58. Nursi, *Sözler*, RNK, 1:241–52; Nursi, *Words*, 557–70. For a brief overview of this treatise, see Turner, *Islam*, 188–97.

59. In quoting the end of this verse, I preferred Asad's English rendering to Abdel Haleem's, since the former brought out its literal sense better; Asad, *Message of the Qur'an*, 653.

60. Nursi, *Words*, 560.

61. Ibid., 477.

62. In fact, Nursi sees *ibdā'* (or creation ex nihilo) and *inshā'* (or creation through composition) within each other. For a helpful summary of Nursi's use of these Qur'anic concepts to offer what we might call a "common sense–friendly" continuous creation approach, see Turner and Horkuc, *Said Nursi*, 73–75.

63. Nursi writes, "For example, a particle located in [your] eye is suitably placed with regard to the blood-vessels like the arteries and veins, and the motor and sensory nerves, and has a wise and purposeful relationship with the face, and then with the head, the trunk, and with the entire human body, and has beneficial duties in relation to each. This demonstrates that only the one who creates all the members of the body will be able to place the particle in that position." Nursi, *Words*, 577. For an extended discussion of the interconnectedness of things in nature, see Nursi, *Sözler*, RNK, 1:268–72; Nursi, *Words*, 619–28.

64. Nursi, *Flashes*, 237.

65. Nursi, *Mektubat*, RNK, 1:483; Nursi, *Lem'alar*, RNK, 1:685.

66. Nursi, *Flashes*, 244 (modified translation).

67. See Nursi, *İşaratü'l i'caz*, RNK, 2:1162–63; Nursi, *Mesnevi-i Nuriye*, RNK, 2:1309, 1372; Nursi, *Muhakemat*, RNK, 2:1998.

68. Nursi, *Muhakemat*, RNK, 2:1999.

69. Nursi, *Mesnevi-i Nuriye*, RNK, 2:1309. Nursi further explains the wisdom of God acting behind the veil of causes in this world; this is very interesting but unfortunately beyond the scope of this work. See, for instance, Nursi, *Words*, 300–301.

70. Nursi, *Muhakemat*, RNK, 2:1999.

71. Nursi, *Letters*, 122–23 (modified translation).

72. Nursi, *Muhakemat*, RNK, 2:1993. Elsewhere, Nursi notes that "exaggeration is implied disparagement." Nursi, *Words*, 749.

73. A similar reconciliation may be drawn from a closer analysis of Ghazali's other theological texts (or even from a dedicated and slightly stretched reinterpretation of Ibn Rushd). Especially in Ghazali's context, his reference to *ijrāʾ al-ʿāda* is capable of offering such a reconciliation between the contingency of natural order and the need to take its consistency seriously. To my mind, Nursi's approach is more straightforward and renders Ghazali's approach more understandable.

74. Nursi, *Sözler*, RNK, 1:105; Nursi, *Words*, 269.

75. Nursi, *Words*, 17; Nursi, *Sözler*, RNK, 1:3.

76. Yazicioglu, "Redefining the Miraculous," 100. For a detailed analysis of this treatise on *bismillah* ("First Word" in *Words*) and its interpretation of Qurʾanic miracle stories, see ibid., 98–100.

77. Ibid. In other words, when Nursi questions natural causality, he is not denying that things happen through natural causes. Rather, he takes his cue, again, from the Qurʾan, which acknowledges the natural causes and refers to divine activity *through* them, as opposed to *without* them. Thus, for instance, the Qurʾan makes reference to God's activity of creating life through water: "We (God) send down *water* from the sky in accordance with a measure [set by Us], and then We cause it to lodge in the earth . . . and *by means of this* [water] We bring forth for you gardens of date palms and vines, wherein you have fruit abundant and whereof you eat." Q. 23:19; translation from Asad, *Message of the Qurʾan*, 520–21 (italics added). See also Q. 13:4, 15:22, 25:48–49, 31:10, etc.

78. For an example of Nursi's more explicit use of the knowledge of natural causes as pointers to God, see his discussion of the scientific description of digestion of food and cleansing of the blood in *Words*, 622n3.

79. For his discussion of the two ways of getting an apple, see Nursi, *Sözler*, RNK, 1:293; Nursi, *Şualar*, RNK, 1:930; Nursi, *Words*, 669; Nursi, *Rays*, 197. For Nursi's use of the term "stealing" [Tk. *hırsızcasına*] as a reference to benefiting from the world without acknowledging the Creator, see Nursi, *Sözler*, RNK, 1:208; Nursi, *Mektubat*, RNK, 1:539; Nursi, *Words*, 486; Nursi, *Letters*, 468.

80. See Nursi, *Sözler*, RNK, 1:11; Nursi, *Words*, 42.

81. Nursi mentions this theme of finitude repeatedly throughout the *Risale-i nur*. For one example, see Nursi, *Lemʾalar*, RNK, 1:584; Nursi, *Flashes*, 29.

82. References to human neediness and vulnerability (*ʿajz* and *faqr*) abound in the *Risale-i nur*. For examples, see Nursi, *Sözler*, RNK, 1:3, 48, 134; Nursi, *Şualar*, RNK, 1:852–53; Nursi, *Words*, 16–17, 141, 336–38; Nursi, *Rays*, 14. I am grateful to Yamina Bouguenaya's explanation of the significance of this concept in the *Risale-i nur*. I'd also like to acknowledge the research talk "The Power of Vulnerability" by Dr. Brené Brown, which indirectly aided my understanding of Said Nursi's references to human vulnerability. The talk can be viewed at http://www.ted.com/talks/brene_brown_on_vulnerability.html.

83. Indeed, reiterating the Sufi vocabulary, Nursi notes that the solution to human problems lies in finding the Giver of the problems. See, for instance, Nursi, *Sözler*, RNK, 1:78–88; Nursi, *Words*, 222–30.

84. Nursi, *Words*, 42, 156, 159.

85. Nursi notes that "it is unanimously agreed the total reversal of truths is impossible. . . . Thus infinite beauty cannot become ugliness, while yet remaining beauty, and, in our example, it is not possible that the beauty of Dominicality [sic (rubūbiyya)], a beauty perceptible and manifest in its existence, should retain its [quality] as the beauty of Dominicality, but become the very essence of ugliness." Nursi, Words, 84n18 (modified translation). In other words, the very fact that we see both mercy and its lack in the case of created beings (for things and persons that reflect mercy also fail to reflect it at other times) points to the genuine source of mercy behind them. And, once one arrives at that source of mercy, she is justified in her certainty that the infinite source may not transform into its opposite. See Nursi, Sözler, RNK, 1:23, 31; Nursi, Words, 67.

86. This is also a point reiterated throughout the Risale-i nur. See, for instance, Nursi, Sözler, RNK, 1:5, 6, 8, 133, etc.

87. Ibid., 1:3, 210–11.

88. Nursi points out that in this day and age, with its widespread attitude of numbing feelings (iptal-i his) and distractions, a believer does not realize the happiness implied within her belief unless she takes a moment to be self-aware. Nursi, Şualar, RNK, 1:1150; Nursi, Rays, 642.

89. Nursi, Words, 17; Nursi, Sözler, RNK, 1:4.

90. Nursi also notes, "However foolish it is to kiss the foot of a lowly man who conveys to you the valuable gift of a king, and not to recognize the owner of the gift—to praise and love the apparent source of bounties and forget the True Bestower of Bounties is a thousand times more foolish. O my soul! If you do not wish to be foolish in that way, give in God's name, take in God's name, begin in God's name, and act in God's name." Nursi, Words, 16.

91. Nursi, Sözler, RNK, 1:212; Nursi, Words, 493–94.

92. Nursi, Lem'alar, RNK, 1:599; Nursi, Flashes, 62.

93. Nursi, Flashes, 62; Nursi, Lem'alar, RNK, 1:599.

94. Nursi, Words, 709; Nursi, Flashes, 246. Nursi also says, "The imagination got deluded into reifying them (the natural laws) [collectively] as 'Nature,' and considered the latter as an external efficacious being and an operative reality, though it is no more than a mental estimation and a theoretical law." Nursi, "Preface to the Al-Mathnawī," 341 (italics added).

95. Thus, for instance, upon repetitive experience of objects consistently falling to the ground when left unsupported, scientists coined the concept of the "law of gravity," which is basically an articulation of the fact that there is a regular pattern in the way things fall down. If we then take this scientific description as the cause of the event of falling itself, we will be guilty of circular reasoning. Mermer, "Induction, Science, and Causation," 244.

96. For instance, Sir Ahmad Khan and Shibli Nuʿmani treated natural laws as logical entities and regarded any interruption in natural laws to be against science and logic. In order to reconcile logic with the word of God, Khan attempted to interpret Qurʾanic miracles symbolically, denying that the passages on miracles suggest anything extraordinary. See Khan, "Khan's Principles," 110, and Khan, "Khan's Principles II," 328. On the other hand, Nuʿmānī recognized that explaining away all the miracle stories in the Qurʾan was quite difficult. He noted that only someone who did not know Arabic well could buy into the argument that the Qurʾan actually does not contain any miracle accounts. Instead, he suggested that the Qurʾanic miracle stories actually refer to extraordinary events that are possible because of some unknown natural laws. See Özervarlı, Kelāmda yenilik, 100–102.

97. Nursi, Lem'alar, RNK, 1:600; Nursi, Flashes, 63.

98. Nursi, Words, 217 (modified translation, italics added); Nursi, Sözler, RNK, 1:76.

99. Nursi, *Words*, 684 (modified translation, italics added); Nursi, *Sözler, RNK*, 1:229.

100. Nursi, *Sözler, RNK*, 1:251, 23n89, 31; Nursi, *Words*, 67.

101. See Nursi's treatise on free will and destiny, entitled "26th Word," in Nursi, *Words*, 477–90. Here, reminiscent of Peirce, Nursi notes that if the world were governed by causal determinism, and if a certain set of causes *necessarily* produced certain results, then there would be no room for human freedom (ibid., 482). See also Yazicioglu, "Said Nursi on Free Will and Destiny."

102. Nursi, *Letters*, 456. For Nursi's understanding of the Qurʾanic audience as including all humanity until the end of time, see his treatise on Qurʾanic interpretation entitled "25th Word" in Nursi, *Words*, esp. 377–78.

103. Nursi, *Words*, 262 (modified translation). The text under discussion in this section is "20th Word" (see the section "Second Station"). For the original text, see Nursi, *Sözler, RNK*, 1:101–9.

104. Nursi, *Words*, 261 (modified translation). Also see Nursi, *İşaratü'l İʿcaz, RNK*, 2:1270.

105. Nursi, *Words*, 262, 264.

106. Ibid., 263.

107. Ibid. Cf. Muhammad Asad, a contemporary interpreter of the Qurʾan, who minimizes the references to miracles in Q. 3:49 by providing an alternative translation and suggesting an exclusively metaphorical reading. Asad, *Message of the Qurʾan*, 74n38.

108. Yazicioglu, "Use of Peirce's Pragmatism."

109. I find it important to note that Nursi does *not* thereby suggest that current science is the exclusive venue for pursuing the horizons of innovation indicated in miracle stories. Rather, his reference to scientific study must be taken in the broadest sense. Thus, for instance, the progress in medicine that Nursi implies need not be conceived exclusively within the framework of mainstream medical science; rather, it can also include alternative therapy methods. The cure for deadly sicknesses such as cancer might be found not in chemical therapy but in herbal medicine, and the emotional basis of many sicknesses can be discovered and healed through spiritual therapy. Nursi's statement that healing wonders can be reached either "physically, or spiritually," as in the case of the spiritual progress of saints, supports this point. See Nursi, *Sözler, RNK*, 1:103; Nursi, *Words*, 265.

110. See (in the Persian translation) Nuʿmānī, *ʿIlm-i kalām-i jadīd*, 61–63, 101–2, cited in Özervarlı, "Said Nursi's Project," 333n68.

111. In this regard, Nursi is closer to Rashid Riḍa, who considered the genuine interruption of natural patterns possible and also saw these stories as pointing toward technological development. Riḍa, *Al-Waḥy al-Muhammadī*, 155, cited in Özervarlı, *Kelâmda yenilik*, 103–4.

112. Cobb frankly notes that to his "own ears that are admittedly conditioned by modernity, it feels a bit strained." Cobb, "Said Nursi and Paul Tillich," 135.

113. Nursi, *Words*, 273. Muzaffar Iqbal characterizes Nursi's works as a precursor to the early modern genre of "scientific *tafsirs*"; Iqbal, *Science and Islam*, 151. This description may be misleading in that, unlike such exegetical works whose main aim was to make connections between modern scientific developments and the Qurʾan, the *Risale-i nur*—a work well over two thousand pages—contains only a handful of references to the Qurʾanic anticipation of scientific discoveries. In fact, to my knowledge, almost all such references occur in a single treatise, the "20th Word" (see the section "Second Station"), which I have used here. (The single page that Iqbal refers to in his description of Nursi's style is from this treatise.)

114. Nursi, *Words*, 251. It is thus important to note that Nursi does not naively think that technological innovation is an objective entity disconnected from cultural attitudes

and a particular worldview. On the contrary, he suggests that according to one's motivations and perspective, the value of the work produced will be different—hence his
emphasis on a worshipful attitude and a worldview that considers the world as a prelude
to eternal life. See ibid., 273.

115. Ibid., 274.

116. Asad, *Message of the Qurʾan*, 495n64.

117. Ibid., 496n64.

118. Nursi, *Words*, 269 (modified translation, italics added); Nursi, *Sözler*, *RNK*, 1:105.

119. Nursi, *Words*, 17; Nursi, *Sözler*, *RNK*, 1:3.

120. Nursi, *Words*, 269; Nursi, *Sözler*, *RNK*, 1:105.

121. Nursi, *Words*, 269. For this description of Abraham, see Q. 2:135, 3:67, 3:95,
4:125, and 16:120.

122. Nursi, *Words*, 269 (italics added).

123. Nursi, *İşaratüʾl İʿcaz*, *RNK*, 2:1269.

124. Cf. Ghazali, who, in his defense of the plain sense of miracle stories in the
Qurʾan, including the story of Abraham's miraculous survival in fire, referred to the
possibility of being protected from fire through a natural means, such as talc. Ghazālī,
Incoherence, 171–72.

CONCLUSION

1. Saleh, *Classical Tafsīr Tradition*, 113.

2. Ibid., 119.

3. Weddle, *Miracles*, 15.

4. He notes that while Ghazali "could hit philosophy where it thought it was the
strongest, in [its] epistemology," contemporary Muslims could not critically engage with
challenges to religion from modern science, and "as a result, contemporary Muslim
debates are only marginally concerned with epistemology." Griffel, review of *Ghazālī and
the Poetics*," 796.

5. For Nursi's insightful distinction between science and its materialist interpretations, see Yazicioglu, "Perhaps Their Harmony Is Not That Simple: Bediuzzaman Said
Nursi on the Qurʾan and Modern Science," *Theology and Science*, forthcoming.

6. For details of how the story was received in the Muslim tradition, see Yazicioglu,
"Engaging with Abraham and His Knife."

BIBLIOGRAPHY

Albayrak, Sadık. *Son devrin İslam akademisi: Daru'l-Hikmeti'l-İslamiye*. Istanbul: İz Yayıncılık, 1998.

Algar, Hamid. "The Centennial Renewer: Bediuzzaman Said Nursi and the Tradition of Tajdīd." *Journal of Islamic Studies* 12, no. 3 (2001): 291–311.

Ali, M. Sami. *Scientific Miracles of the Glorious Qur'an*. Translated by Abdussamad Kyle. Syria, 1997.

Aristotle. *Physics*. In *Aristotle: The Complete Works*, edited by Jonathan Barnes, vol. 1. Princeton: Princeton University Press, 1984. Online edition available from Intelex Past Masters at http://www.nlx.com.

Asad, Muhammad, trans. *The Message of the Qur'an*. Gibraltar: Dar al-Andalus, 1984.

Avicenna (Ibn Sīnā). *Al-Najāt*. Edited by M. S. Kurdi. 2nd ed. Cairo, 1938.

Ayers, Robert. "C. S. Peirce on Miracles." *Transactions of Charles S. Peirce Society* 16, no. 3 (1980): 242–54.

Batak, Kemal. "Tehâfütü'l felâsife ile alakalı genel problemler" [Main issues related to *Tahāfut al-falāsifa*]. *Journal of Islamic Research* 13, no. 3 (2000): 364–400.

Beck, Lewis White. Review of *The Sceptical Realism of David Hume*, by John P. Wright. *Eighteenth-Century Studies* 18, no. 2 (1984–85): 254–57.

Boullata, Issa J. "The Rhetorical Interpretation of the Qur'an: I'jāz and Related Topics." In *Approaches to the History of Interpretation of the Qur'an*, edited by Andrew Rippin, 139–57. Oxford: Clarendon Press, 1988.

Brown, Brené. "The Power of Vulnerability." TEDx Houston talk, 2010. Available at http://www.ted.com/talks/brene_brown_on_vulnerability.html.

Bulut, Halil İbrahim. *Kuran ışığında mucize ve peygamber* [The miracle and the prophet in the light of the Qur'an]. Istanbul: Rağbet Yayınları, 2002.

Burch, Robert. "Charles Sanders Peirce." In *The Stanford Encyclopedia of Philosophy*, edited by Edward N. Zalta. Fall 2007 edition. http://plato.stanford.edu/archives /fall2007/entries/peirce/.

Burnett, Charles. "The Second Revelation of Arabic Philosophy and Science: 1492–1562." In *Islam and the Italian Renaissance*, edited by C. Burnett and A. Contadini, 185–98. London: Warburg Institute, University of London, 1999.

Butterworth, Charles E. "Biographical Sketch of Averröes." In *The Book of the Decisive Treatise Determining the Connection Between the Law and Wisdom and Epistle Dedicatory*, translated and annotated by Charles E. Butterworth, xiii–xxxviii. Provo: Brigham Young University Press, 2001.

———. "Translator's Introduction to the *Decisive Treatise*." In *The Book of the Decisive Treatise Determining the Connection Between the Law and Wisdom and Epistle Dedicatory*, translated and annotated by Charles E. Butterworth, xxxix–xlii. Provo: Brigham Young University Press, 2001.

Capaldi, Nicholas. *David Hume: The Newtonian Philosopher.* Boston: Twayne, 1975.

Cobb, Kelton. "Revelation, the Disciplines of Reason, and Truth in the Works of Bediuzzaman Said Nursi and Paul Tillich." In *Islam at the Crossroads: On the Life and Thought of Bediuzzaman Said Nursi,* edited by Ibrahim M. Abu-Rabi', 129–50. New York: SUNY Press, 2003.

Corrington, Robert. *An Introduction to C. S. Peirce: Philosopher, Semiotician, and Ecstatic Naturalist.* Lanham, Md.: Rowman and Littlefield, 1993.

Courtenay, William J. "The Critique on Natural Causality in the Mutakallimun and Nominalism." *Harvard Theological Review* 66, no. 1 (1973): 77–94.

al-Daghamin, Ziyad Khalil Muhammad. "The Aims of the Qur'an in Bediuzzaman Said Nursi's Thought." In *A Contemporary Approach to Understanding the Qur'an: The Example of the Risale-i Nur, 20th–22nd September, 1998,* 353–79. Istanbul: Sözler Neşriyat, 2000.

Davudoglu, Ahmet. "Bediuzzaman and the Politics of the Twentieth-Century Muslim World." In *Proceedings of the Third International Symposium on Said Nursi: The Reconstruction of Islamic Thought in the Twentieth Century and Bediuzzaman Said Nursi,* 2:286–311. Istanbul: Sözler Neşriyat, 1997.

Dutton, Blake D. "Al-Ghazali on Possibility and the Critique of Causality." *Medieval Philosophy and Theology* 10, no. 1 (2001): 23–46.

Earman, John. *Hume's Abject Failure: The Argument Against Miracles.* New York: Oxford University Press, 2000.

Ess, Josef van. *The Flowering of Muslim Theology.* Translated by Jane Marie Todd. Cambridge: Harvard University Press, 2006.

Fakhry, Majid. *Averroes (Ibn Rushd): His Life, Works, and Influence.* Oxford: Oneworld, 2001.

———. *Islamic Occasionalism and Its Critique by Averroes and Aquinas.* London: George Allen and Unwin, 1958.

Ferreira, M. Jamie. *Scepticism and Reasonable Doubt: The British Naturalist Tradition in Wilkins, Hume, Reid, and Newman.* New York: Oxford University Press, 1986.

Fogelin, Robert J. *A Defense of Hume on Miracles.* Princeton: Princeton University Press, 2003.

———. *Hume's Skepticism in the "Treatise of Human Nature."* London: Routledge, 1985.

———. *Walking the Tightrope of Reason: The Precarious Life of a Rational Animal.* Oxford: Oxford University Press, 2003.

Fowlie, I. M. Review of *Hume's Skepticism in the "Treatise of Human Nature,"* by Robert Fogelin, and *Order and Artifice in Hume's Political Philosophy,* by Frederick Whelan. *Philosophical Quarterly* 39, no. 154 (1989): 124–30.

Gaskin, J. C. A. "Hume on Religion." In *The Cambridge Companion to Hume,* edited by David Fate Norton, 313–44. Cambridge: Cambridge University Press, 1993.

al-Ghazālī, Abū Ḥāmid. *The Clear Criterion for Distinguishing Between Islam and Heresy (Fayṣal al-tafriqa).* In *Freedom and Fulfillment: An Annotated Translation of al-Ghazālī's "Al-Munqidh min al-ḍalāl" and Other Relevant Works of al-Ghazālī,* translated by Richard Joseph McCarthy, 145–74. Boston: Twayne, 1980.

———. *The Correct Balance (Al-Qisṭās al-mustaqīm).* In *Freedom and Fulfillment: An Annotated Translation of al-Ghazālī's "Al-Munqidh min al-ḍalāl" and Other Relevant Works of al-Ghazālī,* translated by Richard Joseph McCarthy, 287–332. Boston: Twayne, 1980.

———. *Deliverance from Error and Mystical Union with the Almighty (Al-Munqidh min al-ḍalāl).* Translated by Muḥammad Abūlaylah. Edited by George F. McLean. Washington, D.C.: Council for Research in Values and Philosophy, 2001.

————. *The Faith and Practice of al-Ghazālī* [translation of *Al-Munqidh min al-ḍalāl*]. Translated by W. Montgomery Watt. London: G. Allen and Unwin, 1967.

————. *Faith in Divine Unity and Trust in Divine Providence* [translation of *Kitāb al-Tawḥīd wa'l-tawakkul*, book 35 of *Iḥyā' 'ulūm al-dīn*]. Translated by David Burrell. Louisville, Ky.: Fons Vitae, 2001.

————. *The Foundations of the Articles of Faith* [translation of *Al-Kitāb Qawā'id al-'aqāid*, from *Iḥyā' 'ulūm al-dīn*]. Translated and annotated by Nabih Amin Faris. Lahore: Sh. Muhammad Ashraf, 1963.

————. *Al-Ghazālī on Divine Predicates and Their Properties: A Critical and Annotated Translation of These Chapters in "Al-Iqtiṣād fī l-i'tiqād."* Translated by 'Abdurrahman Abu Zayd. Lahore: Sh. Muhammad Ashraf, 1970.

————. *Al-Ghazālī on the Ninety-Nine Beautiful Names of God (Kitāb al-Maqṣad al asnā fī sharh asmā' Allāh al-ḥusnā)*. Translated by D. B. Burrell and N. Daher. Cambridge: Islamic Texts Society, 1995.

————. *The Incoherence of the Philosophers: "Tahāfut al-falāsifa"; A Parallel English-Arabic Text*. Translated and annotated by Michael E. Marmura. Provo: Brigham Young University Press, 2000.

————. *Iqtiṣād fī l-i'tiqād*. Edited by A. Cubukcu and H. Atay. Ankara: Nur Matbaasi, 1962.

————. *İtikatta ölçülü olmak* [Turkish translation of *Iqtiṣād fī l-i'tiqād*]. Translated by Hanifi Akın. Istanbul: Ahsen Yayınları, 2005.

————. *Mi'yār al-'ilm* [*Standard of Knowledge*]. Edited by Suleyman Dunya. Cairo: Dār al-ma'ārif, 1961.

————. *On the Boundaries of Theological Tolerance in Islam: Abū Ḥamīd al-Ghazālī's "Fayṣal al-tafriqa."* Translated by Sherman A. Jackson. Karachi: Oxford University Press, 2002.

————. *Al-Qisṭās al-mustaqīm*. Edited by Victor Chelhot. Beirut: Al-Matba'a al-Kāthoulīkīya, 1959.

————. *The Recitation and Interpretation of the Qur'ān: Al-Ghazālī's Theory* [translation of *Kitāb Ādāb tilāwat al-Qur'ān*]. Translated and annotated by Muhammad Abul Quasem. London: Kegan Paul International, 1982.

Giacaman, George J. "Ducasse's Critique of Hume and the Humean Tradition." *Charles S. Peirce Society Transactions* 15, no. 4 (1979): 298–310.

Giacaman, George J., and Raja Bahlul. "Ghazali on Miracles and Necessary Connection." *Medieval Philosophy and Theology* 9, no. 1 (2000): 39–50.

Gianotti, Timothy J. *Ghazālī's Unspeakable Doctrine of the Soul: Unveiling the Esoteric Psychology and Eschatology of the Iḥyā'*. Leiden: Brill, 2001.

Goodman, Lenn E. *Avicenna*. London: Routledge, 1992.

Griffel, Frank. "Al-Ghazālī." In *The Stanford Encyclopedia of Philosophy*, edited by Edward N. Zalta. Fall 2008 edition. http://plato.stanford.edu/archives/fall2008/entries/al-ghazali/.

————. *Al-Ghazālī's Philosophical Theology*. New York: Oxford University Press, 2009.

————. "The Relationship Between Averroes and al-Ghazālī as It Presents Itself in Averroes' Early Writings, Especially in His Commentary on al-Ghazālī's *Al-Mustashfā*." In *Medieval Philosophy and the Classical Tradition in Islam, Judaism and Christianity*, edited by John Inglis, 51–63. Richmond, Surrey: Curzon, 2002.

————. Review of *Ghazālī and the Poetics of Imagination*, by Ebrahim Moosa. *Journal of the American Academy of Religion* 74, no. 3 (2006): 795–98.

Grill, Denis. "Miracles." In *Encyclopedia of the Qur'an*, vol. 3, edited by Jane Dammen McAuliffe. Leiden: Brill, 2004.

Gruender, David. "Pragmatism, Science, and Metaphysics." In *The Relevance of Charles Peirce*, edited by Eugene Freeman, 271–92. La Salle, Ill.: Hegeler Institute, 1983.

Guyer, Paul. "Introduction: The Starry Heavens and the Moral Law." In *The Cambridge Companion to Kant and Modern Philosophy*, edited by Paul Guyer, 1–27. Cambridge: Cambridge University Press, 2006.

Haack, Susan. "Not Cynicism but Synechism: Lessons from Classical Pragmatism." Plenary invited lecture delivered at conference on C. S. Peirce, Virginia Polytechnic Institute and State University, Spring 2004. http://www.as.miami.edu/phi/haack/synechis.pdf.

Halevi, Leor. "The Theologian's Doubts: Natural Philosophy and the Skeptical Games of Ghazali." *Journal of the History of Ideas* 63, no. 1 (2002): 19–39.

Hookway, Christopher. "Abstract of Chapter 11." Published only in the online version of *Truth, Rationality, and Pragmatism: Themes from Peirce*. Oxford Scholarship Online. http://dx.doi.org/10.1093/0199256586.001.0001.

———. *Peirce*. London: Routledge and Kegan Paul, 1985.

———. *Scepticism*. London: Routledge, 1990.

———. *Truth, Rationality, and Pragmatism: Themes from Peirce*. Oxford: Oxford University Press, 2002.

Hume, David. *An Abstract of a Treatise of Human Nature*. In Hume, *Complete Works and Correspondence*.

———. *The Complete Works and Correspondence of David Hume*. Compiled and edited by Mark C. Rooks. Charlottesville, Va.: InteLex, 1995. Online edition available from Intelex Past Masters at http://www.nlx.com.

———. *Dialogues Concerning Natural Religion*. In Hume, *Complete Works and Correspondence*.

———. *An Enquiry Concerning Human Understanding*. In Hume, *Complete Works and Correspondence*.

———. *The Letters of David Hume*. In Hume, *Complete Works and Correspondence*.

———. *A Treatise of Human Nature*. In Hume, *Complete Works and Correspondence*.

Ibn Rushd. *Averroes on the Harmony of Religion and Philosophy* [translation of *Faṣl al-maqāl*]. Translated by George F. Hourani. London: Luzac, 1960.

———. *Averroes' "Tahāfut al-tahāfut" (The Incoherence of the Incoherence)*. Translated and annotated by Simon Van Den Bergh. Vol. 1. Oxford: Messrs. Luzac, 1954.

———. *The Book of the Decisive Treatise Determining the Connection Between the Law and Wisdom and Epistle Dedicatory* [*Kitāb Faṣl al-maqāl wa taqrīr mā bayn al-sharīʿa wa al-ḥikma min al-ittiṣāl; risāla al-ihdā al-mulaqqaba bi-ʾl-ḍamīma*]. Translated and annotated by Charles E. Butterworth. Provo: Brigham Young University Press, 2001.

———. *Faith and Reason in Islam: Averroes' Exposition of Religious Arguments* [translation of *Al-Kashf ʿan manāhij al-adilla*]. Translated by Ibrahim Najjar. Oxford: Oneworld, 2001.

———. *Al-Kashf ʿan manāhij al-adilla fī ʿaqāid al-milla*. 2nd ed. Edited by Mahmud Qāsim. Cairo: Anglo-Egyptian Library, 1964.

———. *Tahāfut al-tahāfut*. Edited by M. Bouyges. Beirut: Imprimerie Catholique, 1930.

Ibn Taymiyya, Aḥmad bin ʿAbd al-Ḥalīm. *Al-Nubūwwāt*. Edited by Muhammad ʿAwad. Cairo, 1985.

Iqbal, Muzaffar. *Science and Islam*. Greenwood Guides to Science and Religion. Westport, Conn.: Greenwood Press, 2007.

Jabre, Farīd, Samih Daghim, Rafiq al-ʿAjam, and Jīrār Jahāmī. *Mawsūʿāt muṣṭalaḥāt ʿilm al-manṭiq ʿinda al-ʿArab*. Beirut: Maktaba Lubnān, 1996.

Jackson, Sherman. Introduction to *On the Boundaries of Theological Tolerance in Islam: Abū Ḥamīd al-Ghazālī's "Fayṣal al-tafriqa,"* translated by Sherman Jackson, 1–82. Karachi: Oxford University Press, 2002.

James, William. *Psychology: Briefer Course.* New York: Henry Holt, 1923.

————. *The Writings of William James: A Comprehensive Edition.* Edited by John J. McDermott. New York: Random House, 1967.

Johnson, David. *Hume, Holism, and Miracles.* Ithaca: Cornell University Press, 1999.

Kant, Immanuel. *Critique of Pure Reason.* Translated and edited by Paul Guyer and Allen W. Wood. 2nd ed. Cambridge: Cambridge University Press, 1997.

Keddie, Nikki R. *An Islamic Response to Imperialism.* Berkeley: University of California Press, 1968.

Khan, Sayyid Ahmad Khan. "Sir Sayyid Ahmad Khan's Principles of Exegesis Translated from His *Tahrir fi ʿusul al-tafsir.*" Translated by Muhammad Daud Rahbar. *Muslim World* 46, no. 2 (1956): 104–12.

————. "Sir Sayyid Ahmad Khan's Principles of Exegesis Translated from His *Tahrir fi ʿusul al-tafsir* II." Translated by Muhammad Daud Rahbar. *Muslim World* 46, no. 4 (1956): 324–35.

Kogan, Barry S. *Averroes and the Metaphysics of Causation.* Albany: SUNY Press, 1985.

Kukkonen, Taneli. "Possible Worlds in the *Tahāfut al-falāsifa*: Al-Ghazālī on Creation and Contingency." *Journal of the History of Philosophy* 38, no. 4 (2000): 479–502.

————. "Possible Worlds in the *Tahāfut al-tahāfut*: Averroes on Plenitude and Possibility." *Journal of the History of Philosophy* 38, no. 3 (2000): 329–47.

Leaman, Oliver. "Nursi's Place in the *Ihya'* Tradition." *Muslim World* 89, nos. 3–4 (1999): 314–24.

Legg, Catherine. "Naturalism and Wonder: Peirce on the Logic of Hume's Argument Against Miracles." *Philosophia* 28, nos. 1–4 (2001): 297–318.

————. "Real Law in Charles Peirce's 'Pragmaticism.'" In *Causation and Laws of Nature*, edited by Howard Sankey, 125–42. London: Kluwer Academic, 1999.

Levi, Isaac. "Beware of Syllogism: Statistical Reasoning and Conjecturing According to Peirce." In *The Cambridge Companion to Peirce*, edited by Cheryl Misak, 257–86. Cambridge: Cambridge University Press, 2004.

MacFarlane, Charles. *Turkey and Its Destiny: The Result of Journeys Made in 1847 and 1848 to Examine into the State of That Country.* London: John Murray, 1850.

Maimonides, Moses. *Guide to the Perplexed.* Chicago: University of Chicago Press, 1989.

Markham, Ian. *Engaging with Bediuzzaman Said Nursi.* Burlington, Vt.: Ashgate, 2009.

Markham, Ian, and Birinci-Pirim. *An Introduction to Said Nursi: Life, Thought and Writings.* Burlington, Vt.: Ashgate, 2011.

Marmura, Michael E. "Avicenna's Psychological Proof of Prophecy." *Journal of Near Eastern Studies* 22, no. 1 (1963): 49–56.

————. "Al-Ghazālī." In *The Cambridge Companion to Arabic Philosophy*, edited by Peter Adamson and Richard C. Taylor, 137–54. Cambridge: Cambridge University Press, 2005.

————. "Ghazālian Causes and Intermediaries." *Journal of the American Oriental Society* 115, no. 1 (1995): 89–100.

————. "Ghazali and Ashʿarism Revisited." *Arabic Sciences and Philosophy* 12, no. 1 (2002): 91–110.

————. "Ghazali and Demonstrative Science." *Journal of the History of Philosophy* 3, no. 2 (1965): 183–204.

————. "Translator's Introduction." In *Incoherence of the Philosophers: "Tahāfut al-falāsifa"; A Parallel English-Arabic Text*, translated and annotated by Michael E. Marmura, xv–xxvii. Provo: Birmingham University Press, 2000.

Masala, Anna. "The Line from Mevlana to Bediuzzaman." In *The Reconstruction of Islamic Thought in the Twentieth Century and Bediuzzaman Said Nursi*, 18–23. Istanbul: Sözler Neşriyat, 1993.

McCarthy, Richard Joseph. Introduction to *Freedom and Fulfillment: An Annotated Translation of al-Ghazālī's "Al-Munqidh min al-ḍalāl" and Other Relevant Works of al-Ghazālī*, translated by Richard Joseph McCarthy, ix–lx. Boston: Twayne, 1980.

Mermer, Yamine Bouguenaya. "Induction, Science, and Causation: Some Critical Reflections." *Islamic Studies* 35, no. 3 (1996): 243–82.

Mermer, Yamine, and Redha Ameur. "Beyond the Modern: Saʿid al-Nursi's View of Science." *Islam and Science* 2 (Winter 2004): 119–60.

Michel, Thomas F. "Muslim-Christian Dialogue and Cooperation in the Thought of Bediuzzaman Said Nursi." Jesuit Interreligious Dialogue and Relations, 2004. http://groups.creighton.edu/sjdialogue/documents/articles/michel_muslim _christian_dialogue.htm.

Misak, Cheryl. "C. S. Peirce on Vital Matters." In *The Cambridge Companion to Peirce*, edited by Cheryl Misak, 150–74. Cambridge: Cambridge University Press, 2004.

Morris, William Edward. "David Hume." In *The Stanford Encyclopedia of Philosophy*, edited by Edward N. Zalta. Winter 2007 edition. http://plato.stanford.edu /archives/win2007/entries/hume/.

Najjar, Ibrahim Y. "Ibn Rushd's Theory of Rationality." *Alif: Journal of Comparative Poetics* 16 (1996): 191–216.

Nasr, S. Hossein. *The Heart of Islam*. New York: HarperCollins, 2002.

Noonan, Harold W. *Hume on Knowledge*. London: Routledge, 1999.

Norton, David Fate. "An Introduction to Hume's Thought." In *The Cambridge Companion to Hume*, edited by David Fate Norton, 1–32. Cambridge: Cambridge University Press, 1993.

Nuʿmānī, Shiblī. "The Fundamental Nature of Prophethood and Miracle: A Chapter from Shibli Nuʿmani's *Al-Kalam*." Translated and annotated by Christian W. Troll. In *Islam in India: Studies and Commentaries*, 1:86–115. New Delhi: Vikas, 1982.

———. *ʿIlm-i kalām-i jadīd* [Persian translation]. Translated by M. Taki Fakhr Dai Kilani. Tehran, 1911.

Nursi, Bediuzzaman Said. *The Flashes: From the Risale-i Nur Collection*. Translated by Şükran Vahide. Istanbul: Sözler Neşriyat, 1995.

———. *The Letters: From the Risale-i Nur Collection*. Translated by Şükran Vahide. Istanbul: Sözler Neşriyat, 1994.

———. "Preface to the *Al-Mathnawī al-ʿArabī al-Nūrī*." Translated by Redha Ameur. In *Islam at the Crossroads: On the Life and Thought of Bediuzzaman Said Nursi*, edited by Ibrahim M. Abu-Rabiʿ, 335–50. New York: SUNY Press, 2003.

———. *The Rays: From the Risale-i Nur Collection*. Translated by Şükran Vahide. Istanbul: Sözler Neşriyat, 2002.

———. *Risale-i nur külliyatı*. 2 vols. Istanbul: Yeni Asya Yayinlari, 1996.

———. *The Words: From the Risale-i Nur Collection*. Translated by Şükran Vahide. Rev. ed. Istanbul: Sözler Neşriyat, 2004.

Ochs, Peter. *Peirce, Pragmatism, and the Logic of Scripture*. Cambridge: Cambridge University Press, 1998.

Özervarlı, M. Sait. *Kelāmda yenilik arayışları*. Istanbul: İSAM Yayinlari, 1998.

———. "The Reconstruction of Islamic Social Thought in the Modern Period: Nursi's Approach to Religious Discourse in a Changing Society." *Asian Journal of Social Science* 38, no. 4 (2010): 532–53.

———. "Said Nursi's Project of Revitalizing Contemporary Islamic Thought." In *Islam at the Crossroads: On the Life and Thought of Bediuzzaman Said Nursi*, edited by Ibrahim M. Abu-Rabiʿ, 317–33. New York: SUNY Press, 2003.

Peirce, Charles. *The Collected Papers of Charles Sanders Peirce*. Vols. 1–6 edited by Charles Hartshorne and Paul Weiss. Vols. 7–8 edited by Arthur W. Burks. Cambridge: Harvard University Press, 1931–58. Online edition available from Intelex Past Masters at http://www.nlx.com.

———. "The Logic of Drawing History from Ancient Documents." In *Historical Perspectives on Peirce's Logic of Science: A History of Science*, edited by Carolyn Eisele, 2:705–62. Berlin: Mouton, 1985.

Pihlström, Sami. "Peirce's Place in the Pragmatist Tradition." In *The Cambridge Companion to Peirce*, edited by Cheryl Misak, 27–57. Cambridge: Cambridge University Press, 2004.

Rahman, Fazlur. *Major Themes of the Qurʾan*. 2nd ed. Kuala Lumpur: Islamic Book Trust, 1999.

———. *Prophecy in Islam: Philosophy and Orthodoxy*. London: George Allen and Unwin, 1958.

———. Review of *Islamic Occasionalism and Its Critique by Averroes and Aquinas*, by Majid Fakhry. *Oriens* 12, no. 1/2 (1959): 232–34.

al-Rāzī, Fakhr al-Dīn. *Tafsīr al-kabīr*. Vol. 14. Cairo: Al-Maṭbaʿa al-Bāhiyah al-Miṣrīya, 1934.

———. *Uṣūl al-dīn*. Edited by Ṭāhā ʿAbd al-Raʾūf Saʿd. Cairo: Maktaba al-Kullīyāt al-Azharīya, 1977.

Riḍa, Muhammad Rashid. *Al-Waḥy al-Muḥammadī*. Cairo: Tabʿat al-Zahra, 1988.

Rosenberg, Alexander. "Hume and the Philosophy of Science." In *The Cambridge Companion to Hume*, edited by David Fate Norton, 64–89. Cambridge: Cambridge University Press, 1993.

Rosenthal, Sandra. "Peirce's Pragmatic Account of Perception." In *The Cambridge Companion to Peirce*, edited by Cheryl Misak, 193–213. Cambridge: Cambridge University Press, 2004.

Russell, Bertrand. *History of Western Philosophy*. New York: Routledge, 2004.

Russell, Paul. "Hume on Religion." In *The Stanford Encyclopedia of Philosophy*, edited by Edward N. Zalta. Winter 2005 edition. http://plato.stanford.edu/archives/win2005/entries/hume-religion/.

———. Review of *Hume's Skepticism in the "Treatise of Human Nature,"* by Robert J. Fogelin. *Mind*, n.s., 95, no. 379 (1986): 392–96.

Saleh, Walid A. *Formation of the Classical Tafsīr Tradition: The Qurʾān Commentary of al-Thaʿlabī*. Leiden: Brill, 2004.

al-Sanūsī, Muḥammad ibn Yūsuf. *Sharḥ Sanūsiyyāti al-kubra*. Edited by ʿAbd al-Fattāḥ Barakah. Kuwait, 1986.

Schmidt, Claudia M. *David Hume: Reason in History*. University Park: Pennsylvania State University Press, 2003.

Sells, Michael. *Approaching the Qurʾan: The Early Revelations*. 2nd ed. Ashland, Ore.: White Cloud Press, 2007.

Sennett, James F., and Douglas Groothuis, eds. *In Defense of Natural Theology: A Post-Humean Assessment*. Downers Grove, Ill.: InterVarsity Press, 2005.

Sheikh, M. Saeed. "Al-Ghazālī: Metaphysics." In *A History of Muslim Philosophy*, edited by M. M. Sharif, 1:581–616. Delhi: Low Price, 1961.

Sheriff, John K. *The Fate of Meaning: Charles Peirce, Structuralism, and Literature*. Princeton: Princeton University Press, 1989.

Stroud, Barry. *Hume*. London: Routledge, 1988.

Turley, Peter. "Peirce on Chance." *Transactions of Charles S. Peirce Society* 5, no. 4 (1969): 243–54.

———. "Peirce's Cosmic 'Sheriff.'" *Journal of the History of Ideas* 36, no. 4 (1975): 717–20.

Turner, Colin. *Islam: The Basics*. 2nd ed. New York: Routledge, 2011.

————. "Renewal in Islam and Bediuzzaman." In *The Reconstruction of Islamic Thought in the Twentieth Century and Bediuzzaman Said Nursi*, 156–63. Istanbul: Sözler Neşriyat, 1993.

Turner, Colin, and Hasan Horkuc. *Said Nursi: Makers of Islamic Civilization*. Oxford: I.B. Tauris, 2009.

Tweyman, Stanley. *Essays on the Philosophy of David Hume*. New York: Caravan Books, 1996.

Vahide, Şükran. *The Author of the Risale-i Nur: Bediuzzaman Said Nursi*. Istanbul: Sözler Yayınevi, 1992.

————. "Toward an Intellectual Biography of Said Nursi." In *Islam at the Crossroads: On the Life and Thought of Bediuzzaman Said Nursi*, edited by Ibrahim M. Abu-Rabiʿ, 1–32. New York: SUNY Press, 2003.

van Ess, Josef. *The Flowering of Muslim Theology*. Translated by Jane Marie Todd. Cambridge: Harvard University Press, 2006.

Watt, Montgomery. *Free Will and Predestination in Early Islam*. London: Luzac, 1948.

————. "Al-Ghazālī." In *Encyclopaedia of Islam*. 2nd ed. Brill Online, 2013. http://reference works.brillonline.com/entries/encyclopaedia-of-islam-2/al-ghazali-COM_0233.

Weddle, David L. *Miracles: Wonder and Meaning in World Religions*. New York: New York University Press, 2010.

Wilson, Fred. *Hume's Defense of Causal Inference*. Toronto: University of Toronto Press, 1997.

Wimbush, Vincent L. "Introduction: TEXTures, Gestures, Power: Orientation to Radical Excavation." In *Theorizing Scriptures: New Critical Orientations to a Cultural Phenomenon*, edited by Vincent L. Wimbush, 1–22. New Brunswick: Rutgers University Press, 2008.

Winter, Tim. Introduction to *The Cambridge Companion to Classical Islamic Theology*, edited by Tim Winter, 1–16. Cambridge: Cambridge University Press, 2008.

Wolfson, Harry Austryn. *The Philosophy of the Kalām*. Cambridge: Harvard University Press, 1976.

Yandell, Keith E. *Hume's "Inexplicable Mystery": His Views on Religion*. Philadelphia: Temple University Press, 1990.

Yazicioglu, Isra. "Engaging with Abraham and His Knife: Interpretation of Abraham's Sacrifice in the Muslim Tradition." In *Interpreting Abraham: Journeys to Moriah*, edited by Bradley Beach and Matthew Powell. Minneapolis: Fortress Press, forthcoming.

————. "A Graceful Reconcilation: Said Nursi on Free Will and Destiny." In *Brill Companion to Said Nursi*, edited by David Goa and Bilal Kuspinar. Leiden: Brill, forthcoming.

————. "Perhaps Their Harmony Is Not That Simple: Said Nursi on the Qurʾan and Modern Science," forthcoming from *Theology and Science*.

————. "Redefining the Miraculous: Al-Ghazālī, Ibn Rushd, and Said Nursi on Qurʾanic Miracle Stories." *Journal of Qurʾanic Studies* 13, no. 2 (2011): 86–108.

————. "Saʿid Nursi." In *The Princeton Encyclopedia of Islamic Political Thought*, edited by G. Bowering, P. Crone, W. Kadi, D. J. Stewart, M. Q. Zaman, and M. Mirza. Princeton: Princeton University Press, 2011.

————. "The Use of Peirce's Pragmatism for Qurʾanic Interpretation." *Journal of Scriptural Reasoning* 8, no. 2 (2009). http://etext.virginia.edu/journals/ssr/issues/vol ume8/number2/ssr08_02_e02.htm.